# Why Do You Need this New Edition?

Each new edition of this classic textbook mirrors our constantly changing world. We reflect on the changes in society and how these changes impact public speaking, and we rewrite material, reorganize sections, and adapt the features that complement the presentation.

*Principles of Public Speaking* has guided students for over eighty years by setting the standard for education in the basic speech course. The combination of commitment to this standard and the latest research in communication theory and recognition of contemporary issues makes this textbook as useful today as it has been through all its editions. Here are some features you will find only in the seventeenth edition.

1. *Special section on assessment of speeches.* This will help you incorporate everything you've learned as you listen to the speeches of your classmates and others. It will help you become a more critical listener.

2. *Focus on speaking in the community.* You will learn about communication as part of civic engagement and service learning. Specific speaking formats are offered to help you in these community contexts.

3. *Unique blend of contemporary and classic public speakers.* Throughout this textbook, you will encounter outstanding examples of public speakers from contemporary life in critical political and social arenas.

4. *Recognition of public speaking as a multimedia event.* Your world is constantly changing, and you'll learn how those changes affect public communication, beginning with the most recent innovations in Web-based research through media support for the speaker's message.

PEARSON

# Principles of Public Speaking

· · · · · · · · · · · · · · · · ·

SEVENTEENTH EDITION

**Kathleen M. German**
Miami University of Ohio

**Bruce E. Gronbeck**
The University of Iowa

**Douglas Ehninger**

**Alan H. Monroe**

**Allyn & Bacon**

Boston     New York     San Francisco
Mexico City     Montreal     Toronto     London     Madrid     Munich     Paris
Hong Kong     Singapore     Tokyo     Cape Town     Sydney

Editor-in-Chief: *Karon Bowers*
Senior Developmental Editor: *Carol Alper*
Series Editorial Assistant: *Susan Brilling*
Marketing Manager: *Suzan Czajkowski*
Production Editor: *Karen Mason*
Editorial-Production Service and Electronic Composition:
    *GGS Higher Education Resources, A Division of Premedia Global, Inc.*
Manufacturing Buyer: *JoAnne Sweeney*
Interior Design: *Susan Gerould*
Photo Researcher: *PoYee Oster*
Cover Administrator: *Joel Gendron*

Between the time Web site information is gathered and then published, it is not unusual for some sites to have closed. Also, the transcription of URLs can result in typographical errors. The publisher would appreciate notification where these errors occur so that they may be corrected in subsequent editions.

Credits appear on page 292, which constitutes an extension of this copyright page.

**Library of Congress Cataloging-in-Publication Data**
Principles of public speaking/Kathleen M. German . . . [et al.]. — 17th ed.
    p. cm.
    ISBN 0-205-65396-0
    1. Public speaking. I. German, Kathleen M.

PN4121.E36 2010
808.5'1—dc22

2008047345

10  9  8  7  6  5  4  3  2  1   RRD-OH   13   12   11   10   09   08

**Allyn & Bacon
is an imprint of**

www.pearsonhighered.com

ISBN-10:  0-205-65396-0
ISBN-13:  978-0-205-65396-6

# Brief Contents

# Contents

Preface    **xvii**

## PART TWO

# Planning and Preparing Your Speech

In Part Two, we get down to the business of building your speeches. Most of you use the Internet, so how can it help you with pieces of the speech-building process? When doing audience analysis, you can find public opinion surveys on beliefs and attitudes relevant to what you are talking about—start at **www.pollingreport.com**. You can also obtain statistics on the demographic composition of your school on your school's Web site. Looking for supporting materials? Pick your favorite search engine, and type in what you're looking for. (Remember that **image.google.com** and **scholar.google.com** will give you a variety of illustrations and solid scholarly research. Some of the research will be accessible only through publication memberships—your library may be able to help you with accessing this material.) While you'll have to organize your speech yourself, the Internet will provide quotations, stories, comparisons, startling facts, and statistics. Make sure to evaluate the information you find and to compare multiple sites. The libraries at Johns Hopkins University and Virginia Tech provide solid advice on evaluating information: **www.library.jgu.edu/researchhelp/general/evaluating** and **www.lib.vt.edu/help/instruct/evaluate/evaluating.html**.

# Presenting Your Speech

Part Three focuses on encoding: putting a speech idea or text into the multiple channels of communication that make up a speech. A speech is made up of the language you use; the characteristics of your voice; your body and the way that you use it through facial display, movements, and stance; and the use of additional visual media that enhance, clarify, and even empower the stream of words, vocal inflections, and embodiment that make up the act of public speaking. When speaking in public, you actually are using varied channels; public speaking is multimediated.

Additionally, audiotaping, videotaping, and using Webcams provide still another communication channel: electronic mediation. Your speeches can be put in an audio archive or broadcast via radio, stored on a DVD or broadcast via network television or local access cable feeds, and uploaded to YouTube or some other digital space for all of the world to search out and see. When that happens, then you must think about how to fit your speaking style to an audio or visual recording. For some advice on speaking when your message will be transmitted through a mass-mediated channel, go to **www.public-speaking.org/public-speaking-tvvideo-article.htm**.

## PART FOUR

# Types of Public Speaking

The world of public information, argument, and even persuasion is dominated by the World Wide Web. So, you're interested in politics: Where do you find the schedule for presidential caucuses and primaries? You go to **www.thegreenpapers.com** or **www.rockthevote.com** to get the list. Debates? The Commission on Presidential Debates at **www.debates.org** is your best bet for history, texts, and directions to good analyses. How about statistics on online hits that each candidate had? Try **www.techpresident.com**. Ads? Each campaign will have them on its Web site, or you just click on **www.youtube.com** to find both ads and creative remakes (mashups) of them. The World Wide Web is, indeed, a spider's invention, drawing you in with seemingly limitless informative, argumentative, and persuasive messages on personal Web sites, blogs, electronic news outlets, streaming video and audio collections, and all the rest. Yet, again, we must emphasize—when push comes to shove in your local groups, associations, affiliative organizations, and civic institutions, public talk is the common denominator. The Web can bring you materials, but you, the voice of one group member or citizen, are still the voice of material, argument, persuasion, and collective memory. You, not the Web, are responsible for what gets done. And so, Part Four will complete your introduction to the role of public speaking in public life.

# Features

# Preface

## A Tradition of Excellence

*Principles of Public Speaking,* Seventeenth Edition, presents the fundamental principles that have helped thousands of students gain the confidence and expertise to speak in public. It combines the latest research of scholars in rhetorical and communication theory with practical advice on how to speak effectively in a culturally diverse society. It retains the core concept of Monroe's motivated sequence that has been its trademark from its inception, and it brings cutting-edge electronic resources and technology to public speaking. Three fundamental principles describe the basic approach of the book:

1. **This textbook gets you on your feet quickly.** You will become acquainted with the communication concepts to prepare and critique speeches, and you will be encouraged to put those concepts into practice early. Chapter 2, "Getting Started," will get you on your feet and speaking to your classmates. Later chapters will discuss ideas in more detail to help you develop your expertise as a public speaker and a critical listener.
2. **This textbook focuses on communication in your college life but also includes examples from the community and beyond.** We recognize that your college environment probably commands your immediate attention, but you're also preparing for a lifetime of public participation. To help you now and in the future, we have incorporated applications and examples from both the college world and the worlds of work, politics, and social activism.
3. **This textbook challenges you technically, intellectually, and morally.** Throughout your life, you will be expected to know how to accomplish goals (technical skills), how to analyze situations and propose courses of action (intellectual skills), and how to interact with others ethically (moral development). This book challenges you not only to develop your skills and thought processes as a speaker and critical listener but also to understand your responsibilities as you participate in an increasingly diverse world.

## The Plan of the Book

*Principles of Public Speaking,* Seventeenth Edition, is organized into four parts, reflecting the four major emphases of most contemporary courses in public speaking. Part One, "Public Speaking in the World of Electronic Culture," provides you with *an orientation to the communication process.* Here, you will encounter the conceptual underpinnings of communication theory; examine the public speaking skills that will enhance your success in school, at work, and in society; and learn how to adapt your ideas to the people who make all the difference—your audience. In Chapter 4, "Public Speaking and Cultural Challenges," you will consider the connection between culture and public speaking so that you will recognize the importance of attending to cultural differences and the challenges you will encounter. The chapters in Part One introduce important ways to think about speechmaking, even as you give your first classroom speeches. Numerous examples show you how the particular skills involved in public speaking apply to a variety of real-world contexts.

Part Two, "Planning and Preparing Your Speech," offers *a step-by-step approach to speech preparation.* You will gain confidence as a speaker by breaking down this complex task into its component parts: setting your purposes, articulating central ideas, finding and assessing supporting materials, organizing and outlining these materials, and building effective introductions and conclusions.

Building a speech is the first half of the speechmaking process. The other half is actually delivering your speech—putting your presentation into words, gestures, bodily actions, vocal patterns, and visual aids. That's what Part Three, "Presenting Your Speech," is all about. Every time you speak, you're communicating by way of four channels: language, sounds, movements, and visuals. The chapters in Part Three will help you master how to send and control the message flowing through each channel.

There are many different kinds of speeches, each with its own demands and conventional rules. In Part Four, "Types of Public Speaking," you will learn about three broad categories of speeches: speeches to inform, speeches to persuade, and argumentative speeches. Studying the characteristics of each of these types of speeches will help you refine your speechmaking skills and learn how to adapt them to particular speaking occasions: speaking in the community and speaking in small groups.

## Features of the Book

- Special attention to Web resources and the MySpeechLab Web site (**www.myspeechlab.com**) provide the latest in online support.

- Oral, face-to-face communication constitutes the core of human relations and culture. Chapter 1 introduces the idea of orality, and the chapters that follow develop the ways that speechmaking builds the bonds of society.

- We live and interact in an increasingly diverse society. Successful public speakers recognize the connections between culture and public speaking and are able to adjust their styles and presentations to their audiences. Chapter 4 focuses specifically on the role of culture in communication.

- Critical thinking is an important part of overall education, including speech instruction. We cover critical thinking throughout the book and highlight the topic in Chapters 3 and 14.

- Chapter 6 guides you through the uses of electronic and Web database technologies to find and assess supporting materials and evaluate the types and uses of computer-generated visual aids. A special section at the end of Chapter 11 offers tips on how to create PowerPoint slides and use them effectively in your presentation.

- Speech ethics is discussed in the first chapter of the book and in a series of boxed features titled "Speaking of . . . Ethics." These boxes examine the moral consequences of communicating and help you explore your own thinking about ethical choices in speechmaking.

- A series of boxed features "Speaking of . . . Apprehension" offer concrete advice to help speakers overcome speaking fears and gain confidence.

- Boxed features "Speaking of . . . Skills" focus on hands-on strategies for preparing and delivering effective speeches. Topics include brainstorming to generate topics and good note-taking skills.

- A boxed feature "Speaking of . . . Surveys" offers advice on how to learn your audience's opinions or demographic information.

- Four hands-on "workshops" cover special topics in depth: "Listening Workshop" at the end of Chapter 3, "Web Workshop" at the end of Chapter 6, "Using Microsoft PowerPoint with Your Presentations" at the end of Chapter 11, and "Information versus Persuasion" at the end of Chapter 12.

- Sample outlines and speeches demonstrate the application of speech-making principles. Annotations on many of the outlines and speeches alert you to the rhetorical principles being used.

- Alan Monroe (1903–1975) and Douglas Ehninger (1913–1979) worked with students and teachers to develop strategies for teaching public speaking to students of diverse backgrounds and talents. With this textbook, you are heir to the pedagogy they built:
  - Monroe's motivated sequence, the greatest formula for putting together a speech—others have copied it, but none have topped it.
  - A critical examination of the forms of supporting materials.
  - Exploration of types of language use, including imagery.
  - Exploration of various kinds of introductions, organizational patterns, and conclusions.
  - Discussion of the factors of attention that help you capture and keep your listeners' interest.
  - Focus on argumentation that teaches you how to build an argumentative speech and analyze the arguments of others.

## Resources for Instructors

For more information about all of the available supplements, as well as sample material, go to www.mycoursetoolbox.com. The ancillary program for *Principles of Public Speaking,* Seventeenth Edition, includes the following instructor supplements:

### Print Resources

**The Instructor's Manual**    This extensive guide to teaching the public speaking course was written by Ferald J. Bryan, Northern Illinois University. For each chapter, it includes an outline of key concepts, questions to check student comprehension and encourage critical thinking, detailed descriptions of classroom activities, impromptu speaking exercises, and a bibliography for further reading.

**Test Bank**    The test bank, written by Cynthia Brown El, Macomb Community College, includes over 1,200 test items—true/false, multiple choice, short answer, and essay questions.

**New Teacher's Guide to Public Speaking, Fourth Edition**    This guide, written by Calvin L. Troup, Dusquesne University and Jayne L. Violette, Eastern Kentucky University, helps new teachers teach the public speaking course effectively. It covers such topics as preparing for the term, planning and structuring your course, evaluating speeches, utilizing the textbook, integrating technology into the classroom, and much more. The new fourth edition features a chapter on how to use and integrate MySpeechLab into your public speaking course.

## Electronic Resources

**Computerized Test Bank**    The printed Test Bank is also available through MYTEST Pearson's NEW computerized testing system. The user-friendly interface allows you to view, edit, and add questions; transfer questions to tests; and print tests. Search and sort features allow you to locate questions quickly and to arrange them in whatever order you prefer. Available online at **www.pearsonmytest.com** (access code required).

**PowerPoint**    This text-specific package, written by Pamela S. Bledsoe, Surry Community College, consists of a collection of lecture outlines and graphic images keyed to every chapter of the text. These are available electronically through Pearson's Instructor's Resource Center at **www.pearsonhighered.com/irc** (access code required).

**MySpeechLab**    (**www.myspeechlab.com**) is a state-of-the-art, interactive and instructive online solution for public speaking courses. Designed to be used as a supplement to a traditional lecture course, or to completely administer an online course, MySpeechLab combines multimedia, video, activities, speech preparation tools including MyOutline and help with topic selection, research support, tests, and quizzes to make teaching and learning fun! Visit **www.myspeechlab.com** (access code required; please contact your Pearson representative to request a demo or for more information).

**VideoWorkshop for Public Speaking, Version 2.0**    This supplement, prepared by Tasha Van Horn, Citrus College, and Marilyn Reineck, Concordia University, is a way to bring video into your course for maximized learning in public speaking. This total teaching and learning system includes quality video footage on an easy-to-use CD-ROM, plus a Student Learning Guide and an Instructor's Teaching Guide. The result? A program that brings textbook concepts to life with ease and that helps your students understand, analyze, and apply the objectives of the course.

The **Allyn & Bacon Digital Media Archive for Communication, Version 3.0** This CD-ROM contains electronic images of charts, graphs, maps, tables, and figures, along with media elements such as video, audio clips, and related web links. These media assets are fully customizable to use with our preformatted PowerPoint outlines or to import into your own lectures (Windows and Mac).

The **Allyn & Bacon Public Speaking Transparency Package, Version II**    This package contains 100 public speaking transparencies created with images and text from our current public speaking texts. The transparency package is useful for providing visual support for classroom lectures and discussion on a full range of course topics.

**Lecture Questions for Clickers**    The Lecture Questions were written by William Keith, University of Wisconsin-Milwaukee. These are an assortment of PowerPoint questions and activities covering a multitude of topics in public speaking and speech delivery. These slides will help liven up your lectures and can be used along with the Personal Response System to get students more involved in the material. Available on the Web at **www.pearsonhighered.com/irc** (access code required).

The **Allyn & Bacon PowerPoint Presentation Package for Public Speaking**, available electronically, includes 125 slides that provide visual and instructional support for the classroom including material on communication theory, visual aids, and tips for organizing and outlining speeches.

## Video Resources

**Pearson A&B Contemporary Classic Speeches DVD**    This exciting supplement includes over 120 minutes of video footage in an easy-to-use DVD format. Each speech is accompanied by a biographical and historical summary that helps students understand the context and motivation behind each speech. Speakers featured include Martin Luther King Jr., John F. Kennedy, Barbara Jordan, the Dalai Lama, and Christopher Reeve.

**Pearson A&B Public Speaking Video Library**    Pearson Allyn & Bacon's Public Speaking Video Library contains a range of different types of speeches delivered on a multitude of different topics, allowing you to choose the speeches best suited for your students. Please contact your Pearson representative for details and a complete list of videos and their contents to choose which would be most useful in your class. Samples from most of our public speaking videos are available at **www.mycoursetoolbox.com.** Some restrictions apply.

## Student Supplements

### Print Resources

**Speech Preparation Workbook**    Prepared by Jennifer Dreyer and Gregory H. Patton of San Diego State University, this workbook takes students through the various stages of speech creation—from audience analysis to writing the speech— and provides supplementary assignments and tear-out forms.

**Preparing Visual Aids for Presentations, Fifth Edition**    This 32-page visual booklet, prepared by Dan Cavanaugh, provides a host of ideas for using today's multimedia tools to improve presentations, including suggestions for planning a presentation, guidelines for designing visual aids and storyboarding, and a walkthrough that shows how to prepare a visual display using PowerPoint.

**Public Speaking in the Multicultural Environment, Second Edition**    Prepared by Devorah A. Lieberman of Portland State University, this booklet helps students learn to analyze cultural diversity within their audiences and adapt their presentations accordingly.

**Outlining Workbook**    Prepared by Reeze L. Hanson and Sharon Condon of Haskell Indian Nations University, this workbook includes activities, exercises, and answers to help students develop and master the critical skill of outlining.

**Study Card for Public Speaking**    Colorful, affordable, and packed with useful information, Pearson Allyn & Bacon's Study Cards make studying easier, more efficient, and more enjoyable. Course information is distilled down to the basics, helping students quickly master the fundamentals, review a subject for understanding, or prepare for an exam.  Because they're laminated for durability, these Study Cards can be kept for years to come and students can pull them out whenever they need a quick review.

**Multicultural Activities Workbook**    This workbook, prepared by Marlene C. Cohen and Susan L. Richardson, Prince George's Community College, Maryland, is filled with hands-on activities that help broaden the content of speech classes to reflect the diverse cultural backgrounds of the class and society. The book includes checklists, surveys, and writing assignments that all help students succeed in speech communication by offering experiences that address a variety of learning styles.

## Electronic Resources

**MySpeechLab (www.myspeechlab.com)**    Where students learn to speak with confidence! MySpeechLab is an interactive and instructive online solution for introductory public speaking.  Designed to be used as a supplement to a traditional lecture course or as a complete online course, MySpeechLab combines multimedia, video, speech preparation activities, research support, tests and quizzes to make teaching and learning fun! Students benefit from a wealth of video clips of student and professional speeches with running commentary, questions to consider, and helpful tips—all geared to help students learn to speak with confidence. Visit **www.myspeechlab.com** (access code required).

**Public Speaking Study Site**    This course-specific website features public speaking study materials for students, including flashcards and a complete set of practice tests for all major topics.  Students also will find links to websites with speeches in text, audio, and video formats, as well as links to other valuable sites. This site has been updated to include a correlation with the Pearson public speaking textbooks, making it even more valuable to your specific course. Visit **www.abpublicspeaking.com**.

**Speech Writer's Workshop CD-ROM, Version 2.0**    This speechwriting software includes a Speech Handbook with tips for researching and preparing speeches, a Speech Workshop that guides students step-by-step through the speechwriting process, a Topics Dictionary that gives students hundreds of ideas for speeches, and the Documentor citation database that helps them format bibliographic entries in either MLA or APA style.

**VideoLab CD-ROM**    This interactive study tool for students can be used independently or in class. It provides digital video of student speeches that can be viewed in conjunction with corresponding outlines, manuscripts, notecards, and instructor critiques.  A series of drills to help students analyze content and delivery follows each speech.

**VideoWorkshop for Public Speaking, Version 2.0**    The VideoWorkshop, prepared by Tasha Van Horn, Citrus College, and Marilyn Reineck, Concordia University, is a way to bring video into your course for maximized learning in public speaking. This total teaching and learning system includes quality video footage on an easy-to-use CD-ROM, plus a Student Learning Guide and an Instructor's Teaching Guide. The result? A program that brings textbook concepts to life with ease and that helps students understand, analyze, and apply the objectives of the course.

**The Allyn & Bacon Classic and Contemporary Speeches DVD**  This DVD presents a collection of over 120 minutes of video footage in an easy-to-use format. Each speech is accompanied by a biographical and historical summary that helps students understand the context and motivation behind each speech.

# Acknowledgments

We owe a great debt to instructors who took the time to review this edition and offer feedback and suggestions:

Pamela S. Bledsoe, Surry Community College
Stacy A. Freed, University of Tennessee–Martin
Brian Kline, Gainesville State College

We would also like to thank the reviewers of previous editions:

Lisa Abramson, *Western Oregon University*
David Airne, *University of Missouri–Columbia*
Robert Arend, *Miramar College*
Eugenia E. Badger, *University of Louisville*
Arlene Badura, *Schoolcraft College*
George Bang, *University of Cincinnati*
Charles Beadle, *Valdosta State University*
Rita Bova, *Columbus State Community College*
Marti Brodey, *Montgomery College*
Michael Butterworth, *College of Lake County*
Mina Casmir, *Pepperdine University*
Rick Casper, *Dawson Community College*
Bonnie Clark, *St. Petersburg College*
William F. Ferreira, *Houston Community College Southwest*
Dennis Fus, *University of Nebraska–Omaha*
Fred Garbowitz, *Grand Rapids Community College*
Carla Gesell-Streeter, *Cincinnati State Technical and Community College*
Richard Harrison, *Kilgore College*
Richard Katula, *Northeastern University*
Michael Leal, *Cameron University*
John Ludlum, *Otterbein College*
Linda Gentry Martin, *Florida Community College at Jacksonville*
Mary L. Mohan, *SUNY Geneseo*
Barry Morris, *State University of New York College–Cortland*
Rhonda Parker, *University of San Francisco*
David Payne, *University of South Florida*
Gayle Pesavento, *John A. Logan College*
Tushar Raman Oza, *Oakland University and Macomb Community College*
Renee Reeves, *Rose State College*
Sam Walch, *Pennsylvania State University, Main Campus*

A special thank you is also due to the thousands of students and instructors who have used this textbook. Their support and suggestions over the years have helped to make *Principles of Public Speaking* comprehensive and enduring. In this way, this textbook belongs to all those who have shared it.

Kathleen M. German
Bruce E. Gronbeck

# 1 | Speech, Speaking, and Training in Higher Education

At first, your body was not constructed for speech. Scientists estimate it was not until about a million years ago that our ancestors developed a throat that was big enough, a larynx that was low enough in the throat, and a neck that was long enough to create a space in our bodies suited to speech. We also needed a rounder, bigger, more agile tongue and a more well-developed nervous systems for the great range of consonants and the stream of contoured air that make up the **phonemes**—the discrete, recognizable sound units of any culture's oral language.[1] The ability to make a range of sounds was followed by developments in the brain that allowed it to process ear data and develop the patterns of neural trails and synapses needed for speaking.

**Human speech,** therefore, is **bio-basic**—sculpted into our skeleton, soft tissues and cartilage, and bodily cavities as well as the central and peripheral nervous systems. **Speaking,** however, as a symbolic transaction between people, is a different matter. It arises out of personal needs, social relationships, and cultural rules for getting along with others.

Maybe you've been wondering, "What am I doing in this class? Why am I taking public speaking?" You've been communicating for most of your life already. You've probably been successful—you've gotten this far, after all—but you can do better. Like training for a sport or mastering a musical instrument, you can improve with expert coaching and practice.

The purpose of this book is to guide you as you learn how to maximize your speaking skills, convey your ideas to others, and operate within the cultural expectations that generally govern your life with others.

## Studying Public Speaking

As a student in a public speaking class, you'll have the opportunity to engage other students while you strengthen your communication skills. Together, you can encourage each other and grow as public speakers. At first, the prospect of speaking in public might seem scary, and you'll probably make a few mistakes. That's natural, too. But, with the support of your classmates and your instructor, you'll learn how to channel your natural feelings of anxiety in positive directions so you come across as poised, prepared, and even persuasive.

At this point, you'll begin to realize that while public speaking is a **personal act,** it's also a **social act**—one involving other people. As you investigate the process of public speaking, you'll realize it is something that well-educated, community-oriented people generally do well. In fact, the importance of speech skills was recognized as long ago as 1964, when the federal government mandated speech training in the Primary and Secondary Education Act. The ability to influence social events and the actions of other people is critical in the twenty-first century.

Because public speaking is a social act, you should think seriously about the culture within which you're speaking. Speaking is also a **culturally governed act.** What are the traditional rules for public talk? What are the expected ways of speaking in specific situations? A pulpit sermon probably differs greatly from a locker room speech at halftime. How do listeners affect the speaker's message? Males and females, whites and people of color, rich and poor, Easterners and

*Studying communication helps you become a more shrewd consumer of messages.*

Westerners—all bring a unique set of expectations to the communication context. There's a lot more to think about than your own sweaty palms and pounding heart. Such rules and cultural influences are a critical part of the speech-making process, and they also account for why public speaking is mandated as a course in higher education.

There are some good reasons for enrolling in a public speaking class in higher education. Consider the following:

1. **A speech classroom is a laboratory and hence an ideal place for trying new behaviors.** You should try to develop new skills in the assigned speeches. Tell a story in the conclusion, use PowerPoint or the Web to make visual aids, or deliver a speech from in front of rather than behind a lectern. The speech classroom is a comparatively safe environment for experimentation.

2. **Practice new speech techniques on friends, in a variety of settings, and in the speech classroom.** Practicing public speaking is every bit as important as practicing musical instruments, soccer formations, or on-the-job interactions. You can't just read about speaking and then do it well. Speaking skills develop through the hit-and-miss process of practice—in the privacy of your own room, in front of friends who are willing to humor you, in other classes, and of course, in your speech classroom. Get feedback wherever you can.

3. **Work on your critical listening skills as well.** In your lifetime, you'll be exposed to thousands upon thousands of public messages in the form of speeches, classroom pitches, TV ads, and chat room exchanges. Practice in listening—trying to accurately comprehend and fairly evaluate what others say publicly—hones skills that are equally as important as speaking skills.

4. **Learn to criticize expertly the speeches of others.** You can use this book as a tool for analyzing speeches you find in print (e.g., with the *Speech Index*),[2] hear in person, or access electronically.

Through activities both inside and outside your speech classroom, speaking and analyzing the speeches of others, you will develop and refine the skills that will make you a more productive and successful member of society.

Public speaking is a primary mechanism for projecting yourself into public spaces, for bringing people together, and for getting them to share perspectives and values so they can recognize who they are and can act together. This component of **orality**—of direct, in-person, spoken connections between people—is the **social imperative.** At the heart of community life is *communication*—the give-and-take of public discussion as community members share resources and determine what actions best serve the public interest. Consider yourself as a member of an educational community. Other students in your classes and your university or college are also part of this community. When the requirements for your education were established, the voices of faculty members, administrators, business leaders, politicians, parents, and students all contributed to the discourse and ultimately to the development of the set of requirements for graduation. As social beings, we engage in communication to enhance our daily lives and resolve our differences.

Public speaking not only enables us to become better makers of messages but also to be more sophisticated receivers of public talk. This component

*Sojourner Truth (Isabella Baurnfree) found a moral basis for speaking in her opposition to slavery prior to the Civil War.*

might be referred to as the **consumer imperative.** It stresses the active role that receivers of messages play in social communities. Communication scholar Roderick Hart has written that a student of speech must engage in both "reflective complaining" and "reflective compliments," that a student must become someone "who knows when and how to render an evaluation."[3] To understand how public communication works, you must have an understanding of basic processes and varied techniques, a vocabulary for talking about both, and standards to use in making value judgments about speeches. Public speaking is as much about listening to as about making speeches.

Finally, there is an **intellectual imperative.** In fact, speech training has been an important part of a liberal arts education since Isocrates made it central to his training of the orator-statesmen of fourth-century B.C.E. Greece:

[T]he power to speak well is taken as the surest index of a sound understanding, and discourse which is true, lawful and just is the outward image of a good and faithful soul.[4]

In this grand conception, the study of human speech is the study of eloquent expressions of the human spirit. The greatest examples of public speaking endure well past the time and place they were given: Pericles' funeral oration in 427 B.C.E. over the dead of the Peloponnesian War; Abraham Lincoln's Gettysburg Address in 1863, soon after Sojourner Truth's identification of black women's problems with those of white women in "Ain't I a Woman?" and Mahatma Gandhi's message of nonviolent resistance in India, inspiring Martin Luther King, Jr.'s "I Have a Dream" speech at the Washington Monument in 1963. You must understand, clearly and unmistakably, that public speaking is about more than you and your problems. In times of crisis and public doubt, it is about the human condition. You take courses in public speaking to improve your self-confidence and sense of personal empowerment, of course, but also for social, self-protective, and intellectual reasons. We begin by looking at the role of orality in social-political life.

## Orality in Social-Political Life

So, then, you might ask, "Why all the stress on public speaking, on oral communication?" You're literate. You can write a letter or e-mail, or call or text someone on your cell phone. You can participate in a blog or chat room with other people who have the same interests that you do, bring up a podcast, or even e-mail your congressional representative. And then there are radio and TV call-in programs, minicams for making movies that you can distribute electronically, fax machines, and on and on. So why do presidents still give televised speeches, teachers still offer classroom lectures, business teams still make oral presentations, and lawyers make opening and closing courtroom speeches?

*There's something essentially, engagingly, powerfully human about speaking publicly to others.* That's it, period. As far back as anyone can trace tribal relationships, human beings have built their relationships with others—from parents to politicians—through face-to-face talk. Speech flows directly out of your mouth and into the ears of others; your movements, vocal tones of sadness or excitement, bodily tensions, and facial displays are directly accessible to those who watch and listen. That sort of person-to-person contact in public, that sheer mutual presence, simply cannot be reproduced on paper, through electronically boosted sound waves, or via video or digital pictures.

The centrality of orality cannot be denied. Edward Hall argued almost fifty years ago that the "biological roots" of "all culture" could be found in speech,[5] while more recently, Walter Ong urged us to remember that the "sounded word" is a tremendous source of "power and action."[6]

It is through words that you act on others—calling them ("Hey you!"), singling them out ("Come here, Eugenia!"), recognizing their group identity ("Remember the Titans!" or the gladiators' "We who are about to die salute you!"). The ancients even practiced word magic—that is, they found supernatural power in oral incantations. Speaking calls up important events by creating an identity and the motivations that flow from them. In past years, the battle cry "Remember the Alamo!" roused Texans to fight Santa Anna's Mexican army. Today, speakers ask us to recall from our memory the events that took place in 2001 when they say "Remember 9/11." These words provide a reason for listeners to act together in particular ways.

What makes face-to-face, oral communication so important to groups? Media theorist Walter Ong has identified a series of characteristics of orality, and his list includes the following items, among others:

1. **Speech tends to be integrative.** In speech, you often draw together ideas or stereotypes held by the group, attaching them to people and events. References in oral speech to "workable" or "practical" plans, "glorious" dawns and "star-lit" skies, and the like come off as clichés in written language but are used regularly in oral language because of their familiarity and shared use across groups. Speech thus integrates members of a society by identifying the values that are shared across peoples. Speeches, therefore, not only are about something, a *policy*, but they simultaneously are about reassembling a group, a *polity*.

2. **Speech tends to be redundant.** You often repeat yourself in public speaking, saying the same thing in more than one way. Notice that the last sentence could have ended at the comma, for the point was presumably clear. In speech, however, the second half likely would have been added, giving listeners a chance to catch the point again in case it wasn't clear in its first phrasing. That's oral language: redundant or repetitious, with backlooping to help people keep up with the flow of the conversation.

3. **Speech tends to be traditionalist.** A group's traditional beliefs and values usually are reflected in public oral language. Sayings such as "A bird in the hand is worth two in the bush" or "Better safe than sorry" capture traditional beliefs for many Westerners: Don't risk what you already have for something that could go wrong. Such sayings live in oral culture and so tend to appear in speeches. Oral communication draws on traditional community beliefs and values, which so often mark speechmaking.

4. **Speech tends to be concrete.** You might write "Relationships between blacks and whites in America are complex," but in a speech, you're more likely to be effective if you get specific: "While blacks and whites in the state of Iowa tend to be separated, in Iowa City the university draws them together, standing in the same lines at John's Grocery, drinking beer at the Sports Column and coffee at the Java House, listening to live music side by side on the Ped Mall. Sharing not only classrooms but life situations means that blacks and whites in Iowa City cannot ignore each other." Here, the concrete references to particular places in the neighboring environment help listeners visualize ideas—an important feature in oral communication.

5. **Speech is agonistically toned.**[7] That is Ong's phrase. It suggests that when people gather together to make decisions, things can get heated. It's as though public speaking is taking the place of ancient rituals of combat. One can disengage when writing, but not so in speech. Speech is personal, flowing out of your mouth and body; it's you who performs it. Writing can be circulated when you're not there and so is more distanced. Speech is immediate, personal—and therein lies its feistiness and its power.

6. **Speech is participatory.** The audience likewise is personally involved. Listeners are part of the speech process. They're often addressed directly, even personally. So you might say, "How many of you have plans to stop at the Bloodmobile at the Student Union today? How many? How about you, Jill—are you going? Jake? Lisa? Maurice?" You cannot make someone else read something, but you have a very good chance of making them listen—of making them participate in public interaction.

7. **Speech is situational.** It occurs in the here and now. You can read a newspaper in the bathroom or a book chapter tonight after supper, but speaking happens right here, right now. At its best, a public speech deals with issues that are visible in the immediate situation, in the actual lives of listeners who are there. If listeners don't know that, you've got to convince them: "So how many of you have stopped for a drink at a fountain in one of the university buildings today? How many times do you stop at a drinking fountain during a week? Three? Four? Even if you take a drink only three times a week, you have about a 1-in-20 chance of ingesting enough lead to make you sick." As a speaker, you must make water quality relevant to your listeners' lives.

So oral culture tends to be dominated publicly by speech communication that is integrative, redundant, traditionalist, concrete, agonistically toned, participatory, and situational. All of these characteristics suggest that public speaking is a dynamic process.

## ■ Basic Elements in the Speech-Making Process

Public speaking is an **interactive process**. That is, it is a transaction or exchange among people in public settings. Four basic elements of speaking work together to create the speech process—a speaker, a message, listeners, and the context (see Figure 1.1). Let's consider each of these four basic elements:

The **speaker** is the source of the message. As the primary communicator in the public speaking situation, the speaker brings an individual perspective, identity, and experience to the communication transaction.

**Figure 1.1** Public Speaking Is an Interactive Process

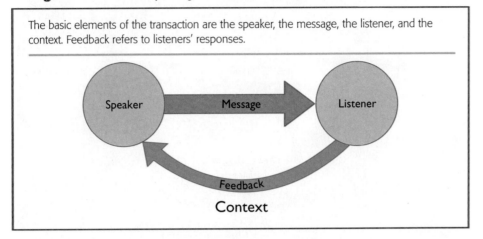

The basic elements of the transaction are the speaker, the message, the listener, and the context. Feedback refers to listeners' responses.

The **message** comprises both the factual content of the speech and the speaker's attitudes and values on the topic. The message is transmitted by selecting words and ideas, then arranging them in a particular pattern.

The **listener** (someone who receives and interprets your message) is also a partner in the speech transaction. You may think of public speaking as communication flowing in only one direction, from speaker to listener, but that is not an entirely accurate picture. Listeners bring prior knowledge, attitudes, and interests to the speech situation. They also provide verbal and nonverbal **feedback**, such as frowns, laughter, yawns, or questions. Feedback refers to messages your listeners send to you before, during, and after your speech. Also, competent speakers always take into account their listeners' central beliefs, attitudes, values, and life experiences when assembling messages.

Speakers and listeners engage each other in a **context**. Some parts of the communication context are obvious, such as the physical setting in which the speech takes place. Other elements, however, are more subtle. The context of the speech also includes the social expectations and cultural rules that come into play when speakers and listeners interact.

To understand how the basic elements function in the communication process, consider a professor teaching an introductory class in, say, social work. As a speaker, that instructor must convey a sense of professionalism (he or she knows the subject matter and participates regularly in professional activities as either a caseworker in the field or a scholar at conventions) and pedagogical expertise (he or she knows how to teach beginners, orally, in a step-by-step fashion). Messages (lectures, discussions) are constructed in such a way that social work practice is clearly outlined, with factual information clearly distinguishable from opinion or judgment. A careful listener can come out of those lectures and discussion sessions with a clear, concrete set of notes. As that last point suggests, the listener—say, you—does have an important role here. You enter into a kind of contract with that professor: If he or she offers relevant material in clear and engaging ways, you agree to record it, question it, and use it to write tests or papers. You agree, at least during that class in that term, to absorb and use the material, at least within the classroom context. You also agree to give the teacher

*A speaker engages listeners in a setting or context.*

feedback—asking questions in class, responding to a course evaluation form, and perhaps even face-to-face comments—just as the professor agrees to read and fairly evaluate your social work and skills.

So professors and students generally have clearly defined communication roles, expectations about messages, and usually shared conceptions of what ought to be going on in classrooms. If both speaker and listener understand what's expected of them in a particular context, the public speaking interaction satisfies both parties.

## Ethical Responsibilities for Speakers

Because public speaking is an interactive process, you have certain responsibilities to your listeners—and they to you. Each time you speak publicly, you are contributing to a process of community building and affecting the lives of others. The act of speaking therefore always involves making ethical choices. You must consider how you are looking, ethically, to your audience; that is the matter of **ethos.** And you have to take into account the **moral frames** of your listeners if you want to convince them of anything.

### Ethos in the Western World

The English word ***ethics*** is derived from the Greek word *ethos*. Actually, we still use that word, to mean something like credibility or reputation. It had a larger meaning, however, in ancient Greece. The speaker was inextricably bound to the community. To Aristotle, a person who had ethos demonstrated while speaking

---

## SPEAKING OF ...
## E T H I C S

### Ethics and Public Speaking

Occasionally, we'll include a boxed area devoted to "ethical moments"—ethical decisions that public speakers must make in preparing and delivering their talks. We hope that you'll take a moment to think about the problems presented and their solutions in your life. You might discuss some of these problems with others to get alternative perspectives.

Here are some typical ethical questions that you might face in the speeches you'll give this term:

1. You read a fascinating article about fund-raising ideas for organizations. Should you borrow these ideas and present them as your own at your next club meeting? Do you need to acknowledge everything you learn from others? Must you always cite sources?

2. An article says exactly what you intended to say about the use of tanning beds. Then you find a more recent article claiming that new research contradicts the first article. Should you ignore the new evidence?

3. An authority whom you wish to cite uses the words *perhaps, probably, likely,* and *often.* Should you strike these words from the quotation to make it sound more positive? After all, you're not tinkering with the ideas, only with the strength of assertion.

Ethical decisions such as these will confront you regularly, both in your speech classroom and throughout the rest of your life. Take a few moments now to consider such situations and to articulate your position. Identify your moral standards before you face ethical dilemmas on the platform.

---

that he or she shared characteristics with others in the community—that is, had good sense, good will, and good morals.[8]

- *Good sense.* To demonstrate to others that one is talking from a position of experience and knowledge, of information tempered by personal experience (i.e., to talk knowledgably).

- *Good will.* To communicate a sense of caring about oneself and more importantly about the audience members, their needs, their status, and their future (i.e., to talk caringly). A speech is a **negotiative process,**[9] one in which speakers are working to offer their views in the hopes of coming to a common accommodation with listeners.

- *Good morals.* To speak in the language of the beliefs and values of the listeners, to share their visions, their fears, their hopes, their cultural imperatives (i.e., to talk morally).

Ethos for the Greeks was thus an orientation to life that individuals shared with their community. They knew and understood what their communities held as important, shared commitments, and lived out those commitments in public talk. Ethos was a multifaceted idea, reflecting what people knew, cared about, and used as guidelines for living.

That such an understanding of ethos is relevant today can be seen in public opinions about President Bill Clinton during the 1990s. In surveys about his personal morals, he tended to score very low; usually fewer than a quarter of the respondents believed that he was personally moral. Yet if those same people were asked who understood the country's needs and knew where to lead them, he was supported by 60 percent or more of the country, and if they were asked which politician cared about them, more than two-thirds of the respondents believed that he did. President Clinton demonstrated that the Greek standards for ethos could sustain a politician in office even if his personal life was questionable.[10]

## The Moral Bases of Public Decision Making

We likewise must understand that the word *moral* comes from the Latin word *mores*, which referred to what most people believed to be important guidelines for shared values and activity. More recently, scholar Stephen Carter calls **civility**—that is, the commitment to a civic life—"the sum of the many sacrifices we are called upon to make for the sake of living together. . . . We should make sacrifices for others not simply because doing so makes social life easier (although it does), but as a signal of respect for our fellow citizens, marking them as full equals, both before the law and before God."[11]

The idea of public morality or civility therefore encompasses ethical commitments to community standards. To act in accordance with community beliefs and values, however, is to work with moral frames—shared values or ways of looking at and valuing the world. Two implications of understanding community beliefs and values as moral frames for handling disagreement or differences are especially important to public speakers:

**1. To be successful, you must find some moral frame you share with your listeners if you're going to convince them that you have their best interests at heart.** Donald Moon calls this the **skyhook principle**.[12] You often speak to people whose backgrounds differ from yours, who hold different—even what have been called incommensurate or absolutely opposed—values. How can you convince people who hold values that are in conflict with yours to do anything? Moon's answer is: Find a skyhook. Find a higher value, a higher appeal, that will transcend your differences.

An excellent example of this principle comes from the world of presidential campaigning. Candidates rolled through state after state in 2007–2008. States in the southwest worried especially about border issues, while states in the midwest were more concerned with the economy, international trade, and job retraining programs. Early on, the war in Iraq dominated conversation, giving way to social-conservative issues when Governor Mike Huckabee made them central to the Republican caucuses and primaries. So how could the candidates find general, moral frames that would carry them across the patchwork of citizens' interests and needs in different parts of the country?

Barak Obama chose a "faith and hope" frame, assembling appeals to citizenry vis-à-vis corporate and political values. Hillary Clinton went for an "experience" frame that valued both citizen consultation and talent in negotiating politically to get things done. Mike Huckabee pushed "conservative values" as a framework for all of his policy proposals, while John McCain presented himself as a long-standing patriot who in practical ways could bring together both Republicans and Democrats to re-energize the country. In Campaign 2008, large moral frames, accompanied by a vision of what the country is and should be like, were of paramount importance.

*More people heard Pope John Paul II (1920–2005) speak than any other human being in history.*

**2. To find a shared moral frame, you must be true to what you believe.** Throughout his lifetime, Pope John Paul II sacrificed none of his own deeply seated, politically democratic beliefs and theologically conservative values even as he reached out to citizens of European Communist countries and to theologians in Central America who found him too anti-progressive. He retained his integrity. You too should always be looking for moral frames that you share with your listeners—not ones that only they accept, but also ones from which you both work. Then you'll be both true to yourself and relevant to your audience.

The moral bases for public speaking therefore are not merely ethical or religious tenets, though these can be a part of the moral bases for community. They are broader than that: They're all of the frames—social, psychological, legal, economic, scientific, philosophical, political, and religious—that human beings in a community generally understand and even largely (though not necessarily universally) accept and live by. In communities as diverse and multicultural as those of the United States, the search for workable moral frames will become one of your most important tasks as a public speaker when you set out to persuade people to change their minds or behaviors.

## Your First Speech

Now it's time to get you started—up on your feet and ready to converse with others in your classroom. Your first speech should follow a few simple guidelines.

## SPEAKING OF . . .
# APPREHENSION

### First-Time Fears

When you get up to speak for the first time, the biggest thing on your mind will most likely be stage fright. Some fears can be overwhelming, interrupting good ideas and stopping otherwise great thoughts dead in their tracks.

The key is to use your anxiety to energize your performance. Expect that you'll be anxious, but don't let it get the best of you. The rush of adrenaline that comes just before you get up to speak should be used to fuel your speech. Below are some tips to help you cope with stage fright:

1. *Prepare ahead of time.* Uncertainty about what you're going to say just adds to the anxiety. You don't need that.

2. *Breathe slowly and deeply.* You can't expect to support your voice and movement without oxygen.

3. *Think about your ideas.* Concentrate on what you're sharing with your listeners, not on how you're feeling.

4. *Don't let your imagination run wild.* A listener who yawns probably didn't get enough sleep last night. Make it your goal to keep that person awake during your speech.

5. *Brace yourself for the natural physical symptoms of adrenaline.* Expect damp palms, a dry throat, or your own peculiar symptoms.

Above all, give yourself a break. Don't expect perfection the first time you speak—or even the second. Speaking well sometimes takes years of practice. Give yourself a chance, and take every opportunity to develop and polish your skills.

Structuring the speech in three main parts—the introduction, the body, and the conclusion—works well. Begin by clearly stating your main or central idea in your introduction. Doing so will help listeners follow your ideas through to the end of your speech. Likewise, your last few sentences should recapture the main idea of your speech to wrap it up and give it a sense of finality. Most speakers draw on their own knowledge as they develop their ideas. Notice how a beginning student, Delores Lopez, used her own experiences in her first speech assignment, "Who Am I?" Delores explains why she is in a public speaking class:

One word that describes my life is "change." Ever since I can remember, things around me have constantly changed. I'm forty-two years old and as I look back, I see lots of change.

When I was a kid, a high school education was enough. My parents didn't go to college; no one in my family did. Although education was respected in my family, there wasn't enough money for us to go on to school. My dad was partially disabled in an industrial accident and we depended on my mom's job to support us. While I was in high school, I had a weekend job and after graduating, I found a full-time job to help support my younger brothers and sisters. At the time, I never considered going to college. It wouldn't have mattered if I had wanted to go. I didn't have the time or money. But things have changed. After I had my oldest son, my mom took care of him and I went back to work. Now he's seventeen and I want him to go to school—to have an opportunity I didn't have. I want his life to be different than mine has been.

My life has changed, too. The corporation where I work has been downsizing and looking for leadership within the ranks. My supervisor has encouraged me to go back to school. She thought I was smart enough to make it, and I know I can study hard. The company is even paying part of my tuition. In this economic climate I realize that to be without higher education is to be more disadvantaged than ever. Maybe those of you who don't have kids don't realize the financial pressures of raising kids.

There is one skill that is in demand in my company. They're looking for leadership qualities in their employees—especially the ability to present oneself and communicate well with others. That's why I decided to take this class in public speaking. As you can see, there has been a lot of change in my life. Some of those changes have come from outside—my job, my family. But, I'm changing inside, too. I am more confident about what I want in my life and I'm finding ways to meet my goals. I'm looking forward to working with all of you; I think we can learn from each other.

Notice how Delores' speech was divided into three main sections. In the introduction, she mentioned the theme of change. She elaborated on that idea by tracing changes in her own life, building on what she knew best, her own experiences. Examples from her family supported and elaborated the theme. Delores answers the question "Who Am I?" by explaining how she has come to be in her public speaking class. The final sentences of the speech summarize the main theme of change. Of course, there's more to consider as you develop your skills in public speaking. Chapter 2 will give you additional advice to get you started.

## Assessing Your Progress

### Chapter Summary

1. Human speech became possible only through the slow development of bodily and brain features and functions—it's bio-basic. Speaking, however, also depended upon symbolic interaction. Sounds and signs had to form oral and written languages.

2. Training in public speaking develops your public identity and helps others work out problems in their communities.

3. The speech classroom gives you a unique opportunity to practice your speaking skills on a live audience, get feedback from listeners, and become a more critical consumer of oral messages and more expert critic of speechmaking in general.

4. There are social, consumer, and intellectual imperatives for studying public speaking.

5. Orality—direct, in-person connections—is central to social life and hence is relevant to your successes even in a print- and electronically oriented world.

6. Oral culture is dominated by public communication that is integrative, redundant, traditionalist, concrete, agonistically toned, participatory, and situational.

7. Speaking is a transaction involving a speaker, listeners, and a message within a context.

8. Listeners attribute ethos, or credibility, to speakers on the basis of their perceptions of the speakers' good sense, good will, and good morals. In turn, speakers must learn to work within listeners' moral frames if they're to succeed.

9. Your first speech should have an introduction, a body, and a conclusion that develop a main or central idea.

## Assessment Activities

Throughout this book, we'll include at least one "Assessment Activity," designed to help your instructor gain a perspective on your public speaking competency levels. In turn, you should be able to get a picture in this way of your strengths and weaknesses as a speech maker, helping you target areas for development and dimensions of speech making where you are moving from levels of basic competency to higher-level proficiency. In this activity, develop a short speech similar to the one by Delores Lopez. Your instructor will not grade but, rather, give you a basic assessment of your ability to construct messages, arrange them in introductions/bodies/conclusions, use appropriate oral language, deliver speeches effectively with voice and body, and take listeners into account in your construction of speeches. Consider this assessment a kind of baseline from which you'll work this semester.

For additional chapter activities, log on to MySpeechLab at www.myspeechlab .com.

## Using the Web

We also will include a web-based exercise. Here's one for starters:

Professor Harry J. Gensler has an interesting Web site on ethics. Go to www .jcu.edu/philosophy/gensler/exercises.htm. Drop down to and click on the segment about the Golden Rule—must reading for public speakers. You even can look at part of a lecture he gave on the topic at Bard College. If you've not had enough, drop down farther on the Web site and check out the Web-based materials on abortion, assessing the ethical appropriateness of arguments and fear appeals used on both sides of that debate.

## References

1. See Susan A. Greenfield, ed., *Human Mind Explained: An Owner's Guide to the Mysteries of the Mind* (New York: Henry Holt, 1996), 134–135.

2. Roberta Briggs Sutton, ed., *Speech Index: An Index to 259 Collections of World Famous Orations and Speeches for Various Occasions*, 4th ed. rev. & enl. (Metuchen, NJ: Scarecrow Press, 1966); and Charity Mitchell, *Speech Index: An Index to Collections of World Famous Orations and Speeches for Various Occasions*, 4th ed. suppl. 1966–1980 (Metuchen, NJ: Scarecrow Press, 1982). Also use Internet search engines to find various collections of speeches. Start at "Speeches and Speechmakers" at www.uiowa.edu/~commstud/ resources/index.html. You might look especially at www.presidentialrhetoric.com for, yes, presidential speeches and www.douglassarchives.org for a much broader range of texts and videos.

3. Roderick P. Hart, *Modern Rhetorical Criticism*, 2nd ed. (Boston: Allyn & Bacon, 1997), 34.

4. Isocrates, *Isocrates II* [including *Antidosis*], trans. George Norlin (Cambridge, MA: Harvard University Press, 1927), 327.

5. Edward T. Hall, *The Silent Language* (orig. pub. 1959; New York: Fawcett World Library, 1966), 37.

6. Walter J. Ong, *Orality and Literacy: The Technologizing of the Word* (orig. pub. 1982; New York: Routledge, 1988), 31.

7. Ibid., pp. 43–45.

8. Aristotle, *Rhetoric*, 1378a.

9. For conceptually solid and practical approach to negotiation as a communication process, see Roger Fisher and Daniel Shapiro, *Beyond Reason: Using Emotions as You Negotiate* (New York: Penguin Group USA, 2006). Their emphasis on the place of emotions in communication relationships will take you directly into the idea of ethos, as based in part on your ability to feel your audience's concerns, taking them into account as you make proposals.

10. When you wish to follow trends in public opinion polls, a good place to go on the Web is www.pollingreport.com, which assembles multiple polls, especially on political topics.

11. Stephen L. Carter, *Civility: Manners, Morals, and the Etiquette of Democracy* (New York: HarperPerennial, 1998), 11.

12. Donald Moon, *Constructing Community: Moral Pluralism and Tragic Conflicts* (Princeton, NJ: Princeton University Press, 1993), esp. 20–21.

# 2 | Getting Started

You learned about your role as a public speaker in our society in Chapter 1. While there's a lot to discover about speech making, you can learn enough about the basics to begin speaking right away. As you prepare to speak, you'll probably ask questions such as these:

- How do I choose a topic?
- What will my listeners want to hear?
- Where do I find the material for my speech?
- What kind of notes should I make?
- What's the best way to practice delivering my speech?

By answering these questions now, you'll be well on your way to success. The key to effective speech-making is planning. You can save time and effort by planning carefully.

There's no magic formula for speaking. However, if you follow the seven steps offered in this chapter—either as they are presented here or in another order that works for you—you'll be ready for your audience. By the end of this chapter, you'll have mastered the basic steps for delivering your first speeches.

## CHAPTER OUTLINE

Selecting and Narrowing Your Subject

*Speaking of . . . Skills: Brainstorming to Generate Topics*

Determining Your Purposes and Central Idea

Analyzing the Audience and Occasion

Gathering Your Speech Material

Making an Outline

Practicing Aloud

Developing Confident Delivery

*Speaking of . . . Skills: Practicing Your Speech*

*Speaking of . . . Apprehension: State and Trait Apprehension*

Assessing Your Progress

## KEY TERMS

# Selecting and Narrowing Your Subject

The most difficult task for many speakers is to choose a subject. Sometimes the subject is chosen for you, but often you will choose your own topic for classroom speeches. Begin by asking yourself questions. What do you know something about? What are you interested in talking about? What topics will interest your listeners? Does the occasion or situation suggest a topic for discussion? It's important to answer these questions carefully. Your answers will help you select and narrow your subject. A well-chosen topic is the first step to a successful speech. Let's examine in more detail the processes of choosing and narrowing a topic.

It's a good idea to begin selecting a topic by listing those subjects you already know something about, choosing the ones you'd like to share with others, and thinking about ways you can relate them to your listeners. If the purpose of your first classroom speech is to inform your classmates about a subject, you might come up with the following list of things you know something about:

Baseball (you played baseball in high school)
Sharks (you did a science project on this subject)
Halloween (it's your favorite holiday and you love to make costumes)
YouTube (you've uploaded several videos of yourself rocking out on your
    electric guitar)
*CSI* (it's your favorite TV show)
Smoking (you quit two years ago)
Careers in accounting (you're considering them now)
Photography (you like taking amateur photos)
Skin cancer (you're worried about the effects of tanning booths)

Next, you need to consider the people who make up your audience. Which topics would interest your classmates most? When you ask yourself this question, you realize that several topics, such as making Halloween costumes, careers in accounting, and photography, are mainly of interest to you. If you can come up with ways to involve your listeners in these topics, they could work, but otherwise, you should probably cross them off your list.

You should also think about your listeners' expectations. What do they already know, and what do they expect to learn? They may already know more than you do about TV shows and YouTube. Unless you plan to do a lot of research, you'll likely want to eliminate these topics from your list. Now you should have a narrower list of potential topics—those that will interest your audience and meet your listeners' expectations.

After some additional thought, you decide to inform your classmates about sharks, because you've done a lot of research on this subject and know that you can arouse their interest. Once you've determined your general subject, you can generate a list of subtopics, including the following:

Types of sharks
Life cycle of the shark
Endangered species of sharks
Shark habitats and habits
Famous shark stories

**Brainstorming to Generate Topics**

Having trouble coming up with possible speech topics? Try this brainstorming exercise:

1. Get a large, blank sheet of paper and a pencil, or open up a blank word processing document on your computer.

2. On the left-hand side of the paper, write the letters of the alphabet in a column. If you're using a computer, create two columns with 26 rows, and put the letters of the alphabet in the first column.

3. Then, as quickly as you can, write down or type single words beginning with each of the letters. Write or type any word that comes to your mind. Repeat until you have the entire sheet filled. You might begin like this: A—apples, alphabet, alarm, alimony; B—bazaar, balsa, baboon, bassoon, balloon; C—comics, cologne, colors, confetti.

4. Next, consider each of the words as a key to potential topics. For example, *apples* might suggest apple pie recipes, Johnny Appleseed and other early American legends, pesticide controversies, fruit in our diets, farm and orchard subsidies, or government price controls of farm produce. This is just the beginning. From one key word, you can derive many possible speech topics.

5. Obviously, not all of these topics would be great speech topics, but this exercise gives you a creative and quick way to generate lots of ideas.

Sharks as a source of human food
Movies about sharks
Shark cartilage as a potential cure for cancer
Shark attacks
Historical evolution of the shark

From this list of subtopics, ask yourself additional questions to narrow the topic even further. How much time do I have to deliver this speech? What do my classmates already know about the topic? Can I group some of these ideas together? After you answer these questions, you may end up with an informative speech focusing on three topics that cluster around the characteristics of sharks:

Types of sharks
Life cycle of the shark
Shark attacks

As you can see from this example, you begin with a broad list of potential topics. Then, you select those that reflect your knowledge, the expectations of your listeners, and the requirements of the occasion. Finally, you consider the possible subtopics and choose several that fit the time limits and that go together naturally. This kind of systematic topic selection is the first step in successful speaking. The next step is to identify your speaking purposes and central idea.

# Determining Your Purposes and Central Idea

Once you know what you want to talk about, you need to ask yourself still more questions. Why do you wish to discuss this subject? Why might an audience want to listen to you? Is what you're discussing appropriate to the occasion? To answer these questions, you must analyze the reasons for your speech. First, think about the **general purpose**, the primary reason you will speak in public. Next, consider your **specific purposes**, the concrete goals you wish to achieve in a particular speech. Finally, focus your thoughts on a central idea, the statement guiding the thoughts you wish to communicate.

## General Purposes

If you examine most speeches, you'll identify one of three *general purposes:* to inform, to persuade, or to entertain. This chart summarizes the general purposes for speaking:

| General Purpose | Audience Response Sought |
| --- | --- |
| To inform | Clear understanding |
| To persuade | Acceptance of ideas or behaviors |
| To entertain | Enjoyment and comprehension |

Throughout this book, we will emphasize speeches to inform and speeches to persuade. These types of speeches dominate the speaking occasions you'll face in life.

*You should practice your speaking skills whenever the opportunity arises.*

**Speaking to Inform** When you speak *to inform,* your general purpose is to help your listeners expand their knowledge—of an idea, a concept, or a process. This is the aim of scientists who gather at the International AIDS Conference to report their research results to colleagues, of presidential press secretaries who make public announcements, of job supervisors who explain the operation of new equipment, and of professors in your college classes.

To create understanding, you must change the level or quality of information possessed by your listeners. They should leave your speech knowing more than they did before they heard it. For example, you might inform your classmates about herbal medicine, photographic composition, laser surgery, Web page construction, tornadoes, Individual Retirement Accounts, anorexia nervosa, the Tet Offensive, or any number of topics. If you talk about laser surgery, for instance, assume that they may already have some knowledge. To increase their understanding, you will need to focus on innovative techniques using lasers, such as LASIK and dental surgery. You might even speculate about how lasers will change standard surgical procedures in the future. By providing explanations, examples, statistics, and illustrations, you expand your listeners' knowledge. Your goal as an informative speaker is to impart both knowledge and overall understanding.

**Speaking to Persuade** If you seek to influence listeners' beliefs and actions, then your purpose is *to persuade*. Celebrities sell us diet plans, cars, and shampoos; lawyers convince jurors to recommend the death penalty; activists exhort tenants to stand up to their landlords; politicians debate taxes.

As a persuasive speaker, you usually seek to influence the beliefs and attitudes of your listeners. You might want to convince them that John F. Kennedy was shot by several assassins, that education is the cornerstone of freedom, or that life exists after death. Sometimes, however, you will want to persuade your listeners to act. You might want them to contribute money to the humane society, sign a petition against a landfill project, vote for a new tax levy, or boycott a local grocery store. In this type of persuasive speech, called a *speech to actuate,* you ask your listeners for specific actions. You might ask your classmates to quit watching TV, cut back on caffeine consumption, donate blood, sign prenuptial agreements, start stock portfolios, or register to vote.

**Speaking to Entertain** Sometimes a speaker's general purpose may be *to entertain.* The goal is to amuse and divert listeners so that they relax and enjoy themselves. After-dinner speeches, travel lectures, and even commencement addresses can be highly entertaining. Gatherings of friends and associates may provide the occasions for such speeches.

Humor is often used, although speeches to entertain are not simply comic monologues. While a lecture on the customs of another culture may entertain an audience with amusing anecdotes, a great deal of information can be presented. As you can see, the skills required are subtle and often difficult to master, because they combine enjoyment with comprehension.

To inform, to persuade, and to entertain are the general purposes of speaking. By thinking about general purposes, you identify your overall speaking goal. The next step is to focus on the specific purposes of your speech.

## Specific Purposes

Your *specific purpose* combines your general purpose for speaking with your topic. For example, if your topic is aircraft and your general purpose is to inform, then your specific purpose might be to inform your audience about the role of aircraft in military combat or to provide them with a history of aircraft design. If your general purpose is to persuade, then your specific purpose might be to persuade your listeners that safety regulations governing air travel ought to be changed. The specific purpose provides a focus for your speech by combining your general purpose with the topic of your speech.

While some specific purposes are public, others are private—known only to you. For example, you probably hope you'll make a good impression on an audience, although you're not likely to say that aloud. Some purposes are short term; others are long term. If you're speaking to members of a local organization about the importance of recycling, your short-term purpose might be to convince them to save their aluminum cans, while your long-term purpose could be to gather support for a citywide recycling program.

You may have several private and public short-term and long-term specific purposes whenever you speak, but it is important to identify one dominant specific purpose to guide your speech preparation. A single specific purpose, one that you can articulate for an audience, focuses you on precisely what you want your audience to understand, believe, or do.

Suppose that you wanted to take on the challenge of getting more of your classmates to use electronic databases. Consider various ways of wording your specific purpose:

- "The purpose of my speech is to explain how electronic retrieval systems can put the resources of other libraries at your fingertips." (understanding)
- "The purpose of my speech is to show my listeners that computers are good for much more than chatting online or playing games." (beliefs)
- "The purpose of my speech is to get my classmates to search electronic databases for their next speech." (action)

All of these purposes involve electronic databases, yet each has a different specific focus, making it a different speech. Locking onto a specific purpose allows you to zero in on your primary target.

## Central Ideas

Once you've settled on a specific purpose for your speech, you're ready to compose a sentence that expresses it. You need to capture the controlling thought of your speech to guide its development. This **central idea** (sometimes called a *thesis statement*) is a statement that captures, usually in a single sentence, the essence of the information or concept you wish to communicate to an audience. For example, your central idea for a speech on diamonds might be "The value of a diamond is largely determined by four factors: color, cut, clarity, and carat."

In a persuasive speech, the central idea phrases the belief, attitude, or action you want an audience to adopt. Your central idea for a persuasive speech on dieting might be "Avoid fad diets, because they create dangerous imbalances in essential nutrients."

The precise phrasing of central ideas is very important, because wording conveys the essence of your subject matter, setting up audience expectations. Examine Table 2.1 for examples of ways to word speech purposes. Then, assume that you've decided to give an informative speech on fixing a leaky faucet. You might phrase your central idea in one of three ways:

- "With only minimal mechanical skills, anyone can fix a leaky faucet."
- "With a few simple supplies, you can fix a leaky faucet for less than $10."
- "Fixing a leaky faucet yourself will give you a sense of accomplishment as well as free you from depending on plumbers for making home repairs."

Note that the phrasing of the central idea controls the emphasis of the speech. The first version stresses the individual audience member's ability to

**TABLE 2.1** Speaking Purposes

This table provides a guide to the relationships among the general purpose, specific purpose, and central idea of your speech.

| General Purpose | Specific Purpose | Central Idea |
|---|---|---|
| To help your listeners understand an idea, concept, or process (to inform) | To teach your listeners about rip currents | "More dangerous than tornadoes, hurricanes, or earthquakes, rip currents claim more lives each year than any other natural hazard." |
| To influence your listeners' actions (to persuade) | To get your listeners to walk to classes this week (short-term goal)<br><br>To get your listeners to develop a fitness program (long-term goal) | "You should start a fitness program today to improve the quality of your life." |
| To influence your listeners' thoughts (to persuade) | To increase your listeners' appreciation of the role of pure scientific research | "Basic scientific research is the foundation for discoveries in medicine, agriculture, business, and everyday life." |

complete the task. Presumably, that speech would offer a step-by-step description of the repair process. The second version suggests a quite different speech, one that is focused on securing the inexpensive supplies. In contrast, the third version concentrates on benefits to the listener.

The process of selecting your subject, determining your general and specific purposes, and phrasing your central idea is the process of narrowing. When you put it all together, here is the result for an informative speech:

SUBJECT: Plumbing repair

GENERAL PURPOSE: To inform

SPECIFIC PURPOSE: To explain how you can fix a leaky faucet

CENTRAL IDEA: Most leaky faucets require a new washer that you can install in less than an hour for about $2.00.

For a persuasive speech, you will probably go through a similar process of determining a topic based on your background and the needs of your listeners. However, your general purpose is different, and this means you must phrase your specific purpose and central idea with the goal of persuading your listeners. Here's an example:

SUBJECT: Saving for retirement

GENERAL PURPOSE: To persuade

SPECIFIC PURPOSE: To convince your listeners that they need a savings plan for retirement

CENTRAL IDEA: Most social retirement plans will fall short of your needs, but you can retire in comfort if you make wise savings decisions now.

Work on your general and specific purposes before constructing your speech. Your speaking purposes clarify your relationship to your audience. They also guide your search for speech materials.

## Analyzing the Audience and Occasion

Communication is a two-way street. That means you need to consider your listeners when you are preparing to speak. It's tempting to focus only on yourself—your goals, your fears, and your own interests. If you want to speak so that you reach others, however, then you must construct the speech from your listeners' viewpoint.

Responsible speakers regularly ask questions such as "How would I feel about this topic if I were in their place?" or "How can I adapt this material to their interests and habits, especially if their experiences or understandings are different from mine?" Putting yourself in your listeners' shoes is what researchers call **audience orientation**—an ability to understand the listener's point of view. Being audience-oriented will push you to construct speeches from the receiving end of the communication process, investigating aspects of the audience's demographic and psychological background that are relevant to your speech. Chapter 5 takes up the topic of audience orientation in detail.

For now, you should find out how much your listeners already know about your subject so that you can adjust to their level of understanding. You should also discover their attitudes toward your subject. If they are apathetic, you must create interest; if they are hostile or favorable, you must adapt what you say. In a public speaking class, this type of investigation is easy enough to conduct—start asking questions. After all, your whole purpose in speaking is to connect with your listeners!

*Your listeners and their expectations should guide your speech preparation.*

It is also important to consider the nature and purpose of the occasion on which you're speaking. The occasion is what brings people together; consequently, it often determines listeners' expectations. Do they expect to hear a comic monologue? Does the situation demand a serious approach, such as a lecture? Will your listeners be tired, wide awake, or distracted by outside noises? Is this a voluntary or a captive audience? How many people will attend? Will the speech be delivered indoors or outdoors? Will the audience be sitting or standing? Will there be other speakers? Will you need to make special arrangements for equipment such as a public address system or an overhead projector?

Throughout the process of developing your speech, always consider your listeners and the occasion. Your listeners' expectations and the reasons they have gathered to hear you will influence your choice of topic and the focus of your speech. As you examine the remaining steps in the process of speech development, remember that your ultimate goal is to communicate with your listeners.

## Gathering Your Speech Material

Once you have considered the subject and purpose of your speech and analyzed the audience and occasion, you'll be ready to gather the materials for your speech. Ordinarily, you'll start by assembling what you already know about the subject and deciding which ideas you want to include. You'll probably find that what you already know is not enough. You'll need to supplement what you know with additional information—facts, illustrations, stories, and examples. You can gather some of this material from newspapers, magazines, books, government documents, radio and TV programs, electronic databases, and the Web. You can acquire other information through interviews and conversations with people who know something about the subject that you do not know.

As you search for materials, if you plan to deal with a current question of public interest, you should consult such sources as the "The Week in Review" section of the Sunday *New York Times, U.S. News and World Report, The Wall Street Journal, Harper's,* and *The Observer.* Many magazines of general interest can be accessed via electronic database searches and the Internet; numerous encyclopedias, yearbooks, government reports, almanacs, and other reference materials can be found in your college library. This important topic—locating supporting materials—will be covered in detail in Chapter 6.

## Making an Outline

Early in your preparation, make a rough list of the points you wish to include in your speech. As you gather information on your topic, you will begin to see a pattern emerging from clusters of information. From these clusters, you can develop a final order for the principal points you wish to present, together with the subordinate ideas that will explain or prove these points. Flesh out your ideas with supporting materials, such as examples, statistics, and quotations.

Remember our speech topic on sharks from the beginning of this chapter? Well, after gathering information on sharks, we're ready to develop an outline. We started with several potential topic areas: types of sharks, life cycle of the shark, and shark attacks. Our research revealed amazing amounts of information on each of these topics—too much for a short speech—so we've narrowed our speech topic to shark attacks. Your outline for a five-minute, informative speech might look like this:

# Shark Attacks[1]

Introduction ────────► I.  Many of us fear shark attacks.
Central Idea ─────────► A.  News stories and films such as *Jaws* sensationalize the threat.
Preview of Main Ideas ─► B.  Let's explore the realities of shark-human contact.
   1.  The risk is minimal.
   2.  There are ways to maximize water safety.

First Idea ───────────► II.  The realities of shark-human contact are quite different from media portrayals.
Subtopic ─────────────► A.  Sharks have more to fear from humans than vice versa.
   1.  There are fewer than 100 shark attacks worldwide per year.
   2.  Fishermen kill between 30 million and 75 million sharks each year.
   3.  Eighty shark species are threatened with extinction.

Subtopic ─────────────► B.  The risk of a shark attack is extremely low—approximately 2 percent worldwide.
   1.  On average, more people are killed by bee stings in the United States than are killed by sharks worldwide.
   2.  Annually, thousands more people are harmed by rat bites, squirrel bites, and even bites by fellow humans than by shark attacks.
   3.  Your own home is a more dangerous place than the ocean in terms of serious and fatal injuries you're likely to sustain.
   4.  Even driving to the beach is fifty times more likely to be fatal than swimming or surfing.

Second Idea ──────────► III.  Education and technology can maximize water safety.
Subtopic ─────────────► A.  Educated surfers and swimmers are smart about using the ocean water.
   1.  They understand shark behavior.
      a. They avoid deep channels or waters that suddenly become deep.
      b. They avoid swimming and surfing at dusk and dawn, when sharks usually feed.
      c. They avoid swimming and surfing where people are fishing or cleaning fish.
      d. They leave watches and reflective jewelry on the beach, because sharks see contrast particularly well.
   2.  They use common sense to minimize danger.
      a. They swim and surf in groups where lifeguards are on duty; safety exists in numbers.
      b. They do not swim too far from shore, because it isolates them from assistance.
      c. They stay out of the water if they have open wounds or during menstrual periods.

Subtopic ─────────────► B.  Technological developments hold promise for making shark-human interactions safer.
   1.  Some companies claim to have developed effective chemical shark repellents.
   2.  The Protective Oceanic Device, or POD, uses an electrical field to discourage aggressive sharks.

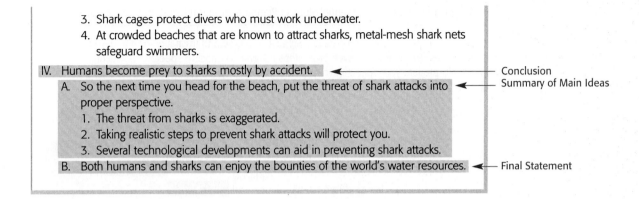

3. Shark cages protect divers who must work underwater.
4. At crowded beaches that are known to attract sharks, metal-mesh shark nets safeguard swimmers.

IV. Humans become prey to sharks mostly by accident. ◄──────── Conclusion
    A. So the next time you head for the beach, put the threat of shark attacks into ◄── Summary of Main Ideas
       proper perspective.
       1. The threat from sharks is exaggerated.
       2. Taking realistic steps to prevent shark attacks will protect you.
       3. Several technological developments can aid in preventing shark attacks.
    B. Both humans and sharks can enjoy the bounties of the world's water resources. ◄── Final Statement

In this outline, we've followed several themes in a topical pattern of organization. When you deliver the speech, you will use linking statements or transitions to guide your listeners. You might say, "Many of our fears of sharks are exaggerated by television and films. Let's examine the facts," or "Now that we've seen the realities of shark attacks, let's look at steps that can help prevent them," or "Here are four technological developments that offer protection for divers and others who must work in the shark's ocean habitat."

In Chapter 7, you'll find a number of additional organizational patterns for arranging the ideas in a speech. There, too, you'll find the form for a complete outline. For now, remember two simple but important rules: (1) Arrange your ideas in a sequence that is clear to your listeners, and (2) make sure that each point is directly related to your specific purpose. If you follow these rules, your speech should be coherent.

## Practicing Aloud

When you have completed your outline, you're ready to practice your speech (see Figure 2.1). Even though you might feel silly talking to yourself, practice aloud to refine the ideas and phrasing of your speech and to work on delivery skills.

Give practice a chance. It can mean the difference between an adequate effort and an outstanding speech. Repeatedly read through the outline until you've made all the changes that seem useful and until you can express each idea clearly and smoothly. Then, write out a notecard with brief cues for each of your main ideas. Next, talk through the speech by looking at your notecards. As you practice aloud, you might inadvertently leave out some points. That's okay. Practice until the words flow easily. Talk at a normal rate, and don't mumble. Finally, if possible, get a friend to listen to your speech, give you direct feedback, and help you practice making eye contact with a real person.

## Developing Confident Delivery

Now you're ready to present your speech. Even if you've prepared fully, you still might be asking, "How can I deal with my nervousness? How can I channel my anxiety into enthusiasm? How can I convey a sense of self-confidence to my

**Figure 2.1** The Essential Steps in Planning, Preparing, and Presenting a Speech

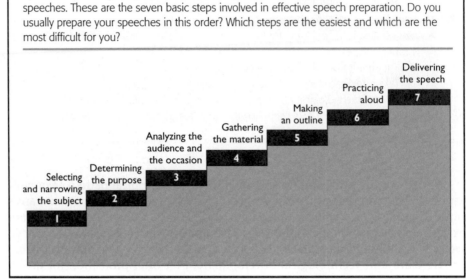

Systematic planning and preparation will save you time and frustration as you develop your speeches. These are the seven basic steps involved in effective speech preparation. Do you usually prepare your speeches in this order? Which steps are the easiest and which are the most difficult for you?

1. Selecting and narrowing the subject
2. Determining the purpose
3. Analyzing the audience and the occasion
4. Gathering the material
5. Making an outline
6. Practicing aloud
7. Delivering the speech

listeners?" Although there's no foolproof program for developing self-confidence, here are some practical ways to communicate confidently:

**1. Realize that tension and nervousness are normal.** They can even benefit you. Remember that tension can provide you with energy. As adrenaline pours into your bloodstream, you experience a physical charge that increases

## SPEAKING OF . . . SKILLS

### Practicing Your Speech

If you've ever learned to play the piano or drive a car with a standard transmission, you know that you can't master it all at once. You must practice to improve. The same principle can be applied to improving your public speaking skills. Remember these guidelines:

1.  *Keep practice sessions brief.* It's better to practice your speech for a few minutes at a time over the course of several days than to go through it repeatedly for two hours the day before it's due.

2.  *Practice in different settings.* Deliver your speech as you walk to class, in front of your friends, or in an empty classroom. This kind of varied practice encourages flexibility.

3.  *After you start your speech, finish it without stopping to correct errors or to restart it.* You aren't going to deliver your speech exactly the same way every time you give it. Expect some changes in your delivery and phrasing.

alertness. A baseball pitcher who's not pumped up before a big game may find that his fastball has no zip. Similarly, a speaker who's not pumped up may come across as dull and lifeless. Practice speaking often so that you learn how you react to stress and develop strategies for coping with it.[2]

**2. Focus on your ideas.** Think about what you want to communicate to your listeners. When you speak, you want their minds to be focused on your ideas, not on the way you're presenting them. Speech anxiety arises in part because of self-centeredness; sometimes you're more concerned with your personal appearance and performance than with your topic. One means of creating confidence is to select topics that you are interested in and know a lot about. By doing this, you make the situation topic-centered rather than self-centered. Have you ever wondered why you can talk at length with friends about your favorite hobby, sports, or political interests without feeling anxious? The fact that you're talking about a subject that interests you may be part of the answer.

**3. Look at your listeners.** If you look at your notes rather than at your listeners, they may get the impression that you don't care about them, that you aren't interested in their reactions to your message, or that you are not prepared. Eye contact with members of your audience will signal your eagerness to communicate with them. In addition, you can watch your listeners' faces for feedback and make minor adjustments as you speak. If you notice looks of puzzlement, for example, you can adjust by further explaining your ideas.

**4. Remember to breathe.** Although this may seem like unnecessary advice, research shows that stress can interfere with your breathing. To counter the effects of stress, breathe deeply using your diaphragm. Your chest should expand, pushing down and out against your waistband. An adequate supply of oxygen will help calm your anxiety and support your vocal apparatus as you speak, so remember to breathe!

**5. Relax your body.** Realize that you are being seen as well as heard and that your body can communicate confidence. In addition, bodily movements and changes in facial expression can help clarify and reinforce your ideas. You might smile as you refer to humorous events or step toward your listeners as you take them into your confidence. Keep your hands free at your sides so that you can gesture easily. As you say, "On the other hand," you might raise one hand to reinforce your statement. As you speak, your body uses up the excess adrenaline it generates. The very act of talking aloud reduces fear.

**6. Speak in public as often as you can.** Public speaking experience will not eliminate your fears, but it will help you to cope. Speaking frequently in front of your classmates is a great way to practice coping with anxiety. Then, as you gain confidence and poise, you'll want to try speaking to different audiences and in different settings. So speak up in class discussions, join in conversations with friends, and contribute to public meetings. You might even decide to run for office!

There are no shortcuts to developing speaking confidence. For most of us, gaining self-confidence results from experience and from understanding the process of communication. The uneasy feeling in the pit of your stomach may always be there, but it need not paralyze you. As you gain experience with each of the essential steps—from selecting a subject to practicing the speech—your self-confidence as a speaker will grow.

## SPEAKING OF . . .
# APPREHENSION

### State and Trait Apprehension

Research distinguishes between two kinds of speech anxiety: state apprehension and trait apprehension. **State apprehension** refers to the anxiety you feel in particular settings or situations. For example, perhaps you can talk easily with friends but are uncomfortable when being interviewed for a job. This sort of apprehension is also known as *stage fright*, because it's the fear of performing that leads to your worries about failure or embarrassment.

Stage fright has physiological manifestations that vary from one person to another. You can probably list your own symptoms—clammy hands, weak knees, dry mouth, and a trembling or even cracking voice. Its psychological manifestations include mental blocks (forgetting what you're going to say), vocal hesitation, and nonfluency.

Some aspects of nervousness are characteristic of the situation, but others are a part of your own personality. This kind of apprehension, called **trait apprehension,** refers to your level of anxiety as you face any communication situation. A high level of anxiety leads some people to withdraw from situations that require interpersonal or public communication with others.

## ◾ Assessing Your Progress

### Chapter Summary

1. Select and narrow your subject, making it appropriate to you and your listeners.
2. Determine your general and specific purposes, then word the central idea to guide your development of the key ideas.
3. Analyze your audience and the occasion to discover what you might say and how you might say it.
4. Gather your material, beginning with what you already know and then supplementing it with additional research.
5. Arrange and outline your points to package your ideas clearly and coherently.
6. Practice your speech aloud, working from outlines and then notecards, first alone and then with an audience.
7. Recognize that self-confidence can be developed by understanding the communication process and through public speaking experience.

### Assessment Activities

Go to the library or use the Internet to find and read several popular magazines and newspapers from the week that you were born. Sort out the events of that week, and write a clear central idea for a brief informative speech. Organize your ideas, and use some illustrations or perhaps some expert testimony from the sources you examined. Follow the rest of the steps suggested in this chapter for developing a speech, and then deliver it to your classmates. After the speech, ask for feedback. Was the central idea clear? Did your listeners follow the structure of the speech easily? Did your delivery convey confidence?

For additional chapter activities, log on to MySpeechLab at www.myspeechlab.com.

## Using the Web

Having trouble finding a speech topic? Visit reputable media sites on the Internet like CNN, ABC, CBS, NBC, or PBS. You can also find regional newspapers online. These sources will provide information that is current. Use various search engines to locate the Internet Public Library or Electronic Newsstand. Browse through thousands of publications from all over the world. These should give you some good ideas for speeches.

## References

1. Materials for this speech outline were obtained from the Web sites for the PBS *NOVA* program featuring shark attacks, the U.S. Office of Naval Research, the American Institute of Biological Sciences, the Florida Museum of Natural History, and the International Shark Attack File.

2. Michael Neer, "Reducing Situational Anxiety and Avoidance Behavior Associated with Classroom Apprehension," *Southern Communication Journal*, 56 (1990): 49–61; John Gorhis and Mike Allen, "Meta-Analysis of the Relationship Between Communication Apprehension and Cognitive Performance," *Communication Education*, 41 (1992): 68–76; and James McCroskey, "Oral Communication Apprehension: A Summary of Current Theory and Research," *Human Communication Research*, 4 (1977): 78–96.

# 3 | Critical Listening

In your daily life, you spend more time listening than you do reading, writing, or speaking. Listening accounts for over 40 percent of your communicative time.[1] You might assume that you're a good listener from all that practice, but you would be surprised to discover how easy it is to miss something important. The fact is, you've probably never had any training in listening, especially for situations such as class lectures, in which you're expected to acquire technical or abstract knowledge primarily through listening.

Conversations, classroom lectures, group meetings, and electronic media expose you to an amazing amount of information every day. If you are to make the best use of all that information, you must hone your listening skills. Both speaker and listener are active partners in the communication process. As a speaker, you reach out to your audience, and as a listener, you respond. Listening is a crucial part of the communication process.

Critical thinking is key to listening well. **Critical thinking** is the process of consciously examining the content and logic of messages to determine their credibility and rationality. Critical thinkers challenge ideas before they accept them. They assess the quality of ideas, judging their merits and faults. Critical thinking is an important feature of the communication process and is vital to good listening.

## CHAPTER OUTLINE

## KEY TERMS

After a more detailed introduction to the process of listening, this chapter will focus on practical listening techniques that you can use in almost any situation. We'll finish by suggesting how you can put new listening skills to work in your classes.

## Hearing and Listening

Hearing is the first step in the listening process. To listen to a message, you first must hear it. **Hearing** is the physiological process of receiving sound waves. Sound waves travel through the air and set up vibrations on the eardrum; in turn, these vibrations are transmitted to the brain through a system of nerves. Hearing is affected by the laws of physics and the neurophysiology of the body. Any number of factors can interfere with hearing—distracting noises, sounds that are too soft, or hearing loss. Some of these conditions can be improved. The speaker can change speaking volume, and audience members can move to better seats to facilitate hearing. Listeners cannot provide feedback to the speaker if their hearing is blocked.

Listening, on the other hand, involves thinking. Listening begins after the nerve impulses that originated as sound waves have been received in the brain. This process of interpretation—registering impulses, assigning them to meaningful contexts, and evaluating them—constitutes listening. **Listening** is the thinking process whereby people generate meaning from the sounds they hear.

## Barriers to Good Listening

Listening is easy to define but hard to practice. Over the years, you've probably developed some barriers to good listening. You'll have to recognize and remove them to become a better listener. At one time or another, most of us experience these five barriers to good listening:

1. **Passive listening.** Many of us are just plain lazy listeners, tuning in and out as our attention dictates. As a result, we often miss important facts and ideas.

2. **Drifting thoughts.** You can comprehend many more words per minute than someone can utter. In fact you probably can process about 400 words per minute, while most speakers produce only about 125 to 175 words per minute. As a result, you may fill the time lag with other thoughts. Your **internal perceptual field** is the world of your own thoughts. While someone is speaking, you may be remembering a television show you saw last night, planning the menu for supper, or thinking about a topic for your next term paper.

3. **Physical distractions.** Sometimes your attention is diverted by elements outside your own thoughts. Your **external perceptual field** is those things in your physical environment that can distract you, such as the buzz of overhead lights, the sun's glare off your teacher's glasses, or a banging radiator. If your attention is sidetracked by physical interference, you will hear and process only part of a spoken message.

**4. Trigger words.** We often bring our emotions into the speech setting. Memories of past events or strong feelings can be triggered by a word or a reference. Many people spend time mentally debating with speakers and remain stuck on one idea while the speaker moves ahead to others. For example, some listeners become hostile when they hear a speaker refer to race or religion or gender. They may spend several minutes fuming and miss the next part of the speaker's message.

**5. Self-fulfilling prophecies.** Preset ideas can get in the way of good listening. If you've heard that Professor Rogers is a dull lecturer, you probably enter the class expecting to be bored. Sometimes previous encounters with a speaker can color your expectations.

Like most people, you probably have predispositions about topics and people. If you let these predispositions get in the way of careful listening, you're likely to miss important parts of speeches. It is important to overcome these barriers to become an active listener and a better participant in the communication transaction. Here are some suggestions for developing your listening skills.

*Often listeners must work through interpersonal, linguistic, and cultural differences.*

## Practical Listening Techniques

Hearing is a natural physiological process for most people, but listening is another matter. You've got to work hard to listen well. The good news, though, is that you can train yourself to listen better. You can begin to practice better listening habits in three ways: (1) determine your purposes for listening, (2) develop techniques that help you comprehend messages, and (3) design questions that help you evaluate speeches.

### Know Your Purposes

To be a good listener, you must figure out why you're listening. This is not as obvious as it seems, because if you think about it, you engage in many different kinds of listening. On any given day, you may listen intently to your instructors to learn new concepts, you may listen to your favorite music to relax, and you may listen attentively to be sure that a car salesperson isn't skipping over essential features of the dealer's guarantee.

Researchers have identified five kinds of listening that reflect the purposes you may have when communicating with others[2]: (1) appreciative, (2) discriminative, (3) empathic, (4) comprehension, and (5) critical.

*Listening well has been a human (and canine) concern for a long, long time.*

**Appreciative listening** focuses on something other than the verbal content of the primary message. Some listeners enjoy seeing a famous speaker. Others relish a good speech, a classic movie, or a brilliant performance. On these occasions, you listen primarily to entertain yourself.

**Discriminative listening** requires listeners to draw conclusions from the way a message is presented rather than from what is said (i.e., the message itself). In discriminative listening, people seek to understand the meaning behind the message. You're interested in what the speaker really thinks, believes, or feels. You're engaging in discriminative listening when you draw conclusions about how angry your parents are with you, based not on what they say but on how they say it.

**Empathic or therapeutic listening** is intended to provide emotional support for the speaker. Although it is more typical of interpersonal than public communication, empathic listening does occur in public speaking situations. For example, when you hear an athlete apologize for unprofessional behavior, a religious convert describe a soul-saving experience, or a classmate reveal a personal problem to illustrate a speech, you're engaging in empathic or therapeutic listening.

**Listening for comprehension** occurs when you want to gain additional information or insights from the speaker. You are probably most familiar with this form of listening, because you've relied heavily on it for your education. When you listen to a radio newscast, a classroom lecture on the principal strategies in an advertising campaign, or an elections official explaining new registration procedures, you're listening to understand—to comprehend information, ideas, and processes.

**Critical listening** is the most difficult kind of listening, because it requires you to both interpret and evaluate the message. It demands that you go beyond understanding the message to interpreting it and evaluating its strengths and weaknesses. You'll practice this sort of listening in class. And as a careful consumer, you'll also use critical listening to evaluate television commercials, political campaign speeches, advice from talk show guests, or arguments offered by salespeople. When you are listening critically, you decide whether to accept or reject ideas and whether to act on the message.

You may have many different purposes for listening, and that's why the first question you should ask yourself is "What's my purpose in listening?" Do you expect to gain information and insight to make a decision? Or are you listening to enjoy yourself, to understand the feelings of another human being, to assess someone's state of mind, or to test ideas? Knowing why you're listening will help you listen more efficiently and effectively. In the rest of this chapter, we'll focus on listening for comprehension and critical listening, because those are the kinds of listening you use primarily in a public speaking situation.

## Listening for Comprehension

Listening for comprehension is the kind of listening you usually do in the classroom. Fully comprehending what's being said requires that you understand the three essential aspects of speech content: (1) *ideas*, (2) *structure*, and

---

SPEAKING OF . . .
S  K  I  L  L  S

### Good Note Taking and Active Listening

One of the easiest ways to practice your listening skills while in college is to work on note taking. As you become a better note taker, you'll also become a better listener. Here are some tips for improving your note-taking skills:

1. *Get organized.* Develop a note-taking system, such as a loose-leaf notebook or word-processing document on your laptop, so that you can add, rearrange, or remove notes. Use separate notebooks or word-processing documents for different subjects to avoid confusion.

2. *Review your notes regularly.* This will prepare you to ask questions while the lecture or readings are still fresh in your mind, and it will help keep you oriented to the class. Research shows that students who review their notes regularly earn higher grades.

3. *Leave a two- to three-inch blank margin when taking notes by hand.* Later, you can add facts, clarification, reactions, and other alterations after comparing your notes with other students' or after doing related reading. Such critical commentary is an important stage in merging the material in the notes with your own thoughts.

4. *Write more.* Making a conscious effort to record more ideas and more words from a speech or lecture will help you remember the important ideas, structure, and supporting evidence. Research shows that most students don't take enough notes. The problem is compounded with long messages; students take even fewer notes as the speech or lecture continues.

5. *Develop a note-taking scheme.* Consider using abbreviations, such as the ampersand (&) for *and*, *btwn* and *w/o* for *between* and *without*, or specialized notations like *mgt* and *acctg* for *management* and *accounting*. Color-code your notes or use highlighter pens to remind yourself of the most important parts of the material.

6. *Pay attention to nonverbal cues.* If your instructor writes something on the chalkboard, copy it in your notes. If your instructor seems especially enthusiastic about an idea, make a note of it.

By taking these steps, you can become an active listener who is engaging in a two-way communication channel.

*Source:* Kenneth A. Kiewra, "Note Taking and Review: The Research and Its Implications," *Instructional Science*, 16 (1987): 233–249.

(3) *supporting materials*. You've got to understand what ideas you're being asked to accept, how these ideas are related to each other, and what facts and opinions underlie them. Asking three questions will help you comprehend a message:

**1. What are the main ideas of the speech?** Determine the central idea of the speech, and look for the statements that help develop it. These main ideas should serve as the foundation on which the speaker builds the speech. The next time you listen to a soap commercial, listen for the main ideas. Are you encouraged to buy it because of its cleaning power, smell, sex appeal, or gentleness to your skin? Before you decide to buy a new brand of soap, you ought to know something about its characteristics. Now transfer this listening behavior to a speech. Always know what ideas you're being sold.

**2. How are the main ideas arranged?** Once you've identified the main ideas, you should figure out the relationships between them. In other words, identify the structure of the ideas and then examine it. If a speaker is explaining child welfare laws, which ideas are highlighted? Does the explanation seem reasonable? Is the speaker limited only to one perspective? What point of view is left out? Who is defined as the victim? Does the speaker express a preference for one point of view over another?

**3. What kinds of materials support the main ideas?** Consider the timeliness, quality, and content of the supporting materials. Are facts and opinions derived from sources too old to be relevant to current problems? Is the speaker quoting recognized authorities on the subject? Ask yourself whether the materials clarify, amplify, and strengthen the main ideas of the speech. For example, if a speaker claims the murders at Virginia Tech in 2007 show that school violence is a growing national problem, ask yourself several questions: How many episodes of school violence occurred during the entire year? Over the past decade, have incidents of school violence increased or decreased? Is this example typical of the kinds of violence in schools?

In other words, to comprehend the content, make sure you know what ideas, relationships, and evidence you're being asked to accept. To be an active listener, you should constantly employ the **RRA technique:** *review, relate,* and *anticipate*.

Take a few seconds to *review* what the speaker has said. Mentally summarize key ideas each time the speaker initiates a new topic for consideration.

*Relate* the message to what you already know. Consider how you could use the information in the future.

*Anticipate* what the speaker might say next. Use this anticipation to focus on the content of the message.

By reviewing, relating, and anticipating, you can keep your attention centered on the message. Using the RRA technique keeps you actively engaged in the listening process. For example, you could just sit in class listening to your instructor drone on about Byzantine art, or you could use the RRA technique and become engaged in the lecture in the following way:

**1. Review.** Your instructor said that the Byzantine Empire, located in the eastern Mediterranean area, lasted from 324 A.D. until the Turks invaded in

1453 A.D. Byzantine art focused on human figures, usually members of the holy family or people represented in the Christian Bible. You might not remember these details, so write them down in your notes. You can review again after the lecture.

**2. Relate.** What do you already know about art that features holy figures? Can you identify any places where such art is used today? Can you imagine eating your meals without the benefit of forks, unknown to the Byzantine world of the fourteenth century?

**3. Anticipate.** What is more important to remember when you study for your next exam? Is your instructor more likely to ask you about forks or about the characteristics of Byzantine art? If your instructor mentions a reading assignment, jot down a note to read the material before the next class. Now you've become an active listener. You're more likely to recall the information presented in class and become engaged in classroom discussions as well.

There are lots of opportunities to use the RRA technique—begin by practicing it as you attend your classes and listen to your classmates speak.

---

## SPEAKING OF . . . ETHICS

### Deliberately Misguiding Listeners

Some advertisers, politicians, sales representatives, and even friends have learned how to misguide their listeners without actually lying. They hope, of course, that you'll draw the conclusions they want you to on the basis of distracting or misdirective statements. You can recognize these situations by thinking and listening critically. Here are some things to listen for:

1. *Percentages rather than absolute numbers.* You're told that women's salaries went up 50 percent more than men's last year. Should you cheer? Maybe not. Even if women got a 3 percent raise when men got 2 percent, if there is a big differential in their salaries to begin with, the actual dollar amount of women's and men's raises was probably about the same.

2. *Characteristics of the sample.* Beware when the manufacturer tells you that "Four out of five of the dentists surveyed preferred the ingredients in Smiles-Aglow toothpaste." How big was the sample? Were the dentists surveyed working in Smiles-Aglow labs or were they in private dental practice? You need to know more about them to know whether this claim is solid.

3. *Hasty generalization.* The neighbor who tells you that "Most folks on this block are against the widening of our street" may have talked to everyone, although that's not likely. He probably means "most folks I know on this block"—and then you'd better find out how many that is. Press him for details before you accept or reject his judgment.

Are speakers lying when they use these distracting or misguiding techniques? Are they acting unethically? Where does ethical responsibility lie—with the speaker or with the audience?

*Source:* Andrew Wolvin and Carolyn Coakley, *Listening*, 5th ed. (Dubuque, IA: Brown and Benchmark, 1995), pp. 3–11 and chaps. 4–8.

## Critical Listening

Once you've figured out why you're listening, how the ideas are arranged, and what supporting materials are being presented, you're in a position to form some opinions. You, after all, are the reason the speech is being given, so you are the one who must decide whether the speaker's ideas are worth accepting. Making such a judgment is a good way to protect yourself from inflated claims, dated information, and unethical speakers. Completely assessing a speech could include asking yourself about the situation, the speaker, and the message. The following questions will help you listen critically:

1. **How is the situation affecting my reception of this speech?** What is the reason for the speech? Is the speaker expected to deal with particular themes or subjects? Am I in sympathy with this speech occasion? Speeches in churches, basketball arenas, and rotary clubs are very different from one another, and you must adjust your evaluation criteria to each situation.

2. **How is the physical environment affecting the speaker and my listening?** Is the room too hot or too cold? Too big or too small? What other distractions exist? The physical environment can have an important impact on your listening. In uncomfortable environments, you might have to compensate by leaning forward, moving up, or concentrating more closely.

3. **What do I know about the speaker?** The reputation of this person may influence you, so think about it. Are you being unduly deferential or hypercritical of the speaker just because of his or her reputation? Do you think the speaker will be fair and honest because he or she represents your interests or is similar to you? Don't let your assumptions about the speaker get in the way of critical listening.

4. **How believable do I find the speaker?** Are there things about the speaker's actions, demeanor, and words that seem either pleasing or suspicious? Does the speaker use adequate and compelling supporting material to reinforce the message? Try to figure out why you're reacting positively or negatively, and then ask yourself whether it's reasonable for you to believe this speaker.

5. **Is the speaker adequately prepared?** Imprecise remarks, repetitions, backtracking, vague or missing numbers, and lack of solid testimony are all signs of a poorly prepared speaker. For example, a speaker who talks about global warming should discuss, among other things, international agreements to curb fossil fuel emissions. If the speaker doesn't discuss this, you'll know that he or she hasn't gotten very far into the topic. Similarly, if the speaker can't clearly explain the causes and effects of global warming, you should question the reliability of other information in the speech.

6. **What's the speaker's attitude toward the audience?** How is the audience being treated: cordially or condescendingly, as individuals or as a general group, as inferiors or as equals? Answering these questions will help you not only to assess your experience but also to form some questions for the speaker after the speech.

7. **How credible are the ideas being presented?** It's crucial for you to assess a speaker's ideas critically, a point we've been stressing throughout this

chapter. Just one warning: You could be mistaken yourself, so don't automatically dismiss new ideas. Listen more carefully to ideas that are new and different or that seem strange. Make sure that you understand them and that they're well supported.

**8. Are the ideas well structured?** Are important concepts missing? For example, anyone who talks about the branches of the federal government but then ignores the Supreme Court has an incomplete set of ideas. Are logical links apparent? The comparisons must be fair, the cause-and-effect links clear and logical, and the proposals for correcting social wrongs practical. Structural relationships between ideas give them coherence.

**9. Is sufficient evidence offered?** The world is filled with slipshod reasoning and flawed evidence. Bad reasoning and a refusal to test the available evidence can lead to mistaken conclusions. Listen for evidence, and write down the key parts of that evidence so you can mull it over, asking yourself if it's good enough to use as a basis for changing your mind. Be demanding; adopt a "show me" attitude. Insist on adequate evidence and logical reasons when a speaker asks you to make crucial decisions.

You might not ask all of these questions every time you hear a speech, because your listening purposes vary considerably from occasion to occasion. However, you will want to ask yourself most of these critical listening questions before you make important decisions, such as whom to vote for, whether to take the job offer, or if you should make a major purchase. You can begin to practice critical listening in your classes right away.

## Developing Skills for Critical Listening

Your speech classroom is set up to teach skills that you can use for the rest of your life. Listening is one of the skills you'll need to survive in your career, your community, and your social life. You'll have to listen to understand your employer's explanation of a new computer system, to make reasonable decisions between two political candidates who offer different views of health care reform, and to follow a neighbor's instructions as she tells you how to rewire a light fixture. The ability to listen can help you make money, be a good citizen, and keep you from frying your fingers on a 110-volt circuit!

Your classes are excellent settings for practicing new listening skills and refining old ones. Review your purposes for listening, and practice the RRA technique as you listen to your instructors and classmates. During this term, we also suggest that you improve your listening in the following ways:

**1. Practice critiquing the speeches of your classmates.** Refine note-taking techniques. Ask questions of the speaker. Take part in post-speech discussions. You can learn a lot from listening well.

**2. Listen critically to discussions, lectures, and student-teacher interactions in your other classes.** You're surrounded with public communication worth analyzing when you're in school. You can easily spot effective and ineffective speech techniques in your classes.

**3. Listen critically to speakers outside of class.** Attend public lectures, city council meetings, religious rallies, or political caucuses. Watch replays of presidential or congressional speeches on C-SPAN. You'll be amazed by the range of talent, techniques, and styles exhibited in your community every week.

**4. Examine the supporting materials, arguments, and language used in newspapers and magazines.** Refine your critical listening skills by practicing critical reading. Together, they represent applications of the skills of critical thinking you need to survive in this world. You will become a vital participant in the communication process when you actively listen to and read others' messages.

Overall, then, listening makes public speaking a reciprocal activity. Listeners seek to meet their diverse needs, ranging from personal enjoyment to crucial decision making, through specialized listening skills designed for each listening purpose. When both speakers and listeners work at making the speech transaction succeed, public speaking reaches its full potential as a partnership in communication.

## Assessing Your Progress

### Chapter Summary

1. Both the speaker and the listener are critical participants in the communication transaction.
2. Critical thinking is the process of consciously examining the content and logic of messages to determine their credibility and rationality.
3. Hearing is a physiological process; listening is a psychological process by which people seek to comprehend and evaluate sounds.
4. There are five purposes for listening: appreciative listening, discriminative listening, empathic or therapeutic listening, listening for comprehension, and critical listening.
5. To improve your listening skills, sort out the essential aspects of speech content: ideas, structure, and supporting materials.
6. The RRA technique—review, relate, and anticipate—can help you listen more efficiently.
7. To improve your speech evaluation skills, practice assessing the situation, the speaker, and the message.

### Assessment Activities

Conduct a class discussion on a controversial topic, such as physician-assisted suicide, multiculturalism and political correctness, the rights of smokers, or fetal tissue research. Establish the rule that before anyone can speak, he or she first must summarize to the satisfaction of the previous speaker what that person said. What conclusions can you draw about people's ability to listen and provide feedback? How do good listening and feedback reduce the amount and intensity of disagreement?

For additional chapter activities, log on to MySpeechLab at www.my speechlab.com.

## Using the Web

Go to the Web site of the International Listening Association (www.listen.org). You'll discover numerous listening tests and exercises for improving your listening skills in public speaking and interpersonal situations.

## References

1. Steven Rhodes, "What the Communication Journals Tell Us about Teaching Listening," *Central States Speech Journal*, 36(1985): 24–32.

2. Andrew Wolvin and Carolyn Coakley, *Listening*, 5th ed. (Dubuque, IA: Brown and Benchmark, 1995).

# L I S T E N I N G

A simple form or rubric will help you focus your listening skills as your classmates present their speeches. Use this speech evaluation form as a checklist to get the most out of your listening experience and to provide a basis for your feedback to the speaker.

| | Excellent | Good | Average | Needs Improvement |
|---|---|---|---|---|
| **The Speaker** | | | | |
| Confident? | | | | |
| Enthusiastic about the topic? | | | | |
| Well prepared? | | | | |
| Use of notes and lectern unobtrusive? | | | | |
| **The Message** | | | | |
| Sufficiently narrowed topic? | | | | |
| Clear general purpose? | | | | |
| Sharply focused specific purpose? | | | | |
| Well-phrased central idea? | | | | |
| Ample support from varied, trustworthy sources? | | | | |
| Introduced adequately? | | | | |
| Concluded effectively? | | | | |
| Major points clear, balanced? | | | | |
| **The Audience** | | | | |
| All listeners addressed? | | | | |
| Ideas adapted to audience segments? | | | | |
| Attitudes toward speaker and subject acknowledged? | | | | |
| Supporting materials tailored to the audience? | | | | |

| | Excellent | Good | Average | Needs Improvement |
|---|---|---|---|---|
| **The Channel** | | | | |
| Voice varied for emphasis? | | | | |
| Conversational style of delivery? | | | | |
| Appropriate rate of delivery? | | | | |
| Nondistracting body movement? | | | | |
| Gestures used effectively? | | | | |
| Face expressive? | | | | |
| Language unambiguous, concrete? | | | | |
| Language vivid, forcible? | | | | |
| **Record your reactions to the following questions:** | | | | |
| Were the audience's expectations met? | | | | |
| What were the strengths of the speech? | | | | |
| List possible improvements. | | | | |
| Write out questions for the speaker. | | | | |

# Public Speaking and Cultural Challenges

Davona was excited about the upcoming informative speech assignment for her public speaking class. She had the perfect topic—the speech on race relations and politics given by Barack Obama in March of 2008 on the presidential campaign trail. She had assessments of the speech's place in the evolution of the presidential campaign, both a printed text and streaming video of it, public opinion polls, expert commentary, and her own memories of watching it on that rainy March morning.

When she told her teenaged brother, Dan, the topic of her speech, however, he stared at her blankly. He had no idea about the political issues featured in the 2008 presidential campaign or the importance of Obama's efforts to detail the frustrations and anger of both black and white communities in the United States. In social studies classes, he had heard a little about the history of U.S. race relations, the economic and social positions of blacks in society, and the sources of white unhappiness over affirmative action and reverse discrimination, but not very much. Her brother, Dan, had no cultural knowledge—no understanding of the ideas underlying Obama's speech. Obama had taken it for granted that listeners knew the world about which he was speaking.

Maybe you've had an experience similar to Davona's, a time when your own view of the world was rocked by others who disagreed fundamentally

## CHAPTER OUTLINE

The Nature of Cultural Processes

Understanding Our Multicultural Society

Strategies for Negotiating Cultural Differences

*Speaking of . . . Ethics: Adapting to Moral Codes*

Assessing Your Progress

## KEY TERMS

with how you saw things or, even worse, a time when others did not know enough about cultural history and daily experiences even to understand what you were talking about. Like Davona, you have run into the complexity of cultural life.

If communication were just a matter of stating facts and ideas, it would be a relatively simple transaction with listeners. Public speaking, however, is more complex. The communication of facts and ideas takes place within a cultural milieu, and negotiating that maze of individual and collective experiences is a challenge every public speaker eventually confronts. This chapter is about speaking in light of cultural challenges that may complicate your job. Let's begin by examining the nature of cultural processes.

## The Nature of Cultural Processes

At its simplest, a **culture** is a social group's system of meanings. We can think of culture as the meanings that we attach to persons, places, ideas, rituals, things, routines, and communication behavior. Since you were an infant, you've been taught who is powerful or not (people), how to act at home and in public buildings (places), what's true and false about your experiences in the world (ideas), how to greet family and strangers (routines), and the most effective—and ineffective—ways to get favors from your teacher or your boss (strategic communication behavior). All this is woven together as part of the fabric of your culture.

This is true for everyone else as well. We've all been taught about the people, places, rituals, ideas, and things that make up our lives. We all participate in culturally constructed knowledge. Your meanings may not be the same as the meanings someone else has learned, however, and your experiences are different from those of others. This happens not only on an individual basis but also on a group basis. In some important ways, men and women have been given different social educations, as have Asians and Hispanics, poor and rich folk, and people who can hear as well as those who cannot. All of our differences in psychological, social, political, economic, and behavioral—which is to say cultural—education can cause speakers some serious problems. And of course those differences are multiplied when you move from one country to another.

Training in public speaking is in part a matter of learning about the cultural expectations of one's audience. Speakers must learn what those expectations are in order to be seen as relevant to others. Speakers who want to affect audiences must learn to be exceptionally good at phrasing ideas and engaging the feelings of others within the communication traditions of their listeners' cultural traditions.

Learning about the cultural practices and expectations of one's listeners, however, is easier said than done. There is a tension between one's self and society and between the individual and the collective—especially in the United States, where children have been taught to maximize their potential and be their own persons. On the one hand, you are you, a unique individual with your own life experiences and your own thoughts about the world. On the other hand, you

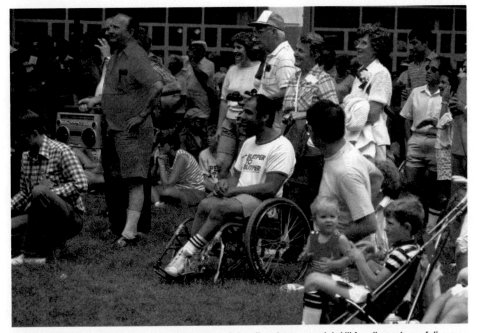

*The ability to communicate across gender, racial, and class lines is an essential skill for all members of diverse communities.*

always are marked by social categories. You are an individual, yes, but you also are reminded regularly that you're gay, of Scottish descent, twenty-something, a Presbyterian, a junior in college who works as a sales clerk, and so on. You are an individual, but part of your self-identity—and certainly a major part of others' perceptions of you—is socially and culturally determined.[1]

In a world where identities are both individually and collectively diverse, you often must meet serious challenges as you prepare to talk publicly:

- Can you respect individual differences and cultural diversity while attempting to get a group of people to think and work together?
- Can you recognize the diversity of your audience's experiences?
- Can you be true to yourself and your commitments while adapting to others?
- Can you successfully negotiate the differences between what audiences expect of you and what you expect of yourself?

These are not easy questions to answer, and you don't think of them every time you rise to say a few words. When you face audiences different from you or have to deal with complicated issues, such as the topic Davona chose, you'll want to examine culture—the shared beliefs, attitudes, values, goals, and desires that turn a group of listeners into a people who are unified in thought and action.[2]

In this chapter, we discuss relationships between public speaking and cultural life. First, we examine the components of culture more specifically. Then, we review some strategies that you can use to address listeners even when they come from diverse cultural backgrounds.

## Understanding Our Multicultural Society

We've defined culture generally. Before you can think about strategies for responding to key points of cultural diversity in your speeches, however, you'll want to think more about how culture affects your everyday life.

Earlier, we raised this question: Can you respect individual differences and cultural diversity while attempting to get a group of people to think and work together? We think that you can, but it's hard work. As we've just noted, to accomplish this, you have to know something about other people's cultural traditions: how they talk to each other, beliefs and values that are important because of their upbringing and families and are relevant to your speech, ways in which they signal disagreement or agreement, how they respond to each other (i.e., their participatory practices), and how they talk in different situations—perhaps one way in families and another in public settings, such as a church or a governmental office.

If you think about all of the different American **co-cultures** (cultures that coexist in a society as relatively complete ways of life, e.g., manhood and womanhood) and **subcultures** (smaller groups of people that define their lifestyles, at least in part, by how they're different from the dominant culture, e.g., bikers or particular religious groups), you can scare yourself. As you think about the black, Hispanic, gay/lesbian/transgendered, and women's empowerment movements of the 1960s and 1970s, the growing emphasis on cultural diversity in the 1980s, and passage of the Americans with Disabilities Act in 1991, you realize that you've got to be very careful when trying to respect cultural orientations of audience members, even in a simple speech. **Multiculturalism**—the recognition that a country such as the United States possesses not a unified culture, but one with several subcultures and powerful co-cultures that interpenetrate yet are separate from one another—is a fact of life.[3]

To reiterate, your cultural life is both acquired and later negotiated face-to-face. To inform, entertain, and persuade others through public speaking, you have to be able to span the gap between your cultural orientations and theirs. But first, you must recognize the diversity.

### Recognizing Diversity

Remember Davona and her brother, Dan? In spite of all they shared, the difference in their experiences with racial history and current events contributed to very divergent ways of thinking. Dan didn't automatically assume that history and black-white frustrations were important, probably because he didn't see how they had affected his life. Davona assumed that everyone had experienced the events in the same way she had—through history classes, news stories about race, and political commentary. In some ways, this is how culture changes. The events that shape the thoughts and responses of one generation or group aren't necessarily transmitted to the next. Davona had not considered any of this before she talked to Dan. You cannot assume that others will share your background and point of view.

An example of this challenge recently occurred on a college campus. In October 2005, the University of St. Thomas in St. Paul, Minnesota, rescinded an invitation for Nobel Peace Prize winner Desmond Tutu to speak on campus at

*As the U.S. House of Representatives' first Muslim, Keith Ellison faced serious political-cultural issues, winning office as a champion of civil liberties for all and with a strong antiwar message—both issues stressing unity over diversity.*

the invitation of its Justice and Peace Studies Program. And the director of the program, Chris Toffolo, lost that position after she publicly challenged the cancellation. Doug Hennes, vice president for university and government relations at St. Thomas, said that Tutu was cancelled because he had said "hurtful" things about Israel and upset parts of the Jewish community. Does challenging Israel's treatment of the Palestinians constitute "hurt"? Well, yes, probably for some, but certainly not for all. (Chris Toffolo assured the press that she, as a Jew, had likewise criticized Israeli policy.)

What were the ideas that ignited such public controversy? Tutu indeed criticized Israel, but he was also accused of comparing the Israeli leadership to Hitler. But did he? The Zionist Association of America said he did, though a look at the speech transcript shows that his mention of Hitler came not in the context of his criticism of Israeli but when saying that powerful forces can be brought down: "For goodness sake, this is God's world. We live in a moral universe. The apartheid government was very powerful, but today it no longer exists. Hitler, Mussolini, Stalin, Pinochet, Milosevic, and Idi Amin were all powerful, but in the end, they bit the dust."[4] The subjects of Israel and the Israeli–Palestinian conflict are so polarizing that you may not be able to find a position on the questions that are considered reasonable by your whole audience. And you'll certainly find various interpretations of arguments that you make.

Often in societies where free speech is protected, unpopular ideas are voiced, and the full extent of cultural difference is revealed. Our history has dulled the edges of controversy over public figures like Martin Luther King, Jr., Susan B. Anthony, William Lloyd Garrison, Cesar Chavez, and Malcolm X. Each of these people alarmed other members of their society, started contentious public debate, and suffered censure and discrimination as a result of their opinions.

Today, we have come to accept them and their ideas as part of our cultural heritage, even though each was reviled during his or her lifetime.

In similar ways, the basic ideas and actions of cultures constantly undergo evolution. It may be hard for us to imagine that at one time in our history the possession or distribution of birth control devices was a criminal offense, or that human beings could be bought and sold at auction, or that women could not vote, or that Native Americans were not considered American citizens. Through confrontation, often led by eloquent and impassioned public speakers, cultural practices such as these were reformed. And in every case, people could be found on both sides of the controversy, exposing the rich diversity of our culture.

As you survey your own daily life, recognize the diversity that exists there. You may fundamentally disagree with your parents, friends, or teachers. You'll probably see a wide range of opinions as you tune into television, from shock jock Howard Stern to televangelist Pat Robertson. The diversity of experience is compounded when you consider that although we may use the same language, we may express very different meanings. To understand this, let's turn to identifying the values that surface in our culture.

## Identifying Multiple Values

Because audiences often form groups on the basis of the diverse characteristics of the individuals composing them, it's likely that different segments see the world in different ways, using some of the same words as others but meaning quite different things. This is because people's **value orientations**—their habitual ways of thinking about positive and negative grounds for human thought and action—tend to become materialized in highly idiosyncratic ways. Consider the phrase *family values*. Almost everyone supports family values, but varied value orientations—we can call them liberal, middle-of-the-road, and conservative ideologies—underlie people's use of that label (see Table 4.1).

That *family values* can mean such different things to people shouldn't be surprising, because the issue is a strongly divisive one in American society today. The differences are so great that you can't ignore them when talking about this topic, either. Rather, you're better advised to recognize the differences and define the phrase *family values* carefully, so that your listeners know exactly what you're talking about. Even then, you may well want to negotiate among the varied definitions. You might have to say, "All right, then, on what do we agree? How far can we go together in helping parents raise their children?" It was precisely this kind of thinking that got liberals, conservatives, and those somewhere in the middle together in 1993 to form a coalition in Congress. That coalition passed the Family and Medical Leave Act in the name of both fostering traditional families (by requiring businesses to pay a parent who stayed at home with an infant) and recognizing a child's needs (by guaranteeing him or her parental support in the earliest stages of social life).

Not all questions of cultural difference are settled as easily. Some are much more controversial and entangle many segments of our society in their resolution. Understanding the different values at the base of any public discussion means to identify the complexities of culture and to uncover the different positions that people can take in public debate.

Consider, for example, the culturally determined set of practices and beliefs that are associated with the end of life. Such practices and beliefs have varied dramatically among cultures across time—from the view that the end of one's

**TABLE 4.1** The Diversity of "Family Values"

| Conservative Ideology | • America is in moral decline and must return to older family values.<br>• We've become a permissive society characterized by divorce, illegitimacy, juvenile crime, and spoiled children.<br>• We must bolster the traditional, two-parent, heterosexual family as the best environment for children and eliminate governmental (including school) interference with the family's operations. |
|---|---|
| Liberal Ideology | • America has to give parents more aid in raising their children.<br>• Everyone, not just parents, has a stake in making sure that children are cared for, supported, and raised to be good citizens.<br>• Because financial resources are so varied in this country and so many families are troubled, government at the local, state, and national levels must help parents with child care, health care, paid parental leave when children are infants, and other forms of financial assistance.<br>• It is better to help all forms of family—single- and dual-parent, traditional and nontraditional—with their children than to deal with juveniles in prisons later. |
| Middle-of-the-Road Ideology | • Raising children should primarily be a matter of parental responsibility but with governmental safety nets in place.<br>• Parents must be made more responsible for the growth and actions of their children yet should have help available in the form of family planning agencies, subsidized adoption and abortion services, and sex education in the schools.<br>• If parents fail or abuse their children, the state should rescue children from such situations; but if not, parents should be made to take responsibility for their children's care, feeding, and nurture. |

life is a choice that each individual must make, to the view that others like rulers or communities hold the right to determine the end of a life, to the view that God is the only arbiter of human life. In the United States, the termination of life continues to be the subject of great cultural and political debate.

In 1976, the New Jersey Supreme Court permitted the parents of Karen Ann Quinlan to turn off her respirator. In 1990, the U.S. Supreme Court recognized the rights of Nancy Cruzan's guardians to forego unwanted treatment. In 1997, the Oregon legislature passed an assisted suicide law, letting doctors prescribe medication to end life at the request of their terminally ill patients. The case of Terri Schiavo, however, dominated public attention for months and reflected how multiple voices continue to shape cultural practices.

Terri Schiavo collapsed in 1990 at the age of twenty-six. Although the cause has not been determined, many think that chemical imbalances triggered by an eating disorder were responsible for the collapse. Schiavo was able to breathe on her own but was unable to engage in any other normal bodily motion. For fifteen years, Schiavo remained in what was described as a persistent vegetative state, depending on a feeding tube to remain alive. After an extended legal battle between her husband and her parents, and even a legislative debate, her feeding tube was removed. She died on March 31, 2005.

Shiavo did not have a living will, a document that specified what medical measures to take at the end of life, and she did not leave specific written instructions regarding her wishes about ending her life. As a result, her husband, Michael, fought a series of legal battles with her parents, Robert and Mary Schindler, who sought custody in order to prevent the removal of Schiavo's feeding tube. Their struggle produced a searing national debate about the rights of incapacitated people, the role of parental custody, and the end of life. During its last few months, the battle involved the Vatican, the George W. Bush administration, Congress, Governor Jeb Bush of Florida, and dozens of court hearings, although the U.S. Supreme Court, which was petitioned, declined to hear the case.

The range of public values regarding the termination of life can be seen in the statements made by various individuals and groups. Hundreds of Americans, from politicians to medical personnel, from members of the clergy to ordinary citizens, expressed their viewpoints on the case. A sample of their positions reflects the influence of multiple cultures and cultural values on the debate[5]:

- David Gibbs, a lawyer representing Terri Schiavo's parents, said, "She had a life that was worth saving."

- Florida governor Jeb Bush said to reporters, "Her experience will help us to be aware of the importance of families dealing with end-of-life issues and that is an incredible legacy."

- Dr. Diane E. Meier, New York's Mount Sinai School of Medicine, said, "We've always said that autonomy and self-determination does not trump the infinite value of an individual life, that people have the right to control what is done to their own body."

- President George W. Bush stated, "I will continue to stand on the side of those defending life for all Americans, including those with disabilities."

- Andrea Albanese asked for extension of life: "In the Catholic perspective, we can offer up our sufferings to Christ."

- Tony Perkins, president of the Christian conservative Family Research Council, said, "It shows just how much power the courts have usurped from the legislative and executive branches that they now hold within their hands the power of life and death."

- Judge Stanley Birch, 11th Circuit Court of Appeals, stated, "The legislative and executive branches of our government have acted in a manner demonstrably at odds with our Founding Fathers' blueprint for the governance of a free people—our Constitution."

- Marilyn Saviola also requested heroic measures: "We're a very disposable society, and I don't want to be considered disposable."

- Betty Miller wrote on her Web site, "Abortion, suicide and euthanasia are all sins."

- Dr. Shahid Athar advocated following the Koran, which forbids euthanasia but also discourages prolonging the dying process.

- Burke Balch, of the National Right to Life Committee, said, "Terri Schiavo's death is a gross injustice and it marks a sad day in our history when our society allows Terri and others like her who have severe disabilities to be discarded in such a cruel and inhumane manner."

- David North, journalist for *World Socialist* wrote, "The controversy surrounding the fate of this unfortunate woman and her beleaguered husband is a prism through which the malignant social contradictions of the United States are being refracted."

- Like other public events, the Schiavo case rippled through our society, stimulating an examination of medical practices, legal rights, and religious convictions. It provoked debate at all levels and spawned legislation regarding the end of life as well as a surge of interest in living wills. And the debate continues today, shaped by the voices of many cultural groups. As students of public communication, we need to understand the strategies for negotiating cultural differences.

## Strategies for Negotiating Cultural Differences

One of any speaker's primary jobs is to acknowledge relevant cultural experiences or expectations affecting listeners' reception of a message, even while calling for unified thought and action. Relevance is an important concept here. If you're giving a speech on how to recycle old cell phones, for example, your audience's racial background probably is irrelevant, but if you're talking about federal programs for housing or business start-up loans or police profiling, you need to take background of your audience members into consideration. Race is irrelevant to recycling, but race is highly relevant to questions about profiling and distribution of federal mortgage money. So how can you recognize cultural difference or diversity while seeking to get people to work together? You might have to understand the difference between your personal speaking style and those styles that are known and understood by your audiences (see Table 4.2).

### Accepting Multiple Paths to Goals

Among the strategies for negotiating cultural differences is the recognition that there are many ways to reach a shared goal. Thus, for example, some colleges and universities allow students to meet a foreign-language requirement in varied

**TABLE 4.2**  What's Your Conversational Style?

| | |
|---|---|
| There are cultural preferences for varied conversational styles. Researchers have identified four dimensions that govern these preferences. Which of the following is more comfortable for you? | |
| **Direct/Indirect** | 1. "Can I borrow your pen?" (direct)<br>2. "I didn't bring a pen to class today." (indirect) |
| **Elaborate/ Succinct** | 1. "Your eyes have a blue tone that picks up the color in your blouse." (elaborate)<br>2. "You look good in blue." (succinct) |
| **Personal/ Contextual** | 1. "I think it's your fault." (personal)<br>2. "The time limits for the meeting won't allow for further discussion." (contextual) |
| **Instrumental/ Affective** | 1. "When I finish my homework, I'll be able to watch television." (instrumental)<br>2. "I hate Mondays!" (affective) |

For additional information, see William Gudykunst and Stela Ting-Toomey, *Culture and Interpersonal Communication* (Newbury Park, CA: Sage, 1988), 99–116.

*Latino/a speaking styles often must combine characteristics learned in their local communities with those needed for talking to broader multicultural*

ways, such as a demonstration of skills (oral or written test), life experiences (having grown up in a household that spoke the language), and in-class instruction (taking enough classes to become proficient). Likewise, American medical pain control protocols often allow you to try different regimes, such as self-hypnosis, psychotherapy, electrotherapy (TENS machines), acupressure and acupuncture, psychic aura readings, and any number of drug therapies.

Suppose you're in a situation, however, in which people tend to say, as some parents do to their children, "There's only one way to do this: the right way!" In such situations, how can speakers create a sense of tolerance and acceptance of multiple paths leading to common goals? Metaphors and allegories (see Chapter 9) are useful ways of letting people see the utility of allowing multiple paths to shared goals. In his speech at the Atlanta Exposition in 1894, black social activist Booker T. Washington used the metaphor of the hand, whereby individual ethnic groups (i.e., the fingers) were depicted as attached to and part of the same social system (i.e., the hand). The metaphor of colors—with their blue-and-orange uniforms, the Denver Broncos defensive team recently was called "The Orange Crush"—is also useful.

Pursuing multiple policy options focused on a single goal can blend varied resources and kinds of expertise, helping forge bonds between efforts that usually aren't associated with each other. Anyone conversant with energy problems has seen this strategy at work. For example, in early 2008, when Susan Hockfield, President of the Massachusetts Institute of Technology (MIT), keynoted a conference on "Energy and Inspiration: Inventing the Future in Time," she first set out the problem:

> [W]e need to work on two [energy] tracks at once: We need to focus on transformational technologies, that will allow us one day to leap to the other side of that chasm [between now and a day when we have "perpetually renewable energy"], and at the same time, we need to work on a host of innovations that will dramatically improve today's energy systems. These are the innovations that will buy us time until we are ready for the leap.

Then, President Hockfield outlined multiple paths to the goal of perpetual renewable energy:

> At MIT, we're working hard and creatively on both tracks, both on near-term innovations and long-term transformations, from sources including the sun, wind, waves, tides, geothermal energy, and biomass and biofuels. For those more distant transformational solutions, the centerpiece of MIT's work will be solar.

She justified MIT's primary commitment to solar energy as the best and ultimately most powerful renewable fuel. She then moved on to talk about the short-term work needed on nuclear power, oil, gas, and coal, the big "four fuels" of today. Next, she threw in what she metaphorically called a "fifth fuel" and summarized again the goal of MIT's multipath approach to an energy policy:

> At the same time, we need to elevate "efficiency" to the status of a "fifth fuel." Especially in our buildings and vehicles, the potential gains from efficiency are tremendous. In the U.S., of all the energy we use, our buildings consume about 40 percent of it, and they use 70 percent of our electricity. As scientists and engineers, the waste in those systems should entice us to want to make it right.
>
> All of these routes to a sustainable energy future remain beyond our grasp without intense, targeted investment and active partnerships among universities, industry, government, and the public. If we could bring the critical forces to bear, however, I believe that a bright, clean energy future is within reach, in time.[6]

If you're going to successfully get past those matters that divide listeners into distrustful groups, teaching people to accept multiple paths or cooperative arrangements to shared goals is a technique that you must learn to use almost daily in your speech.

## Choosing a Rhetorical Frame

Another good strategy to use when speaking to multicultural audiences is to think about **rhetorical frame**—that is, conceptual borders that orient information in a particular way—and then choose those that will most likely be attractive and understandable to your listeners.

Belinda volunteered to help raise money for the day-to-day operations of her local humane society. When she asked her boss to donate money, she talked about the "partnership" that the company had formed with the community and reminded her boss that part of the responsibility of a partnership is to share with others. Belinda relied on the metaphor of partnership to convince her boss to give money. When she asked her roommate for money, however, Belinda told the story of Sparky, the little dog she had adopted from the humane society. The exploits of Sparky had her roommate laughing and crying—and writing a check to the local humane society. And when Belinda asked her classmates for donations, she reminded them that everyone deserves a chance, even abandoned animals. Her reliance on the value of life over death netted several contributions from her classmates.

For each of her audiences, Belinda relied on the careful choice of an appropriate rhetorical frame. As Belinda realized, a variety of conceptual borders or rhetorical frames can be put on factually equivalent messages. The idea that human beings come to perceive, comprehend, and ultimately evaluate aspects of the world through cognitive frames is essential for successful communication. It demands that speakers be highly sensitive about how they tell their audiences to look at the world. Two kinds of cognitive frames can help you deliver the facts to your listeners.[7]

**Narrative Frames** Just as Belinda discovered when she used the heartwarming story of Sparky, narratives can elicit tremendous emotional responses from listeners. Stories of tragedy and hope, romance and danger, can capture attention and hold interest even when the story does not directly involve the listener. Studies of front-page news stories reveal that narrative form appears more often than any other form. Researcher Jay Rosen examined the front-page news stories of seven major national newspapers and discovered that only 16 percent of the stories were straight news accounts of the who-what-when-where-why-how variety. Most (30 percent) were combative stories of conflict, winners, and losers, while the remainder combined minor narrative forms with other forms, such as explanatory. Additional studies of the 2000 election campaign found that over 60 percent of the news coverage of leading candidates in major newspapers dealt with the candidates' personalities and activities, not with the issues or policy stands they were taking.

Think about the upset election of bodybuilder and film star Arnold Schwarzenegger, who challenged incumbent California Governor Gray Davis in 2004. Schwarzenegger enacted the stories of his film roles as media spectacles during his campaign in everything from his Total Recall Committee to "Hasta la Vista, Davis" and "Terminator for Governor" buttons. His narrative strategy worked, as voters were reminded of his tough-guy film character.

**Valuative Frames**   Issues can also be framed by values—by looking at them ethically, economically, socially, and aesthetically. Dominant community values, such as fair housing and job opportunities, are often emphasized on local news broadcasts. More abstract values, such as freedom, justice, and democracy, become the standards by which policy makers determine if American troops should be committed on foreign soil. And both sides in the debate on abortion stress human rights—the right to life versus the right to choice. There is evidence to suggest that arguments featuring positive values are more persuasive than those featuring negative values. So it's probably wise to stress the positive values of "freedom" and "peace" over the negative values of "enslavement" and "conflict."

Suppose that you want your classmates to pressure Congress to pass a more aggressive policy on protecting gay rights in governmentally funded charity programs. In that case, you might say:

> Now, for many, perhaps even most, people in this class, the issue of gay rights in government-subsidized, faith-based charities seems irrelevant. You're not gay, right? And you don't plan on working for the Salvation Army, do you? You say, "Why worry?" Well, there are plenty of reasons to worry. If charitable organizations can dictate the sexual lifestyle of their employees with the endorsement of the federal government, then such government tolerance for exceptions to antidiscrimination laws in the states can expand. If faith-based charities drive out gay employees with Washington's blessing, then they're weakening civil rights in this country as well as closing employment doors to about 10 percent of our population. If Washington allowed exceptions to antidiscrimination laws in areas of welfare, why not do it as well for companies that bid on federal construction contracts or serve as vendors to the American military? And if your sexual orientation can be dictated, how about dress codes, mandatory overtime, and the work week? Even those of you who are straight, therefore, have to deal with important social and legal questions flowing from the Salvation Army's request for exceptions to government policy.

In this kind of argument, you work through a fundamental difference that most members of the audience do not experience, yet you do it in a way that asks them to see how it's relevant to their own lives.

## Maintaining Self-Identity in the Face of Difference

The third strategy for effective communication with a multicultural audience deals with your own self-identity. Most of the time, you probably won't be willing to surrender your self-identity—your own life experiences and culture. This creates a quandary: How can you be true to yourself while managing to work effectively with others?

SPEAKING OF...
E  T  H  I  C  S

## Adapting to Moral Codes

The stated theme of this chapter is simple: You must learn to adapt your ways of talking to the cultural orientations of your listeners to achieve your goals as a speaker. What, however, are the moral limits of that requirement?

1. Must you use profanity if talking about opponents of your position just because members of your audience do?

2. Is it ethical to play to the fears a Jewish audience might have of Arabs in a speech on the evils of population control?

3. When talking to an audience of Indians about birth and population control, must you confront the practice in some of the poorer parts of India of aborting female fetuses just because of the cost of dowries?

4. What sorts of appeals to motivation and hard work should you use when talking to an audience of people whose unemployment rate has been about 40 percent for the last fifteen years?

5. What if you want to talk about a subject that is taboo (i.e., unspoken) in your family? Suppose one or both of your parents drink too heavily: How can you talk about it constructively? Or can you?

Set up some discussions in class in which you tackle these and similar problems that members of your group have encountered. Moral judgments become even more difficult to render when the participants have significantly different cultural backgrounds.

---

One technique is to recognize your similarities with others even while maintaining your own identity. This is what President Lyndon Johnson did in 1965 when urging Congress to pass civil rights legislation: "There is no Negro problem. There is no Southern problem. There is no Northern problem. There is only an American problem. And we are met here tonight as Americans—not as Democrats or Republicans—we are met here as Americans to solve that problem." [8] Johnson was searching for a transcendent identity with which, he hoped, all in his audience could associate.

Identity also can become a complicated issue when speakers see themselves as having multiple identities that sometimes seem to conflict. Speaking to the 1996 Republican National Convention, Mary Fisher had a potential identity problem. She had AIDS and was speaking as an AIDS advocate. Even though Fisher had eloquently addressed members of the GOP at their 1992 convention four years earlier, she was speaking to an audience in which the more conservative members especially wanted little to do with AIDS patients or with federal programs for help. Fisher phrased the potential identity problem early in the speech: "I mean to live, and to die, as a Republican. But I also live, and will die, in the AIDS community—a community hungry for the evidence of [political] leadership and desperate for hope." To make use of that distinction and to overcome it, Fisher chose to strip away the conservative political culture of her listeners to demand their action: "The question is not political. It's a human question, sharpened by suffering and death, and it demands a moral response." Thus, she could argue, by the end of her speech, that political action should be undertaken not for ideological reasons but for social and cultural ones. Hugging a 12-year-old

African American girl named Heidia, who had been born with AIDS, Fisher concluded her speech as follows:

> The day may come when AIDS will have its way with me, when I can no longer lift my sons to see the future or bend down to kiss away the pain. At that moment Max and Zack will become the community's children more than my own, and we will be judged not through the eyes of politics but through the eyes of children. I may lose my own battle with AIDS, but if you would embrace moral courage tonight and embrace my children when I'm gone, then you and Heidia and I would together have won a greater battle, because we would have achieved integrity. [9]

To find ways of affirming your own self, your own ethos, while also recognizing and complementing your listeners' sense of self is a search that you'll continue throughout your lifetime when you speak publicly. Finding ways of achieving unity in the midst of social diversity is a central challenge to all who would inform and persuade others. You'll often find yourself saying such things as these:

- "Now I'm not a small business person myself—I teach school right here at this college. But I spend enough time in your store to see the struggles of someone hanging on in this community. I know you put in ridiculous hours in the store, not counting the after-hours when you're working the books, your suppliers, and the employment office looking for help. I know that you face safety regulations, fire regulations, health inspections, tax evaluations, new sewer levies, Social Security payments for your employees, and bank loan reviews. I'm sure you hope that you can stay afloat, save money for your kids' college education, and get some time off with your spouse for a little vacation. You're facing the struggles of every small, low-income occupation in this country."

- "Now, I'm not from Arizona or Nevada or southern California, yet I can understand how the stereotyping that makes us laugh in a popular sitcom like *My Name Is Earl* can bother you a little. The broad portrayal of lower/middle-class people from the Southwest like Earl, Randy, Joy, and Patty is so over-the-top that the show makes us aware of how full of stereotypes it is. However, can even exaggerated comedic characters like these backfire? Do we come away from sitcoms having unintentionally reinforced those very ideas we know to be exaggerated and oftentimes untrue?"

- "Okay, so college athletes not only get a free ride through school, but many also gain enough notoriety to have a leg up on job hunting when they're done. But have you ever stopped to think about what they pay in time, stress, and physical problems for that glory? I never did until last fall, when I became the roommate of a football player."

One final point: Just as you'll often reinforce your own identity in the face of different others, so will you want to urge them to act from their own convictions. This is the final challenge of cultural life: recognizing the importance of letting other people, not necessarily like you, keep their self-identities.

This is not to say that you'll always accept the lifestyle choices of others. There will be times when you'll find it important to confront the socially dangerous or personally destructive behaviors of, for example, a drug or online gambling addict. There may be lifestyle choices that others have made that don't appeal to you, and you may find it impossible to accept appeals for cultural consistency. Sometimes appeals to male bonding or sisterhood, to your whiteness or brownness, to your youth or status as an elderly person, get nowhere. Some questions will transcend cultural practices in your mind, and you'll be forced to face them. Even then, however, it's vitally important to understand all you can about others' cultures so you can select confrontational strategies that have a chance of actually moving listeners to change their life patterns.

Throughout much of this book, you'll find us returning to questions of cultural life, multiculturalism, and the search for social unity. We do not approach what are essentially the cross-cultural dimensions of social life for political reasons. Although multiculturalism assuredly has strong political dimensions, our focus is cultural, not political. If you don't understand that speakers must adapt to their listeners' cultural moorings, you'll have great difficulty speaking to any but your own close circle. Social life—and hence public communication—is rooted in cultural practices.[10] Thus, it becomes your job to understand those practices and adapt your public speaking strategies to them.

## Assessing Your Progress

### Chapter Summary

1. Culture is a social group's system of meanings.
2. Given cultural differences between and among people, a central question every speaker must answer is this: Can you respect individual differences and cultural diversity while attempting to get a group of people to think alike and work together?
3. To understand our multicultural society, we must first recognize the diversity and then identify multiple values within that diversity.
4. At least three primary strategies for communicating with multicultural audiences are available to public speakers: (1) accepting multiple paths to goals, (2) choosing a rhetorical frame, and (3) maintaining self-identity in the face of cultural differences.
5. Speakers can choose from two rhetorical frames: narrative or valuative.

### Assessment Activities

Take one of the following topics, and by yourself or in a team, identify three or more value orientations that might be held by ideologically liberal, conservative, and middle-of-the-road people. (See the discussion of values in Chapter 5 for help.) Then, suggest at least two shared goals that you think might be acceptable to most people in all three groups. Work with one of the following topics:

a. Undocumented (illegal) aliens
b. Legalization of same-sex marriages
c. Federal subsidies to faith-based charities
d. Tuition as the basic method for financing higher education
e. Federal funding of stem cell–based medical research

Your instructor will assess your identification of value orientations and shared goals as unsatisfactory, competent, or proficient.

For additional chapter activities, log on to MySpeechLab at www.myspeech lab.com.

## Using the Web

Intercultural communication exercises are some of the best ways to learn how to apply the advice given in this chapter. Many games/exercises are available for purchase on the Internet. Some are available for no cost. Look at three suggested at www.globaledge.msu.edu/academy/ExerciseSimulations/index.asp. Phil Darg's "A Visit with Amberana" is particularly appropriate for this class.

## References

1. To explore the role of social categories of human beings is to begin dealing with the "consequences of differences and divergences, boundaries and borders," in the words of Angie McRobbie, *Postmodernism and Popular Culture* (New York: Routledge, 1994), 6. Differences and divergences should not be thought of as tools for shattering societies—as so often happens when scholars begin thinking about "the postmodern"—but rather as a phenomenon that enriches your life experience and provides you with interesting challenges when you're trying to alter other people's worlds in positive ways. For a contemporary discussion of relationships between social categories and power—especially the power to affect how one sees others—go to Ramaswami Mahalingam, "Essentialism, Power, and the Representation of Social Categories: A Folk Sociology Perspective," *Human Development,* 50 (2007): 300–319.

2. What is here called *common ground* is termed *radical categories* by cognitive scientist George Lakoff. A radical category is a variation on some central model. In one of his examples, the category "mother" can have different radicals or variations in interpretation: "(1) The birth model: the mother is one who gives birth. (2) The genetic model: the mother is the female from whom you get half your genetic traits. (3) The nurturance model: your mother is the person who raises and nurtures you. And (4) the marriage model: your mother is the wife of your father" (*Moral Politics: What conservatives Know that Liberals Don't* [Chicago: University of Chicago Press, 1966], (8). Radicals categories thus represent different ways of looking at a particular phenomenon or idea. For an update on common ground studies, see Benny P. H. Lee, "Mutual Knowledge, Background Knowledge and Shared Beliefs: Their Roles in Establishing Common Ground," *Journal of Pragmatics,* 33 (2001): 21–44.

3. For a discussion of co-cultures, see the introduction and essays in Alberto González, Marsha Houston, and Victoria Chen, eds., *Our Voices: Essays on Culture Ethnicity and Communication,* 4th ed. (New York: Oxford University Press, 2007). How these ideas play out publicly is explored in Clint C. Wilson II, Félix Gutiérrez, and Lena M. Chao, *Racism, Sexism, and the Media: The Rise of Class Communication in Multicultural America,* 3rd ed. (Thousand Oaks, CA: Sage, 2003).

4. See www.insidehighered.com/news/2007/10/04/tutu.

5. To follow the entire public debate, see, among other sources, Abby Goodnough, "Schiavo Autopsy Says Brain, Withered, Was Untreatable" *New York Times,* June 16, 2005, pp. 1, A25; John Schwartz and James Estrin, "Many Seeking One Final Say on End of Life," *New York Times,* June 17, 2005, pp. 1, A12: Sheryl Gay Stolberg, "A Collision of Disparate Forces May Be Reshaping American Law," *New York Times,* April 1, 2005, p. A17: and www.nrcl.org/euthanasia/Terri/index.html.

6. President Susan Hockfield, "Energy and Inspiration: Inventing the Future in Time," AAAS conference address, February 14, 2008. Available at web.mit.edu/hocked/speeches/2008-aaas.html.

7. William L. Benoit, "Framing Through Temporal Metaphor: The 'Bridges' of Bob Dole and Bill Clinton in their 1996 Acceptance Addresses," *Communication Studies,* 52 (2001): 70–84; Jerusha B. Detweiler, Brian T. Bedell, Peter Salovey, Emily Pronin, and Alexander J. Rothman, "Message Framing and Sunscreen Use: Gain-Framed Messages Motivate Beach-Goers," *Health Psychology,* 18 (1999): 189–196; Shanto Iyengar, *Is Anyone Responsible? How Television Frames Political Issues* (Chicago: University of Chicago Press, 1991); Shanto Iyengar and Richard Reeves, eds., *Do the Media Govern? Politicians, Voters, and Reporters in America* (Thousand Oaks, CA: Sage, 1997); Jay Rosen and Princeton Survey Research Associates, "Framing the News: The Triggers, Frames, and Messages in Newspaper Coverage." Available at www .journalism.org/framing/html; and Herbert W. Simons with Joanne Morreale and Bruce Gronbeck, *Persuasion in Society* (Thousand Oaks, CA: Sage, 2001).

8. President Lyndon Baines Johnson, "We Shall Overcome," delivered to a joint session of Congress, March 15, 1965. Reprinted in Theodore Windt, ed., *Presidential Rhetoric 1961 to the Present* (Dubuque, IA: Kendall/Hunt, 1994), 67.

9. Mary Fisher, address to the Republican National Convention, August 12, 1996. Transcription done from the C-SPAN broadcast of the address.

10. See ch. 8 on social criticism in Malcolm O. Sillars and Bruce E. Gronbeck, *Communication Criticism: Rhetoric, Social Codes, Cultural Studies* (Prospect Heights, IL: Waveland Press, 2001).

# Understanding Your Audience

Every time a salesperson gets ready to call on a client, every time a lawyer prepares to address a jury, every time a teacher plans a lecture, and every time you get ready to give a speech, audience analysis comes into play. Successful salespeople, lawyers, teachers, and speakers know that effective public speaking is audience-centered. You improve your chances of getting the desired response by tailoring your communication to your listeners—whether a client, a jury, a classroom, or an audience. People understand things in terms of their own experiences. To be most effective, you must analyze your listeners and select experiences that help them relate to you.

As you know by now, you need to interact with the people you address. Because of the richness and diversity of the American population, you can't assume that everyone thinks and acts exactly as you do. Think about your listeners as you select your speech topic, establish your purpose, and narrow your subject. Each of the remaining steps in speech preparation—selecting supporting materials, arranging the sequence of ideas, and developing introductions and conclusions—also requires that you keep your audience in mind. Your effectiveness as a speaker depends on how you adapt to your audience.

Obviously, you can't address your speech to each person individually, but you can identify common features among your listeners. Think of your audience as an onion. You peel away one layer, and you find others. The most effective way to understand your audience may be to peel away as many layers as possible. Identifying those layers or characteristics is the key to audience analysis. Once you have determined the primary features of your listeners, you can begin to adapt your ideas to them. This chapter discusses the demographic and psychological features of listeners, how to find out about your audience, and how to use what you learn. Let's first turn to demographic analysis.

## ■ Analyzing Your Audience Demographically

**Demographic analysis** is the study of observable characteristics in groups of people. In any audience, you will notice traits that group members share. You should determine your listeners' general age, gender, education, group membership, and cultural and ethnic background. Let's examine each of these factors individually.

### Age

Are your listeners primarily young, middle-aged, or older? Does one age group seem to dominate a mixed audience? Is there a special relationship between age groups—parents and their children, for instance? Are your listeners your peers, or are they much younger or older?

Watch how nursery school teachers adapt to their young listeners or risk chaos. They simplify their vocabulary and shorten their sentences. If you've ever

*Demographic groups' beliefs, attitudes, and values often are grounded in their shared experiences. Age can be an especially important grounding.*

read a story to a child, you know that you can command their attention through animation. If you talk like a wizard or a teapot or a mouse, you can see children's eyes widen. The point is this: Even if your listeners are very different from you, you can still engage them by recognizing what captures their attention. In this way, you are using audience analysis to make your message more effective.

## Gender

Is your audience predominantly male or female, or is the group made up of both genders? Do your listeners maintain traditional gender roles, or do they assume different roles? Ted chose date rape as the topic for a classroom speech. He was concerned about the lack of information about date rape on his campus and wanted to provide his classmates with the facts, but two things bothered Ted. First, it seemed that date rape might be seen as an inappropriate topic for a male speaker. Second, Ted wondered how he could interest both the male and female members of his class in the subject.

Ted decided first to convince his listeners that date rape is not an issue that affects only women. Everyone should be concerned. To reveal the extent of the problem, Ted planned to present statistics showing the rising number of date rapes. Then, he told the story of a good friend who had been raped by another student who offered to walk her back to her apartment after a party. By using a personal example, Ted was able to convince his classmates that he was legitimately concerned about the problem—and that they should be concerned, too. Ted's awareness of gender as a demographic variable allowed him to deal with his audience effectively.

## Education

How much do your listeners already know about your subject? Does their experience allow them to learn about this subject easily and quickly? Obviously, people who have worked with a particular software program, for example, will learn its new features more quickly than people who have not.

Knowing the educational background of your audience can guide your choice of language, supporting material, and organizational pattern. Assume that you are addressing the faculty senate as a student advocate of expanded student parking on campus. This audience will be familiar with the school and the issues and likely be supportive of your position. You can express complex arguments without defining technical terms or providing a lot of background information. When you are invited to speak to a local citizens' group about the proposal for expanded student parking, however, you will have to broaden your language, supporting material, and organization for a more diverse audience that may not be as familiar with the issues or as supportive of the proposal.

## Group Membership

Do your listeners belong to groups that represent special attitudes or identifiable values? Are they part of a formal organization, such as a church, chamber of commerce, or scouting group, or have they spontaneously come together? Can you pick out common traditions or practices within the organization? What is the cultural climate of the organization?

In many ways, those of us living in the United States are joiners. We join churches, fan clubs, support groups, hobby organizations, professional organizations, online groups, social networking sites, and chat rooms—the list seems endless. You can find a group to join for almost any purpose. We come together to share common values and to express feelings. Often, group members share demographic characteristics as well. For example, doctors, lawyers, and dentists join professional societies based on occupational similarities. Members of labor unions have jobs and economic welfare in common. Homeowners' groups share geographic features. Tee-ball clubs, high school reunions, and associations of retired persons unite people who are similar in age. Identifying these common interests is an important element of assessing your audience, as the following example illustrates.

The city council in Abby's hometown wanted to build an incinerator for the disposal of solid waste in order to save money. Abby was against the incinerator project, and she found herself representing a grassroots group of local homeowners. Abby attended the next city council meeting and told the council members that more money could be saved by recycling household plastics, selling aluminum cans, and mulching grass clippings. Those simple steps would reduce the waste significantly and make a new incinerator unnecessary. Abby's clinching argument was to remind council members that several of them were up for reelection. Her arguments hit a nerve; the incinerator project was canceled. As members of a group, the city council was dependent on the homeowners' approval for their jobs.

## Cultural and Ethnic Background

Are members of your audience predominantly from particular cultural groups? Do your listeners share a special heritage? Can you identify common origins among listeners? More and more, the United States is becoming a multiracial, multicultural society. Currently, over 25 percent of all Americans identify themselves as multiracial, and that number is expected to grow rapidly in the next ten years. Many Americans celebrate their roots in other countries or cultures, and these strong cultural heritages may bear on your speechmaking experience. It is important to recognize the cultural and ethnic diversity of your listeners.

Brad, a district health coordinator, was invited to talk about childhood immunizations to a group of Lakota parents. He realized that kinship ties and blood relationships are important to this Native American plains people, because the idea of family responsibility is deeply rooted in the origin stories of their culture. It is important for Lakota children to be guided by the experience and wisdom of their families, which includes many people in addition to parents, as they grow. Because of this understanding, Brad was able to appeal to the cultural sense of communal accountability shared by his listeners.[1]

## Using Demographic Information

Recognizing the variables that are present in an audience is the first step in audience analysis. The key is to decide which of these demographic factors will affect your listeners' reception of your message. In other words, you must shape your message with your audience in mind.

Sometimes several factors may affect your message. For example, if you've been asked to talk to a local kindergarten class about your baseball card collection, you must take age and education into consideration. You should adapt to your young listeners by using simplified concepts—talking about the number of hits rather than ERAs, for example. You should also keep your talk brief to accommodate shorter attention spans. And most importantly, you should involve children by using visual aids. Bring several cards for them to hold and examine.

If you were to talk about your baseball card collection to a group of local business owners, on the other hand, your message would be very different. Since your listeners are older and better educated, they can understand more complex ideas. For example, you might focus on the investment potential of baseball card collections. You could use a chart showing the relative value of your collection as it increases over time. As owners of businesses, their group membership suggests that your listeners would be interested in the commercial aspects of your collection.

Demographic analysis helps you adapt your message to your listeners more effectively. If you know who is listening to your speech, you can better select and develop your key ideas.

## Analyzing Your Audience Psychologically

Careful psychological analysis of your audience may provide clues about how they think. This is especially important when your general speaking purpose is to inform or to persuade. Before you can hope to increase understanding, alter their thoughts, or prompt action, you need to know what ideas your listeners already hold.

To analyze your audience psychologically, you can use **psychological profiling.** That is, you identify what your listeners already think and feel, much as you would discover their demographic characteristics. Beliefs, attitudes, and values are the key concepts in discussing the psychology of listeners. After we have examined each of these concepts, we'll discuss ways in which you can use them to tailor your message to your listeners.

*Beliefs, attitudes, and values are key concepts for understanding listeners.*

### Beliefs

The first task of psychological profiling is to understand your audience's beliefs. **Beliefs** are convictions about what is true or false. They arise in many ways—from firsthand experiences, from public opinion, from supporting evidence, from authorities, or even from blind faith. Beliefs are held with varying degrees of conviction. For example, you might believe that calculus is a difficult course on the basis of your own experience. At the same time, you might also believe that calculus is important for your career because of what your parents and high school teachers have told you. Each of these beliefs is supported by different kinds of external evidence, and each belief can be held with a different degree of conviction.

Beliefs also are supported by varying degrees of external evidence. When you say, "Thermal vents on the ocean's floor are rich sources of unusual marine life forms," you're very sure of that belief, because you know that marine biologists have proven that such vents and life forms exist. You hold this belief with certainty, because there is hard evidence to support it. Other beliefs, however, might not have strong external evidence to support them. As a speaker, you can indicate to your listeners the kind of evidence you have chosen to support your claims. You might say, "Marine biologists agree that . . ." to convey the strength of your facts. Or you can indicate that your beliefs are based on personal observations by saying, "In my opinion . . ."[2]

Once you have investigated your audience's beliefs, how can you use this information? You need to determine which beliefs will help you and which beliefs are obstacles to be overcome. Imagine that you are explaining facets of Malay culture to a North American audience. Most of your listeners probably don't believe in *hantu,* the malicious spirits that take the form of beasts or old men in Malay culture, so you will have to make a special effort to help them understand this cultural difference. Until your listeners appreciate the importance of spirits in Malay culture, they may have difficulty comprehending it.

## Attitudes

The second goal of psychological profiling is to identify audience attitudes. **Attitudes** are tendencies to respond positively or negatively to people, objects, or ideas. Attitudes express our individual preferences and feelings, such as "I like my public speaking class," "Classical music is better than country music," and "Prague is a beautiful city." In other words, they are emotionally weighted. Attitudes often summarize our personal reactions to our beliefs about the world (see Table 5.1).

Attitudes often influence our behavior. One dramatic example of the strength of attitudes occurred when the Coca-Cola Corporation introduced "New Coke," a refigured formula, with disastrous results. Although extensive blind taste tests indicated that people preferred New Coke's flavor, consumers reacted negatively because of their loyalty to the classic formula. Their attitudes influenced their purchasing behavior, and the corporation wisely "reintroduced" Coca-Cola Classic.

As a speaker, you should consider the dominant attitudes of your listeners. Audiences may have attitudes toward you, your speech subject, and your speech purpose. Your listeners may think you know a lot about your topic, and they may be interested in learning more. This is an ideal situation. If, however,

**TABLE 5.1**  Beliefs and Attitudes

| Beliefs and attitudes are psychological constructs held by individuals or by groups. | |
| --- | --- |
| **Beliefs** | **Attitudes** |
| Seat belts save lives. | Fastening my seat belt takes too much time. |
| Vegetables contain important minerals and vitamins. | Broccoli tastes good. |
| AARP represents the interests of older Americans. | I love Grandfather. |

they think you're not very credible and they resist learning more, you must deal with their attitudes. For example, if a speaker tells you that you can earn extra money in your spare time by selling unused items on eBay, you may have several reactions. The thought of extra income is enticing, but you might be reluctant to devote much time to this project. These attitudes toward the speech topic, purpose, and speaker will undoubtedly influence your final decision.

## Values

The third component of psychological profiling is understanding audience values. **Values** are the basic concepts organizing one's orientation to life. They underlie an individual's particular attitudes and beliefs. For many Americans, life, freedom, family, and honesty are basic values. These are deeply ingrained and enduring; as a result, they are very resistant to change. Imagine trying to convince a friend to renounce his or her citizenship. No matter how noble your cause, you will likely meet with powerful resistance, because you are attacking a fundamental value.

Values are more basic than beliefs or attitudes. They serve as the foundations from which beliefs and attitudes may spring (see Figure 5.1). For example, a person may hold the value "Human life is sacred." That value can be expressed in multiple attitudes, such as "Capital punishment is wrong" or "Mercy killing is immoral." That value may also be expressed in beliefs, such as "A fetus is a human being," "Most Americans are opposed to war," or "Religious authority ought to be respected on questions of morality."

Values, then, underlie an individual's particular attitudes and beliefs. Former Representative Barbara Jordan, the first African American woman to give the keynote address at the Democratic National Convention, identified basic values that her audience shared. Among them, she listed "equality for all and privileges for

**Figure 5.1**  Beliefs, Attitudes, and Values Are Interdependent

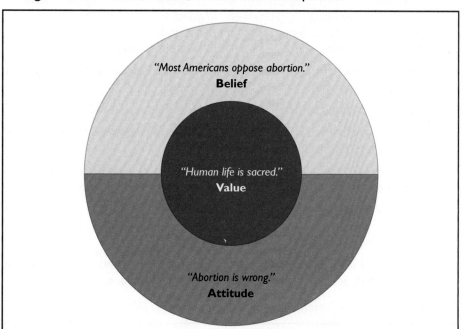

none."[3] Her speech is highly regarded, because she highlighted common ground—shared values that organized and influenced the beliefs and attitudes of her listeners.

## Discovering Demographic and Psychological Factors

Now that you understand which demographic and psychological factors are important to consider in developing a speech, you should think about how you're going to discover this information. You can ask your listeners for their opinions, and you can observe your listeners and draw inferences from your observations.

### Surveying Your Listeners

The best source of information about your audience is often your listeners themselves. Ask them. You may not have the services of a professional pollster, but you can conduct informal interviews with members of the group or develop a more formal survey to assess their beliefs, attitudes, and values.

---

SPEAKING OF . . .
S U R V E Y S

#### Using Surveys to Obtain Information

Surveys or questionnaires are a good way to gather information from a large number of people when you can't interview them individually. You have several choices when designing your survey. You can use yes-no questions, often referred to as *closed-ended questions,* when you are looking for overall attitudes or experiences. For a measurement of agreement on specific issues, you should choose *scale questions* that ask for a level of agreement, such as: Strongly Agree__ Agree__ Neutral__ Disagree__ Strongly Disagree__. *Open-ended questions,* such as "What do you think is the most important challenge facing our nation today?" allow for elaboration.

Keep the following suggestions in mind while designing your survey:

- Determine what you need to know, and avoid asking questions for which you already have answers.

- Keep your survey short to increase the chances that people will complete it.

- Consider whether you will keep the individual survey responses confidential, and tell your respondents if you will use their names.

- Think about blending your questions to evoke more inclusive responses. Use closed-ended questions, scale questions, and open-ended questions.

- Carefully word your survey questions. For example, avoid asking, "Do you drink plenty of water every day?" For a more specific response, ask "How many eight-ounce glasses of water do you drink every day?"

- If you need demographic information from your respondents, such as sex, age, income level, and so on, be sure to include these questions.

For more information, see Internet resources like www.surveymonkey.com

---

Suppose you are concerned about the rapidly rising number of sexually transmitted diseases among local teenagers. As the parent of a teenager, you are convinced that every effort should be made in the schools to halt this trend, including making condoms available to all students. If you intend to convince the school board to take action on this issue, you need to know how the members of the board currently feel about the issue. Your plan is clear: You will talk to the members of the board individually and find out.

You may, however, also have to convince the local Parent–Teacher Association to support your plan. This presents an entirely different problem, because there are thousands of parents in your school district. Even if you spent hours on the phone, you still probably couldn't interview every parent in the district. Your alternative is to talk to parents who are active in the organization or call a representative sample of parents to get an accurate profile of their views.

In each case, your questions should be basic. You will need to know whether parents vote at all. You will need to find out whether they regularly attend meetings. You will need to understand why they feel the way they do about the issue.

---

SPEAKING OF...
S K I L L S

### Handling Hostile Audiences

How do you gain a positive response from people who disagree with you? While it is unreasonable to expect to convert every member of a hostile audience, you can improve your chances of getting them to listen with the following strategies:

1. *Establish good will.* Let them know you are concerned about the issues or problems you're discussing.

2. *Start with areas of agreement.* Develop some common ground before you launch into controversial territory.

3. *Offer principles of judgment.* Determine the basis on which you and your listeners can evaluate ideas.

4. *Develop positive credibility.* If your listeners respect you, they are less likely to reject your ideas.

5. *Use experts and supporting material to which your audience will respond.* Choose your supporting material with your audience in mind.

6. *Disarm your listeners with humor.* Mutual laughter establishes positive rapport.

7. *Use a multisided presentation.* Recognize more than one perspective on the issues.

Above all, be realistic when addressing a hostile audience. Remember that the more strongly an audience opposes your position, the less change you can reasonably expect to occur.

For more information, see Herbert Simons, *Persuasion in Society* (New York: Random House, 2001), 150–160.

By asking questions that get at some of these answers, you'll be able to identify the basic points of commonality and conflict.

## Observing Your Listeners

Sometimes you don't have direct access to members of your audience. If this is the case, then you must rely on indirect observation and inference for your audience analysis. Occasionally you'll have public statements, earlier conversations, voting behaviors, purchasing decisions, and other information on which to base your analysis. At other times, you will have to rely on indirect information from others.

If you aren't closely tied to the group you will address, you'll want to (1) talk with program chairpersons and others who can tell you who is in the audience as well as something about their interests, (2) ask speakers who have addressed this or similar audiences what you can expect, (3) attend a few meetings of the group yourself, (4) read the constitution of or other literature about the group, and (5) check out the group's Web page on the Internet. In combination, the information you obtain from some or all of these sources will help you adjust your speech to your listeners.

Finally, you can consult published sources that provide demographic and survey information on broad segments of our society. Opinion polls, market surveys, political profiles, and demographic shifts are all available in your library or on the Internet in sources such as *Statistical Abstract of the United States, Survey of Current Business, Business Conditions Digest, Bureau of Labor Statistics News, Statistics of Income Bulletin,* and *Facts on File.*

## Using Your Psychological Profile

After you have developed a profile of your audience's beliefs, attitudes, and values, how can you use this information? Understanding your audience's beliefs, attitudes, and values will help you make decisions about three aspects of your speech: your ideas, your supporting materials, and your phrasing. Your psychological profile can help you do the following:

1. **Frame your ideas.** For example, if your listeners believe that childhood is a critical time of development, you can move from this belief to recruit volunteers for a day care co-op. If they value family life, you can touch on this theme to solidify their commitment. On the other hand, if your listeners are apathetic about childhood development, you must establish the critical nature of the early years of child development before you can hope to persuade them to support a co-op.

2. **Choose your supporting materials.** If your audience analysis shows that your listeners consider statistics to be reliable, you should use scientific studies or numerical data in your speech. On the other hand, if your audience believes in the divine inspiration of sacred religious texts, such as the Bible, you can cite biblical testimony to sway them.

3. **Phrase your ideas.** You can choose your words to reflect the intensity of your audience's convictions. If your listeners are ready to picket a local video rental store, then your language should show the urgency of immediate action. Demand action now. On the other hand, if they are reluctant to take up placards, then you should use less forceful words.

# Using Audience Analysis in Speech Preparation

Audience analysis helps you search for clues to the way your listeners think and act. Identifying the demographic and psychological characteristics of your listeners is an important step toward good communication. Using these characteristics helps you discover what might affect the audience's acceptance of your ideas. Consider how audience analysis helps you develop your speaking goals, your specific purpose, and the appeals you will use.

## Developing Your Speaking Goals

As you develop your speaking goals, it is important to consider both the demographic and psychological dimensions of your listeners, because these affect what your listeners will comprehend as well as how they will interpret your message.

Demographic factors, such as age, gender, education, group membership, and cultural and ethnic background, will help you understand your listeners' familiarity with your topic, motivation to listen, and ability to understand your message. If your goal is to explain new tax laws, your message will take a very different form for part-time, teenage workers than for senior citizens. Now imagine the same informative speech for an audience of tax accountants. As you can see, the demographic nature of your audience is critical as you think about the complexity of the information you will share as well as the ways in which your listeners will probably use that information.

Your listeners' beliefs, attitudes, and values can be important clues to how they will perceive what you say. For example, in speaking to a local Parent–Teacher Association about a new after-school program of foreign language and culture instruction, you're addressing an audience of school administrators, teachers, and parents.

## SPEAKING OF...
## ETHICS

### Using Audience Analysis Ethically

Marketers can often determine the underlying emotions and values that drive consumer choices using a process called psychographics. This ability to understand consumer behavior based on demographic and psychological profiling gives marketers an impressive tool. It also raises some ethical concerns. Consider the following uses of audience analysis:

1. Research suggests that many people who suffer from alcoholism feel deep social inadequacy and alienation. Advertisers often associate alcohol with social situations, such as parties. Is this attempt to target alcoholics by tapping their need for companionship an ethical use of audience analysis?

2. Some fixed beliefs are **stereotypes,** the perception that all individuals in a group are the same. Is it appropriate for speakers to use stereotypes? For example, a speaker might say, "We all know the rich cheat on their taxes. Let's raise the tax rates in the higher income brackets to compensate" or "You can't trust him—he's a politician!"

3. Should advertisers of security devices, such as pepper sprays, alarm systems, and handguns, play on women's fears of rape and assault?

4. Tobacco companies target young people by offering inducements to purchase cigarettes, such as free gifts. Is this ethical?

*As you work on your classroom speeches, consider thoughtfully what common beliefs, attitudes, and values you can draw on. And don't be afraid to conduct an informal survey—ask about some of them before you speak!*

Each of these groups has varying beliefs, attitudes, and values that will affect their perception of the program. School administrators may believe that its cost is prohibitive, teachers may think the program will enhance the current curriculum, and parents may want to know how the program will affect their children. Probably most audience members value education. As you think about how you will present your information, you should consider framing it within the broad value of education while at the same time addressing the practical problems of cost and implementation.

Be realistic about the degree of change you can expect from your listeners. How intensely can you motivate an audience to react to a topic? If your listeners are strongly opposed to downtown renovation, a single speech—no matter how eloquent—will probably not reverse their opinions. One attempt may only neutralize some of their objections. For a single speech, this is a more realistic goal than completely reversing opinions.

How much action can you expect after your speech? If your prespeech analysis indicates that your listeners strongly support after-school programs, you may be able to recruit many of them to work long hours lobbying and participating in telephone marathons. If, however, they only moderately support such programs, you might ask for a small monetary donation rather than an actual commitment of time. Audience analysis should help you set realistic communication goals.

## Developing Your Specific Purposes

Suppose you have a part-time job with your college's Career Planning and Placement Office. As part of your job, you speak to various student groups about building a résumé. Audience analysis should help you determine appropriate, specific purposes. If you were to talk to a group of incoming students, for example, you would know that they probably:

- Know little about the functions of a résumé (have few beliefs on the subject).
- Are more concerned with such short-term issues as registering for classes and finding a major (are motivated by practical values).

Given these audience considerations, you would probably provide basic rather than detailed information about résumés. You might phrase your specific purpose as follows: "To brief incoming students on the functions of a good résumé." This orientation will include a brief description of what is included in a résumé and an appeal to your listeners to choose college classes and extracurricular activities to build their résumés.

If you spoke to a group of graduating college seniors on the same subject, you would address your listeners differently. You would discover that they:

- Are familiar with the functions of résumés, because roommates and friends have used them (have beliefs that are based on personal experience).
- Tend to think of the résumé as a tool for getting a good job (have a practical perspective on the topic).

Given these audience considerations, you would offer more specific details about building a résumé. Because your listeners are probably aware that they will soon need one as they enter the work force or apply for graduate school, you might describe the specific features of a successful résumé rather than simply outlining its general functions. You might also reassure your listeners that their job search will be more productive when they allow ample time for résumé development and that a good résumé will define their skills and focus their job search. You might phrase your specific purpose as follows: "To inform graduating seniors about the features of a good résumé and about the steps they should take in creating the resume that will land them their dream job." Audience analysis will help you shape your specific purposes and determine which are most appropriate to your listeners.

---

I. **General Description of the Audience:** The library board comprises 10 members appointed to office. Citizens sometimes attend and speak at board meetings.

II. **Demographic Analysis**
  A. *Age:* Most of the board members are between thirty and sixty-five.
  B. *Gender:* The council is composed of two men and eight women.
  C. *Education:* All but four of the board members have finished college.
  D. *Group Membership:* All listeners are politically active and registered voters. Although they do not necessarily share party affiliation, they all value participation in the democratic process.
  E. *Cultural and Ethnic Background:* Ethnic background is mixed but predominantly African American, European, and Hispanic.

III. **Psychological Profile**
  A. *Factual Beliefs:* Sexually explicit Web sites are easily accessible on the Internet.
  B. *Attitudes:* Members of the board agree that everyone, including children, should have free use of library Internet facilities.
  C. *Values:* Members of the board are committed to the importance of family. They take pride in their city as a safe place to raise kids.

## Developing Your Appeals

So far, we've focused on how audience analysis helps you target your listeners as a large group. Using an approach called **audience segmentation**, you can divide your listeners into a series of subgroups or "target populations." A typical college audience, for example, might be segmented by academic standing (incoming students through seniors), by academic major (art through zoology), by classroom performance (A+ to F), or even by extracurricular activity (ROTC, SADD, Young Republicans, Pi Kappa Delta). You can direct main ideas to each of these subgroups.

Suppose you were to give a speech to members of a local community club urging them to fund a scholarship. Through audience analysis, you discover that the club is composed of social service personnel and businesspeople. By thinking of the club as segmented into these subgroups, you are in a position to offer each subgroup some reasons to support your proposal. For example, you might appeal to social service workers by saying, "The social-team concept means educating others who will contribute to the improvement of the community." For the businesspeople, you might declare, "Well-educated citizens contribute more to the financial resources of the community as investors, property owners, and heads of households."

You can see how each statement is directed to segments of your audience. These main ideas implicitly refer to the commitment of social services to helping people from all strata of life and to business leaders' commitment to financial responsibility and success.

Understanding your audience is a key step in speech preparation. Demographic and psychological analyses of audience members will help you make decisions about your topic, specific purposes, and phrasing for central ideas and main ideas. If you learn all you can about your listeners and use relevant information to plan your speech, you'll improve your chances for success.

## ■ A Sample Audience Analysis

In this chapter, we have surveyed various factors that you will consider as you analyze your audience and occasion. If you work systematically, these choices will become clearer. Suppose you want your local library board to purchase software that filters computer access to inappropriate materials. You might prepare the following analysis of your audience as you plan your speech.

With this audience analysis completed, you can begin to craft your speech. From your analysis, you conclude that the board will probably favor purchasing software to filter sexually explicit Internet materials, because they wish to protect children from such Web sites. However, they may not realize the urgency of the need. Therefore, you can choose among several approaches:

1. Stress your listeners' commitment to the welfare of the community and their responsibility to protect children in locations such as libraries, where parental guidance may not be available.
2. Emphasize the importance of the public library to the community by sharing data about the increasing number of children who use its facilities after school and on weekends.
3. Reassure board members that about 40 percent of all public libraries use such filtering software, including all libraries in Georgia and West Virginia.

As you can see, when you understand the demographic and psychological characteristics of your listeners, it's much easier to tailor a specific message for them.

# Assessing Your Progress

## Chapter Summary

1. Public speaking is audience-centered.
2. The primary goal of audience analysis is to discover the demographic and psychological characteristics of your listeners that are relevant to your speech purposes and ideas.
3. Demographic analysis is the study of audience characteristics, such as age, gender, education, group membership, and cultural and ethnic backgrounds.
4. Psychological profiling seeks to identify the beliefs, attitudes, and values of audience members.
5. Beliefs are convictions about what is true or false.
6. Attitudes are tendencies to respond positively or negatively to people, objects, or ideas.
7. Values are basic concepts organizing one's orientation to life.
8. Audience segmentation allows you to identify audience subgroups for more effective selection of main ideas.

## Assessment Activities

Choose the text of a speech from this textbook, from *Vital Speeches of the Day* (or another anthology of speeches), or from a newspaper, such as the *New York Times*. Identify statements of fact and opinion in the speech. Determine the speaker's attitudes and values from statements in the speech. Develop a profile of the audience, and assess the effectiveness of the speech for this group of listeners.

For the text of over 100 historic and contemporary speeches and additional chapter activities, log on to MySpeechLab at www.myspeechlab.com.

## Using the Web

Locate a home page for an organization. What insight does this page give you into the nature of the organization? From the material provided, determine who is likely to belong to the group. Speculate about age, gender, education, and cultural or ethnic background. What attitudes, beliefs, and values do you think members of this organization might hold in common? Explain your conclusions.

## References

1. For more about the Lakota culture, see Albert White Hat, Sr, *Reading and Writing the Lakota Language* (Salt Lake City: University of Utah Press, 1999).

2. For more discussion, see David L. Bender, ed., *American Values* (San Diego, CA: Greenhaven Press, 1989); Milton M. Rokeach, *Beliefs, Attitudes, and Values: A Theory of Organization and Change* (San Francisco: Jossey–Bass, 1968); and Rokeach, *The Nature of Human Values* (New York: Collier–Macmillan, Free Press, 1973).

3. See Wayne Thompson, "Barbara Jordan's Keynote Address: Fulfilling Dual and Conflicting Purposes," *Central States Speech Journal*, 30 (1979): 272–277.

# 6 | Finding and Using Supporting Materials

The twentieth century, called by many the Communications Century, has generated the miracles of information technology: the telegraph, the telephone, film, television, the computer chip, satellites, fax machines, e-mail, cell phones, and digital sound and video reproduction. The twenty-first century promises to produce even more astonishing communication technologies. You have at your disposal staggering amounts of information that can be accessed more easily than ever before. As you put your speeches together, you will need to find and sort through this information, choosing the supporting material that works best for your speech.

We have more information at our disposal than at any other point in history, but more information does not automatically mean better information. Instead, the mountains of facts and ideas available to us require an understanding of how to access these materials, sophisticated research strategies, and critical thinking to determine their quality.

This chapter explores the challenge of finding and assembling the materials relevant to your speech, your audience, and the speech occasion. Your challenge, ultimately, is to turn information into knowledge—to transform streams of facts into something your listeners can use in their daily lives. Devoting careful thought to how you will organize your search for supporting materials, and then to how you will put those

## CHAPTER OUTLINE

Determining the Kinds of Supporting Materials You'll Need

*Speaking of . . . Skills: How Much Is Enough?*

Finding Supporting Materials

*Speaking of . . . Ethics: What Is the Ethical Response?*

Sources of Supporting Materials

Forms of Supporting Materials

*Speaking of . . . Skills: Choosing Supporting Materials*

Functions of Supporting Materials

A Word About Plagiarism

*Speaking of . . . Skills: Citing Sources*

Sample Outline for a Problem-Solution Speech: The Heartbreak of Childhood Obesity

Assessing Your Progress

**Web Workshop**

## KEY TERMS

materials to use, will make your preparation time more productive. First, we will examine the sources of supporting materials, and then we'll suggest some ways of using these materials.

## Determining the Kinds of Supporting Materials You'll Need

To guide your choice of supporting materials, you need to consider your main topic, your audience, and the ideas you intend to discuss. Thinking about these elements should help you decide what kinds of supporting materials you will need. Consider the following critical questions before you begin your search process:

**1. What support does your topic require?** Specific topics require certain sorts of supporting materials. It's obvious that you wouldn't use the same kind of supporting material to describe your experience volunteering at an orphanage in Lima, Peru, as you would to report your international relations club's financial status. The rational requirements of your speech topic should suggest the appropriate forms of supporting material.

**2. What does your audience need to know?** No matter what forms of supporting material you choose, merely citing the findings of research is not enough. You also need to think about what your audience already knows and what they need to know. Your search for supporting materials should reflect your listeners' needs.

If you give a speech on skin cancer to a group of students in your communication class, your audience is probably most interested in knowing their chances of getting it. They may be unaware that certain practices, such as the use of tanning beds, increase the risk of skin cancer, and they probably don't know about the latest treatment methods. Your search for supporting material on this topic should uncover this information.

**3. Which form of support will be most effective for your topic?** Different forms of supporting material accomplish different results. Explanations, comparisons, and statistics will help you develop the topic so that your listeners can better understand it. Examples and testimony will lend interest to the topic. In an introduction to a speech on fire alarms, you might use an example of a local house fire to stimulate audience interest and then, in the body of the speech, use statistics to establish the importance of installing fire alarms.

**4. How objective is your supporting material?** To read and think critically, you must be able to distinguish among sources of information. One way to differentiate is to distinguish between **primary sources** (eyewitness/firsthand accounts) and **secondary sources** (accounts based on other sources of information). The diary of a soldier serving in Iraq would be a primary source; a *Washington Post* story about the war in Iraq would be a secondary source. Obviously, each type of supporting material reflects a different perspective on the war.

These initial questions about your topic (1) help you decide what supporting materials your topic requires, (2) guide your selection of supporting materials in light of your audience demands, (3) determine which forms of supporting material are most effective for your topic, and (4) indicate what supporting material will be most objective.

### How Much Is Enough?

Have you ever found yourself wondering, "How much supporting material should I use in my speech?" While there's no absolute rule governing the number or kind of supporting materials, you need enough support to establish your points. This varies according to the quality and kind of supporting materials. Here are some guidelines:

1. *Complex or abstract ideas are enhanced by concrete supporting materials, such as visual aids and specific examples.* A graph or example from daily life would clarify a speech on chaos theory.

2. *Controversial points require a lot of authoritative evidence.* This means that a speech that supports raising income taxes would benefit from statistics, budget trend information, and well-respected testimony.

3. *Speakers with low credibility need more supporting material than speakers with high credibility.* If you plan to speak on educational reform for the next century but your only experience has been as a student, you should use a lot of supporting material.

4. *If your topic is abstract or distant from your listeners' experiences, use concrete supporting material to establish identification with listeners.* A speech on life in a space station doesn't come alive until you insert specific details and concrete examples.

5. *If your audience's attention or comprehension is low, use more examples.* Enliven a speech on accounting procedures with a story or a specific instance.

## Finding Supporting Materials

So, where do you find the materials you'll need for your speeches? You'll find those materials in several places—in print and online and in interaction with others who have specific knowledge or information to share.

Obviously, your research strategy will vary with the topic of your speech, because your topic will determine the questions that you'll ask. If you decide to speak about the pre–Civil War construction of the canal system linking Lake Erie with the Ohio River, you'll probably want to know why and how the canals were constructed. You might even want information about where the ruins of the canal system are located so that you can tell your listeners to visit those sites. Your primary and secondary sources of information will probably come from historical archives and newspapers from the era as well as from general books on the subject.

On the other hand, if you intend to advocate limiting stem cell research, you'll need to consult very different resources. You'll probably need medical sources and contemporary news sources. Historical and archival materials are often found in library print collections, state and local historical societies, or through interviews, while contemporary medical information and news can be accessed online. In each case, you'll save yourself time and effort if you know where to look for supporting materials appropriate to your speech topic.

## Finding Print Resources

Most of the time, your university or college library will house the print sources you need to consult during your research. Print materials are especially useful if you need an in-depth, authoritative account such as books and reference sources can provide. Your library collection contains thousands of volumes of reference books and specialized works that you can search. Most libraries have shifted from manual card catalogs to online catalogs that list everything in the library collection by author, title, or subject. This listing will also provide the Library of Congress call number or Dewey decimal number to help you locate the material.

Print resources are often highly authoritative. Editors and publishers provide control over the material published, offering some assurance that the facts presented in print form are accurate, and books, newspapers, and magazines are checked for factual accuracy before publication. If the newspaper or magazine was published before 1980, you should check for print copies. While some of this early material has been digitized and is available in electronic form, much of it still remains available only in print form. Your librarian can help you locate newspapers and magazines through indexes such as the *New York Times Index* or the *Reader's Guide to Periodical Literature* (*Readers' Full Text* is the electronic version), which includes publications of general interest. Interlibrary loan arrangements are usually available if the print material is not in the collection of your library.

Special collections of materials, such as diaries, photographs, art work, memorabilia, and other items, are sometimes only accessible through local library archives and the collections of county and state historical societies. For a speech on the pre–Civil War Ohio canal system, you would most likely find photographs, topographical charts, and engineering instruments for its construction in county libraries, historical societies, and museums. An online search would give you the list of items in each collection as well as the operating hours of and maps to each library or museum. You may even discover material that no one else has worked with before.

## Finding Electronic Resources

Your university library most likely catalogs its collection electronically. Your reference librarian will be able to provide you with instructions for accessing the electronic resources. Generally, online catalogs will conduct searches by key words, author, title, or topic. So, as you're thinking about where to begin your search, you should jot down key terms and phrases.

Learning to narrow your searches through precise specification of topic or through subcategorization will make those searches less frustrating. Most search sites offer you **Boolean searches**, in which you use such words as *and, or,* and *not* to control the subject matter. So "medieval *or* architecture" gets you all references with either word, "medieval *and* architecture" pulls up references to all works with both words in them, and "medieval *and* architecture *not* England" highlights medieval architecture everywhere except England. Knowing authors and titles will help even more.

Finally, find out what databases your university can access. These are collections of materials that usually have a central focus such as popular periodicals, medical information, or journals published within a specific academic discipline (e.g., science, history, law, or mass media). The reference librarian can help you find the database that is most useful for your research. Some of the most popular general databases include the following:

*Computerized database searches can yield vast information rapidly and efficiently.*

- *InfoTrac* is a collection of databases through which your library might subscribe to databases in specialized disciplines like psychology or management.

- *Readers' Guide Full Text* provides full texts for over 100 popular publications and abstracts for many more.

- *EBSCOhost* provides periodical articles, often in full text.

- *FirstSearch* is an extensive listing of other databases, such as *WorldCat* and *ArticleFirst,* both of which include library collections and journal articles.

- *Academic Search* provides full texts of articles from more than 3,000 popular and scholarly periodicals like the *Wall Street Journal* and the *Christian Science Monitor.*

- *ProQuest Research Library* indexes approximately 2,000 periodicals and academic journals, providing full texts for about half of its entries.

- *LexisNexis Academic Universe* includes full texts for about 5,000 public and commercial business, legal, newspaper, and media sources with television broadcast transcripts.

- *ERIC* provides articles, citations, and abstracts for education and humanities journals as well as unpublished documents collected by a government clearinghouse.

- *MLA Bibliography* contains references to articles, books, and dissertations on literary criticism.

- *PsycInfo* is a comprehensive database of psychological research.

- *MEDLINE* will get you into psychosocial and physiological studies of disease and associated medical problems.

This is the most general place to begin your research. If you are looking for these reference materials in your library, use the electronic catalog. However, you might want to expand your search to include specialized resources or materials from other libraries, research institutes, or international sources. To access these specialized resources, you'll need to know about search engines, directories, and virtual libraries.

## Search Engines

A **search engine** is a computer program that allows you to search multiple databases using specific words or phrases. They allow you to explore in hundreds of thousands of places very quickly. Search engines take your search terms and look among millions of bits of online data for matches. Then, they list those sources on your computer screen for you to explore further. You should realize that no single search engine is capable of searching the entire Web; it's just too extensive. Because each search engine has a different way of organizing and accessing the information on the Web, it's a good idea to try more than one search engine when you're researching a topic. By varying the search engines that you use, you'll generate multiple sources.

Different search engines have different virtues. Large databases include Google, Yahoo!, All the Web, AltaVista, HotBot, Excite, InfoSeek, and Lycos. Advanced search features allow you to search in special ways—for example, Ask.com asks you questions in natural language, Simpli.com has pull-down menus to help you focus, and both InfoSeek and AltaVista help you refine questions. Annotated directories, such as the Britannica Internet Guide, LookSmart, Snap.com, and the Mining Company, tell you how to get into the search process. Included among business directories are Livelink Pinstripe, Dow Jones Business Directory, SearchZ, and Northern Light Industry Search. A nice online guide to search engines, *The Meta Search Engines: A Web Searcher's Best Friends* by Daniel Bazac, will help you even further as you make your way through these and other tools.[1] See Table 6.1 for advice on which search engines to use for which approaches to information finding and retrieving.

**Metasearch engines** allow you to compensate for the limitations of individual search engines, because they send your search request to a number of search engines simultaneously. For example, a popular metasearch engine is MetaCrawler. It searches in Google, Yahoo!, Ask.com, About, LookSmart, Overture, and Find What. So, you can access several search engines with this single metasearch engine. You should be careful when using a metasearch engine, however, because you will multiply the number of hits that you would generate with a single search engine. Therefore, metasearch engines work best for obscure topics or very specific search parameters.

Just like individual search engines, each metasearch engine will scan differently. Because they are searching more broadly, the searches are often limited in both time and the number of hits for each individual search engine that is included. Among the better metasearch engines are MetaCrawler, Dogpile, ProFusion, IxQuick, Metasearch, Hog Search, Mama, Wakweb, Veoda, SurfWax, Turbo10, and Vivisimo. You can locate them by conducting a search using the name of the engine. Since both search engines and metasearch engines change rather frequently, you can keep updated on the latest additions and their capabilities through www.allsearchengines.com, www.searchenginewatch.com, or www.searchengineguide.com.

**TABLE 6.1** Internet Search Engines

| Information Needed | Characteristics of the Search Engine |
|---|---|
| Overview of topic | DMOZ and Yahoo! organize information in "trees" from general to specific topics; All the Web and Google are the largest, fastest search engines. |
| Relevant hits only | Excite has excellent summaries, and you can ask for "more documents like this one." Teoma has great relevancy. |
| Review of what's available on the Internet | MetaCrawler works across engines; Inference Find searches engines, merges the results, and removes redundancies. |
| Pinpoint research | AltaVista is massive yet has a fast indexer of full texts; MSN and Ask.com work well on subcategories. |
| Common words | HotBot is fast and powerful, and ranks results as well as other options for searches; Excite, Yahoo!, and Lycos are tailored to less-experienced searchers. |
| Have a date | HotBot Super Search limits by date. |
| Scientific information | AltaVista has the best rating among general engines. |
| Proper names | AltaVista and InfoSeek are sensitive to capital letters; HotBot can search names in regular or reversed order (Sam Jones; Jones, Sam). |
| Images, sounds, media types (Java, VRML), extensions (e.g., .gif) | Try Lycos Media, HotBot Super Search, Yahoo! Computers and Internet, Google Image Search, and American Memory. |
| Email discussion groups | LISZT is a directory of mailing lists and those who run them. |
| Quotations | Go to The Quotations Page, Bartlett, Land of Quotes. |

Information taken from material prepared by Debbie Abilock (1996), updated April 10, 2008, at nuevaschool.org/~debbie/library/research/adviceengine.html and Jennifer Tanaka, "The Perfect Search," *Newsweek*, September 27, 1999, pp. 71–72. See also commentary by Danny Sullivan at SearchEngineWatch.com.

## Directories

Unlike search engines that are programmed to seek matches without regard to quality, directories have been developed by information specialists. **Directories** also seek information, but they have arranged Internet sites by topic, such as sports, shopping, entertainment, finance, and news. You can choose the directory that is most likely to generate specific matches to your search goals. If you are interested in a specific topic and don't want to be bothered with irrelevant hits, you should consider using a directory. Some general search engines, such as Google and Lycos, also offer the option of conducting a search through a directory.

You'll want to consider using a directory to conduct your search if you are seeking scholarly work rather than material from popular sources. For example, if you are planning an informative speech on autism and use a general search engine to locate materials, you'll be overwhelmed by thousands of hits. Your general search will yield material that includes popular press stories about autistic children, chat rooms, personal Web sites, and hundreds of other sites.

To avoid wasting time with irrelevant material, you should refine your search through a directory. Use directories like ArgusClearinghouse, Internet Scout Project, Librarian's Index to the Internet, or World Wide Web Virtual Library to generate a more useful, authoritative list of available materials.

## Virtual Libraries

As you will soon discover when you conduct Internet research for your speeches, the problem is not the quantity but the quality of the materials available to you. Anyone can post anything on the Internet—and they do. To fuse the quality found in the traditional library print collection with the unlimited potential of the Internet, libraries have been created. **Virtual libraries** are usually nonprofit, smaller than commercial search engines, and hosted by academic or scholarly organizations, such as universities and research groups. They combine the advantages of technological speed with traditional library methods of organizing and cataloging information.

The advantage of the virtual library is that the accessible materials have been screened for quality. They also include many databases and other resources that are overlooked by commercial search engines. These databases and other resources are referred to as the **invisible Web,** because they are not indexed by commercial search engines and thus escape notice with generic searches. *This is why a general search is only the beginning of your research.* With virtual libraries, you gain quality of materials as well as an expanded search capacity. Here is a partial list of virtual libraries to get you started:

- Librarian's Index to the Internet (www.lii.org)
- Education Virtual Library (www.csu.edu.au/education/library.htm)
- Internet Public Library (www.ipl.org)
- Infomine (infomine.ucr.edu)
- Invisible Web Directory (www.invisible-web.net)
- Academic Information (www.academicinfo.net)
- Social Science Information Gateway (www.sosig.ac.uk)

The value of virtual libraries can be seen rather dramatically when you consider what happens if you begin with a random search through a generic search engine and then tailor your search using a virtual library. Let's take the popular myth that George Washington wore wooden dentures. How would you discover if this is true? Using the search phrase "George Washington," you search the Internet using the metasearch engine MetaCrawler. In twelve seconds, your search generates hits in eighty-six different places, from eBay to Expedia.com. You've turned up references to Washington, D.C., hotels and to George Washington University. This didn't work very well, so you try Google, a single search engine. In 0.06 seconds you have 50,400,000 hits. This isn't working either. Finally, you use Librarian's Index to the Internet, a virtual library, and find forty-eight authoritative biographies on George Washington within seconds. If you had used the search phrase "wooden dentures," you would have turned up several specific biographies instead of forty-eight separate books. Still, in each case, you've completed your initial searches in less time than it would take to find your car keys, put on your coat, and go to the local library. Choosing the best search engine and refining your search phrase can save you even more time.

SPEAKING OF...
ETHICS

### What Is the Ethical Response?

What is the most ethical response in each of the following situations?

1. You can't find exactly the right testimony from an expert to prove a point you want to make in a speech. Is it okay to make up a quotation to use if you know it will result in a better grade?

2. Should you rip out a page from a magazine in the library if it contradicts something you plan to say in your speech? If the page is missing, nobody will know about the contradiction.

3. If you are a spokesperson for a company, is it okay to suppress facts about the side effects of a new fat-free product? What if the side effects

aren't fatal and the product will let thousands of people lose weight?

4. If you can sell more life insurance when you exaggerate the death benefits, should you do it? What if your job depends on increasing your monthly sales? Is it okay to distort facts to keep your job?

5. Should you post a message on the Internet that you know isn't supported by facts? What if it's just a joke?

6. Should you deliberately conceal the source of a fact because you know it's not credible? What about attributing the fact to another, more credible source?

## Sources of Supporting Materials

Whether you walk to your library or sit down in front of your computer to begin your research, you'll find a variety of quality resource materials available to you both in print and online. Your search for resources will probably begin with general sources and then become more specific as you decide what aspects are most interesting. For that reason, we'll start with general reference works and then discuss more specialized reference works.

### General Reference Works

General reference works can be good place to start your research once you've chosen a speech topic, because they offer basic facts and general orientations to a variety of topics. Usually you'll use general reference works to provide a background before you move on to more specialized sources. Resist the temptation to rely on *Wikipedia*, a popular online encyclopedia, since it posts contributions without screening them. Anyone who has access to a computer and the Internet can post an entry, and they often do! Instead, you might read *Encyclopedia Americana* or *The New Encyclopaedia Britannica* to get started. Most encyclopedias provide a broad view of an extensive array of topics, summarizing information found elsewhere. Somewhat narrower in scope, there are also specialized encyclopedias, such as the *Encyclopedia of Religion* and the *Encyclopedia of Physical Education, Fitness, and Sports*. *The Oxford English Dictionary* or *Webster's New Biographical Dictionary* will help you with any unfamiliar words. *The World Almanac and Book of Facts* and *National Geographic Atlas of the World* can provide answers to specific questions about people, times, and places. Once you've investigated the background for your speech topic, you'll be ready to dig deeper into more specialized references, such as newspapers, magazines and journals, specialized yearbooks and encyclopedias, government publications, biographies, and collections.

## Newspapers

Newspapers are obviously a useful source of information about events of current interest. Your school or city library undoubtedly keeps on file copies of one or two highly reliable papers, such as the *New York Times, The Observer,* the *Wall Street Journal,* or the *Christian Science Monitor,* as well as the leading newspapers of your state or region. Through the *New York Times Index,* you can locate the paper's accounts of people and events from 1913 to the present. Another useful and well-indexed source of information on current happenings is *Facts on File,* issued weekly since 1940. Almost all major newspapers will run their own Web sites as well, and LexisNexis gives you electronic access to more than 200 major and local newspapers.

## Magazines and Journals

The average university library subscribes to hundreds of magazines and journals. Some, such as *Time, Newsweek,* and *U.S. News & World Report,* summarize weekly events. *The Atlantic* and *Harper's* are representative of monthly publications that cover a wide range of subjects of both passing and lasting importance. *The Nation, Vital Speeches of the Day, Fortune, Washington Monthly,* and *The New Republic,* among other magazines, contain commentary on current political, social, and economic questions. More specialized magazines include *Popular Science, Scientific American, Ebony, Sports Illustrated, Field and Stream, Ms., Better Homes and Gardens, Rolling Stone, Byte, Today's Health, National Geographic,* and *The Smithsonian.*

Indexes are available for most publications. A reference librarian can show you how to use them.

## Yearbooks and Encyclopedias

The most reliable source of comprehensive data is the *Statistical Abstracts of the United States,* which covers a wide variety of subjects ranging from weather records and birth rates to steel production and election results. Information on Academy Award winners, world records in various areas, and the "bests" and "worsts" of almost anything can be found in *The World Almanac and Book of Facts, The People's Almanac, The Guinness Book of World Records, The Book of Lists,* and *Information Please.* The *Gale Encyclopedia of Multicultural America* provides information about the culture, history, and contributions of minority groups in America. You can also find additional material to supplement your knowledge of diverse groups by examining *The Asian American Almanac, The Muslim Almanac,* the *St. James Press Gay and Lesbian Almanac, The African American Almanac, The Hispanic American Almanac,* and *The Native American Almanac.*

## Government Publications

The U.S. Government Printing Office collects, prints, and distributes information produced by federal agencies such as the executive branch of government, the House of Representatives, the Senate, the Census Bureau, and the Environmental

Protection Agency. Much of this material is provided free of charge in print form or online. The *Guide to U.S. Government Publications* (both in print and online) provides a step-by-step tutorial to take you through the process of finding government publications. FirstGov.gov (www.firstgov.gov) and the University of Michigan Document Center (www.lib.umich.edu/govdocs) provide direct access to federal and international government information and services. You can also search sites maintained by individual offices, such as the Census Bureau, the White House, or state governments.

Many state universities publish reports on issues related to agriculture, business, government, engineering, and scientific experimentation. Endowed groups, such as the Carnegie, Rockefeller, and Ford Foundations, and special interest groups, such as the Foreign Policy Association, the Brookings Institution, the League of Women Voters, Common Cause, and the U.S. Chamber of Commerce, also publish reports and pamphlets. Although it is not comprehensive, *The Vertical File Index* serves as a guide to some of these materials.

## Biographies

The *Dictionary of National Biography,* the *Dictionary of American Biography, Who's Who, Who's Who in America, Current Biography,* and more specialized works organized by field contain biographical sketches that are especially useful in locating facts about famous people and in documenting the qualifications of authorities whose testimony you may quote. A number of multicultural biographies, such as *African American Biography, Hispanic American Biography, Asian American Biography, Arab American Biography,* and *Native American Biography,* are excellent sources of material often neglected in traditional biographies.

## Collections

Collections of poetry, maps, charts, quotations, and other facts can be useful if you are looking for specialized information. For example, the *Columbia Granger's Index to Poetry* will provide the text of a poem if you know only the first line or author's name. *Bartlett's Familiar Quotations* is a popular collection of statements and phrases that can be used by public speakers. The *Guinness Book of World Records* and *The People's Almanac* provide useful information of all kinds. And, if you're looking for a map or chart, you should consult the *Rand McNally Commercial Atlas and Guide* or the *National Geographic Atlas of the World.* All of these sources are available in print and online.

## Finding Information Through Interviews

When looking for material, many of us forget the easiest and most logical way to start: by asking questions. The goal of an **informational interview** is to obtain answers to specific questions. Interviews increase your understanding of a topic so that you will avoid misinforming your audience, drawing incorrect inferences from information, and convoluting technical ideas. Your interviewee may be a content expert or someone who has had personal experience with the issues you wish to discuss. If you're addressing the topic of black holes, who is better qualified to help you than an astronomer? If you're explaining the construction of a concrete boat, you might contact a local civil engineer for assistance. If you wish to discuss anorexia nervosa, you might interview a person who has suffered through the disorder. Interviews can provide compelling illustrations of human experiences that can be woven into the text of your speech.

Conducting a successful interview requires planning. You need to observe these general guidelines in preparing an informational interview:

**1. Determine your specific purpose.** What do you hope to learn from the interview? Can the person you are interviewing provide precise information from a unique perspective? Determine what you would like to glean from the interview, and communicate that purpose directly to the person you plan to interview.

**2. Structure the interview in advance.** Plan your questions in advance so that you have a clear idea of what to ask. The interview may not follow your list exactly, so you'll need to remain flexible and free to deviate from your interview plan to clarify or elaborate on a previous response. Begin the interview by setting limits on what will be covered during the session. End the interview by recapping the main ideas and expressing your appreciation.

**3. Remember that interviews are interactive processes.** Adept interviewers should be good listeners. You should listen carefully to what is said and accurately interpret the significance of those comments. Follow a pattern of "turn taking," as you would in any conversation. And if you don't understand something, ask additional questions to allow plenty of opportunity to clarify remarks and opinions.

**4. A good interviewer builds a sense of mutual respect and trust.** Feelings of trust and respect are created by revealing your own motivation, by getting the person to talk, and by expressing sympathy and understanding. Good communication skills and a well-thought-out set of questions build rapport in interview situations.

**5. Be courteous.** Arrive on time, and use the interview period productively. Always follow up the interview with a note or letter expressing your appreciation for the person's shared time and expertise.

## ▌ Forms of Supporting Materials

After you've located your supporting materials, you need to choose among them. The supporting materials that are used to clarify, amplify, or strengthen your ideas fall into four categories: (1) comparisons and contrasts, (2) examples, (3) statistics, and (4) testimony (see Figure 6.1).

### Comparisons and Contrasts

Comparisons and contrasts are useful verbal devices to clarify ideas—to make them distinctive and focused. Pointing out similarities and differences helps listeners comprehend your ideas and opinions.

**Comparisons** connect something already known or believed with ideas a speaker wishes to have understood or accepted. Comparisons therefore stress similarities; they create analogies. In the early hours of September 11, 2001,

**Figure 6.1** The Forms of Supporting Materials

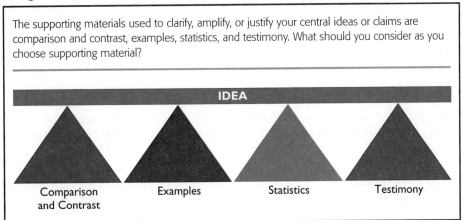

The supporting materials used to clarify, amplify, or justify your central ideas or claims are comparison and contrast, examples, statistics, and testimony. What should you consider as you choose supporting material?

during the terrorist attacks on the World Trade Center and the Pentagon, many journalists and politicians compared the unfolding events to the 1941 attacks on Pearl Harbor. This comparison created an analogy between the terrorist attacks and the aerial bombing that precipitated the U.S. entry into World War II. Both were surprise attacks that resulted in tremendous loss of American lives.

**Contrasts** help clarify complex situations and processes by focusing on differences. A speaker explaining professional football would want to contrast it with the more familiar rules governing interscholastic football. To illustrate the severity of the huge tsunami that hit Indonesia and other coastal areas in 2004, the news networks contrasted the loss of life with that in other natural disasters.

Contrasts can be used not only to clarify unfamiliar or complex problems but also to strengthen the arguments you wish to advance. One student speaker

### SPEAKING OF...
### SKILLS

#### Choosing Supporting Materials

Recent research compared qualitative and quantitative supporting material. *Qualitative supporting material* includes examples, anecdotes, and analogies, such as "a friend of mine was in a car crash, and a seat belt saved her." *Quantitative supporting materials* are statistical or numerical information, such as "a recent investigation found that people are 50 percent more likely to be injured if they are not wearing a seat belt."

The research found that both qualitative and quantitative supporting material are equally effective in changing attitudes initially. However, qualitative supporting materials worked much better over time. There are two reasons that qualitative supporting materials strengthen long-term attitude change:

1. Qualitative supporting materials are more vivid, and the impact of vivid images is greater than that of numbers.

2. We can more easily remember qualitative supporting materials than numerical information.

See Dean C. Kozoleas, "A Comparison of the Persuasive Effectiveness of Qualitative Versus Quantitative Evidence," *Communication Quarterly,* 41 (1993): 40–50.

argued that regulations governing ocean vessels should be strictly enforced. Explaining the reasons for the huge federal fine against Royal Caribbean Cruise Lines in July 1999, she said, "While crew members wore 'Save the Whales' buttons, ships discharged hazardous chemicals into their ocean wakes." This speaker brought the issue of enforcement into sharp focus by stressing the contradictions in an actual instance. Contrasts can cut to the heart of issues quickly and dramatically.

You can use comparisons and contrasts together to double their impact on your audience. For example, a student speaker focused on the messages in cartoons. To help his listeners understand how cartoons provide commentary, he compared and contrasted *Rocky and Bullwinkle* with *Beavis and Butthead:*

> Both cartoons have stirred up considerable public controversy. In the 1960s, some people boycotted *Rocky and Bullwinkle* just as some refuse to watch *Beavis and Butthead* today. There are major differences, however. *Rocky and Bullwinkle* episodes pitted the pair against Boris and Natasha, mimicking the Cold War conflict between the United States and the Soviet Union. *Beavis and Butthead,* on the other hand, avoids political commentary while focusing on the struggle of the main characters with adolescence.

Whenever using comparisons and contrasts, try to make sure at least one of the items is familiar to listeners. Comparing professional football and interscholastic football will make no sense to an Irish listener, who probably doesn't know anything about either one. You'd have to compare and contrast professional football and European rugby to clarify the game for her.

## Examples

Examples can be powerful ways to involve an audience in your topic, because they make abstract or general ideas easier to comprehend. Examples take various forms—they can illustrate concepts, conditions, or circumstances; they can narrate events; or they can be listed as undeveloped specific instances.

**Types of Examples**  **Hypothetical examples** are made up. **Factual examples** (or real examples) are recitations of events that actually happened or of people, places, and things that actually exist. If you were giving a speech on why homeowners should move into apartments, you might narrate a "typical" homeowner's day: a leaky faucet to fix, a lawn to mow, real estate taxes to pay, and a neighbor's dog to chase out of the flower garden. Although not all of these events occurred in the same day, asking listeners to imagine what life would be like if they did would help you convey the carefree life of an apartment dweller. For many audiences, factual examples are more potent. Many speakers have been highly successful using facts from their own lives. For instance, some actors, such as Michael J. Fox and the late Christopher Reeve, have used their struggle with life-threatening conditions to argue for increased funding for medical research.

While some speakers glean examples from their own lives, others illustrate ideas with the lives of others. Former Minnesota governor Jesse Ventura advocated extending rights to gay partners with this example: "I have two friends who have been together for forty-one years. If one of them becomes sick, the other one is not even allowed to be at the bedside. I don't believe government should be so hostile, so meanspirited . . . Love is bigger than government."[2] Notice how Ventura drew his conclusion immediately after the example. This helps listeners grasp the point of the example, strengthening your argument.

Sometimes speakers use a list of specific instances. Their power comes from cumulative effect rather than from vivid detail. You can use a single, specific instance if you only need a quick example—for instance, "You're all familiar with the windows in this classroom, but you might not have noticed their actual construction. I want to talk about those windows—those double-glazed, low-emissivity, gas-filled windows—and how the use of such windows contributes to reduced energy consumption."

More often, though, speakers pile up specific instances to help establish a point. In the famous passage of his 1941 declaration of war, President Franklin Delano Roosevelt listed the islands attacked by the Japanese Imperial forces. In 1992, Mary Fisher spoke at the Republican National Convention about AIDS. She said to the delegates: "[T]he AIDS virus is not a political creature. It does not care whether you are Democrat or Republican, it does not ask whether you are black or white, male or female, gay or straight, young or old." She continued by adding details to the series of specific instances:

> Tonight, I represent an AIDS community whose members have been reluctantly drawn from every segment of American society. Though I am white, and a mother, I am one with a black infant struggling with tubes in a Philadelphia hospital. Though I am female, and contracted this disease in marriage, and enjoy the warm support of my family, I am one with the lonely gay man sheltering a flickering candle from the cold wind of his family's rejection.[3]

With these accumulated instances, Fisher demonstrated to her listeners the impact of the disease on all Americans.

**Choosing Examples** When selecting examples, whether hypothetical or factual, you should keep three considerations in mind:

1. **Is the example relevant?** If the connection is vague, it won't accomplish its goal. If your hypothetical story about a spring break road trip is fun to listen to but not related to your speech on saving the Florida Everglades, you're in trouble!

2. **Is it a fair example?** An audience can be quick to notice unusual circumstances in an illustration or story; exceptional cases are seldom convincing. Having your grandmother who uses a walker but surfs on weekends in your story, for example, would stretch the credulity of your listeners.

3. **Is it vivid and impressive in detail?** Be sure your extended examples are pointed and visual. When a student argued for more humane treatment of animals raised for slaughter, he described the procedures at a local auction barn, traced typical routes to processing plants, and detailed the handling of animals in the holding pens. This example was specific and detailed enough to convince listeners that there was cause for change.

## Statistics

**Statistics** are numbers that show relationships between or among phenomena—relationships that can emphasize size or magnitude, describe subclasses or parts (segments), or establish trends. By reducing large masses of information into

*Compile complex information in a form that your listeners can easily understand.*

generalized categories, statistics clarify situations, substantiate potentially disputable central ideas, and make complex aspects of the world clear to your listeners.

**Magnitude**  We often use statistics to describe a situation or to sketch its scope or seriousness—that is, its size or **magnitude.** The effect on listeners can be especially strong if one statistical description of the size of a problem is piled up on others. Notice how a student used multiple statistical descriptions of magnitude while urging her classmates to consider the problem of wildlife-related car accidents:

> Wildlife-related automobile accidents are a growing problem on rural roads around the country. From 1990 to 2004, such accidents increased by fifty percent, killing more than 2,800 people. Almost 2 million accidents involving wildlife during this fourteen-year period injured thousands of drivers and cost more than $8 billion. Ninety percent of these accidents happen in rural areas and deer are usually involved. The average cost of car repair is $8,000, and medical expenses are almost four times higher. In Pennsylvania, with the most vehicle-wildlife crashes, drivers struck nearly 97,000 deer in 2006. As deer habitats are overrun by housing developments and more of us take to the road, the problem will only get worse in the coming decades.

Not all uses of magnitudes, of course, need such piling up of instances. Simple, hard-hitting magnitudes sometimes work even better. For example, Brenda Theriault of the University of Maine, arguing that there is "very little nutritional value in a hamburger, chocolate shake, and fries," simply noted that "of the 1,123 calories in this meal, there are 15 calories of carbohydrates, 35 calories of protein, and 1,073 calories of fat."[4] These were all the numbers the listeners needed in order to understand the nutrition in a typical fast-food meal.

**Segments**  Statistics that are used to isolate the parts of a problem or to show aspects of a problem caused by separate factors or parts are statistical **segments.** In discussing the sources of income for a college or university, for example, you would probably segment the income by percentages coming from tuition and fees, state and federal money, gifts and contributions, special fees such as tickets, and miscellaneous sources. Then, you would be in a position to talk reasonably about next year's proposed tuition hike. In one case, a student speaker used survey results to show how people shop on the Web:

> People spent a total of $10.7 billion dollars on products and services they found via the Web during the holiday season at the end of 2007. Electronic and computer products sales comprised 27 percent of this total and travel another 24.3 percent, making up over half of all Web sales. The remainder of the sales is divided almost equally among adult entertainment, general entertainment, food/drink, gifts/flowers, and apparel.[5]

As this example illustrates, the most important value of statistics doesn't lie in the numbers themselves but in how you interpret and use them. In using statistical data, always answer the question "What do these numbers mean or demonstrate?" In this case, it's clear that electronic and computer products dominate Web site sales.

**Trends** Statistics often are used to point out **trends,** or indicators that tell us about the past, the present, and the future. The comparison of statistical data across time allows you to say that a particular phenomenon is increasing or decreasing (see Table 6.2). If you were arguing for stricter controls on chewing tobacco, you might cite Federal Trade Commission statistics revealing that chewing tobacco sales have increased steadily. Over the ten-year period from 1989 to 2007, revenues grew by more than $100 million annually, exceeding $2.2 billion in 2007.[6] This upward trend suggests that something should be done to control smokeless tobacco. You could make your case even stronger by citing a corresponding upward trend in cancers of the lips, gums, and tongue and an increased number of deaths from oral cancer.

**Using Statistics** When you use statistics to indicate magnitude, to split phenomena into segments, or to describe trends, you can help your listeners by "softening" the numbers. You can use the following four strategies to do this:

1. **Translate difficult-to-comprehend numbers into more understandable terms.** In a speech on the mounting problem of solid waste, Carl Hall illustrated the immensity of 130 million tons of garbage by explaining that trucks loaded with that amount would extend from coast to coast three abreast.[7]

2. **Don't be afraid to round off complicated numbers.** "Nearly 400,000," is easier for listeners to comprehend than "396,456," and "just over 33 percent," or, better yet, "approximately one-third" is preferable to "33.4 percent."

3. **Use visual materials to clarify statistics whenever possible.** Use a computer-generated graph; hand out a photocopied sheet of numbers; prepare a chart in advance. Such aids will allow you to concentrate on explaining the

**TABLE 6.2** Types of Statistics

In a speech to inform, a speaker might use three types of statistics to describe students at Central University. What other forms of supporting material could complement these numbers?

| Magnitudes | Segments | Trends |
|---|---|---|
| "Three-fourths of all Central University students come from the state." | "Sixty percent of all Central University students major in business; twenty-five percent are humanities majors; the remaining fifteen percent are in fine arts." | "Since 1975, enrollment at Central University has increased by ninety percent every five years." |

significance of the numbers rather than on making sure the audience hears and remembers them.

**4. Use statistics fairly.** Arguing that professional women's salaries increased 12.4 percent last year may sound impressive to listeners until they realize that women are still paid less than men for equivalent work. In other words, provide fair contexts for your numerical data and comparisons.

**Testimony** When you cite the opinions or conclusions of others, you're using **testimony.** Sometimes testimony merely adds weight or impressiveness to an idea, as when you quote Mahatma Gandhi or Mother Teresa. Other times, it lends credibility to an assertion, especially when it comes from expert witnesses. When Janice Payan addressed the Adelante Mujer Conference, she used testimony in another way. She cited her favorite poem as a source of inspiration for her listeners. She urged them to seek success as she quoted the poet: "I wish someone had taught me long ago, How to touch mountains."[8]

Testimony should relate to and strengthen the ideas you are discussing. When you use quotations in your speech, they should accomplish more than simply amplifying or illustrating an idea.

Testimony also should satisfy four more specific criteria:

**1. The person quoted should be qualified, by training and experience, to speak on the topic being discussed.** Athletes are more credible talking about sports equipment or exercise programs than they are endorsing breakfast food or local furniture stores.

**2. Whenever possible, the authority's statement should be based on firsthand knowledge.** A Florida farmer is not an authority on an Idaho drought unless he or she has personally observed the conditions. Veterinarians aren't usually experts on human diseases, and Hollywood stars may not know much about international DVD sales.

**3. The judgment expressed shouldn't be unduly influenced by personal interest.** Asking a political opponent to comment on the current president's performance will likely yield a self-interested answer.

**4. Your listeners should perceive the person quoted to be an actual authority.** An archbishop may be accepted as an authority by a Roman Catholic audience but perhaps not by Protestant or Hindu listeners. When citing testimony, don't use big names simply because they're well known. The best testimony comes from subject-matter experts whose qualifications your listeners recognize.

Finally, always acknowledge the source of an idea or particular phrasing. Give your source credit for the material, and give yourself credit for having taken the time to do the research.

## Functions of Supporting Materials

As you choose supporting materials for your speech or listen to others speak, you should be conscious of the role of supporting material. There is no absolute rule about how each kind of supporting material functions, but there is general agreement about what supporting materials accomplish in your speech. Here are some guidelines for choosing your supporting materials:

**1. Complex and abstract ideas benefit from the use of specific information.** Use examples to clarify complex or abstract ideas. Compare the relationship of subatomic particles to balls on a billiard table, for instance. Such simplification is especially useful when your listeners have little background or knowledge about your topic or when the subject matter is complex. Examples also provide more vivid details and make ideas more immediate. Thus, they can stimulate your listeners' enthusiasm for complex or abstract material.

When your audience has only minimal knowledge of a concept, you should use comparisons, examples, and statistical magnitudes and trends to help you amplify the idea. These forms of support expand on your idea so that your audience can more easily comprehend and examine it.

**2. If your idea is controversial or members of your audience are hostile, use supporting material such as statistics and testimony.** These forms of supporting material are generally regarded as highly rational and credible, so they work well with controversial topics or hostile listeners. When there is disagreement among experts on the issue, you will need an abundance of supporting material.

**3. Supporting materials can enhance your credibility as a speaker.** While your listeners may question your ability to understand the complex nature of the International Monetary Fund, they will respect authorities on the subject. They will also probably be reluctant to question supporting material such as statistical information. You should always use supporting materials when you are not an expert or when your status is lower than that of your listeners.

**4. Supporting materials provide audience members with ammunition for later discussions.** When you ask for a raise, you are more likely to get it by providing information about your job performance. Your supervisor can use this information in defending your raise to others. If you are asking your listeners to make sacrifices or to accept ideas that are unfamiliar to them, use plenty of supporting material. It provides the reassurance they need to take a risk and embrace a new thought.

**5. Generally, examples create human interest, while statistics provide reasonable proof.** Listeners tend to respond subjectively to narratives. On the other hand, their response to statistics is often more detached and objective. In a speech on street children in Brasilia, you would establish the significance of the problem by providing statistics, but you would involve your listeners by telling them about the danger and hunger suffered by Emilio, who lives on the streets.

## A Word About Plagiarism

Now that we've discussed locating and generating material for your speeches, we come to a major ethical issue: plagiarism. **Plagiarism** is defined as "the unacknowledged inclusion of someone else's words, ideas, or data as one's

SPEAKING OF...
S K I L L S

### Citing Sources

When you cite your speech sources in written form, as in endnotes or a bibliography, you will probably use one of the more popular citation styles. Usually you'll include the author, title of the article and book, location of the publisher, name of the publisher, and date of the publication. Notice the differences in these two common styles:

#### APA (American Psychological Association) Style

O'Donnell, V. (2007). *Television criticism*. Thousand Oaks, CA: Sage.

#### MLA (Modern Language Association) Style

O'Donnell, Victoria. *Television criticism.* Thousand Oaks, CA: Sage, 2007.

When you cite sources orally in a speech, your goal is to add credibility to your ideas. The rules for oral citation of sources are less strict than those for written citations. Usually the location and name of the publisher aren't as important as the qualifications of the author. Sometimes the publication date is important if you want your listeners to know that you are using recent information. You might say, "According to Victoria O'Donnell, a well-known television scholar, . . ." or "Last year Professor O'Donnell studied entertainment television and reached this conclusion." You could also say, "In her recent analysis of television, critic Victoria O'Donnell wrote in her book *Television Criticism . . .*" Each of these oral citations emphasizes the qualifications of the source, adding weight to your speech.

own."[9] In speech classes, students occasionally take material from a source they've read and present it as their own. Even if listeners have not read the article, it soon becomes apparent that something is wrong: The wording differs from the way the person usually talks, the style is more typical of written than spoken English, or the speech is a patchwork of eloquent and awkward phrasing. In addition, the organizational pattern of the speech may lack a well-formulated introduction or conclusion or be one not normally used by speakers. Often, too, the person who plagiarizes an article reads it aloud badly—another sign that something is wrong.

Plagiarism is not, however, simply undocumented verbatim quotation. It also includes undocumented paraphrases of others' ideas and undocumented use of others' main ideas. For example, you are guilty of plagiarism if you paraphrase a movie review from *Newsweek* without acknowledging that source or if you use economic predictions without giving credit to *BusinessWeek*. Check with your university or college Web site for its policy on plagiarism.

## ▌ Sample Outline for a Problem-Solution Speech

Study the following outline. Notice that a variety of supporting materials are used to strengthen each of the points in the speech. Although the proof of a single point may not require as many different supporting materials as are used in this outline, the variety of support shows how a number of different forms can be combined in a speech.

## The Heartbreak of Childhood Obesity

I. Childhood obesity is an increasing problem in our society. ◄──────
    A. Michelle is a typical American child—fifteen percent overweight.
    B. U.S. Department of Health and Human Services survey reveals that childhood obesity has nearly doubled between 1983 and 2008.
    C. The prediction for the future is even more bleak, as even younger children are weighing more and more.
    D. After defining the nature of obesity, let's examine the causes of obesity in children, look at its dangers, and then investigate some solutions we can implement.

*This speech starts with an illustration and trend statistics.*

II. Obesity is defined as a positive energy balance. ◄──────
    A. This means that more energy is conserved than expended.
    B. Over time, the excess energy is stored by the body in fat cells.
    C. Approximately 2,500 extra calories become an extra pound of body weight.

*An explanation clarifies what is meant by obesity.*

III. There are three primary causes for childhood obesity. ◄──────
    A. Some children inherit the tendency to acquire extra weight.
      1. Parents who are obese tend to have children who are also obese.
      2. Experiments with mice have located genetic triggers for overeating.
      3. According to experts, the genetic predisposition to gain extra weight is a contributing factor in childhood obesity.

*The problem of obesity is developed as a three-part explanation.*

    B. Eating style also contributes to obesity. ◄──────
      1. Dr. Daniel A. Kirschenbaum, who specializes in childhood obesity, reports that obese children typically show a "high-density" eating style.
      2. A high-density eating style refers to both the quantity and frequency of eating among children.
      3. High-density eating is a behavior that contributes to obesity.
      4. Emotional stress may trigger a high-density eating style.

*To develop the problem, the speaker provides a comparison with lab mice, testimony of Dr. Kirschenbaum and Dr. Dietz, an explanation of high-density eating style, and magnitude statistics.*

    C. Television viewing is also a culprit among obese children.
      1. Dr. Steven Gortmaker of Harvard University says that many children watch over 30 hours of television weekly.
      2. Inactivity, including television watching, results in a positive energy balance and, over time, leads to obesity.
      3. In addition, Dr. William Dietz of Tufts University notes that children's eating habits are influenced by television commercials for food that is high in sugar and fat.

IV. What are the dangers of obesity?
    A. Sixty percent of overweight children already have one risk factor for heart disease.
    B. Obesity dramatically increases the risk of type II diabetes.
      1. Eighty-five percent of children diagnosed with type II diabetes are obese.
      2. Among obese children, twenty-five percent show early signs of type II diabetes.
      3. Since 1990, new cases of type II diabetes have averaged four percent per year, mostly among obese children.
    C. Obesity complicates the treatment of other diseases, such as asthma.

V. You can control weight gain in children with four steps. ◄──────
    A. Don't assume the child will grow out of it.
      1. If your family has a history of weight problems, be alert for them in your children.
      2. Four out of five children can be helped with intervention before the problem gets worse.

*In the solution section, the speaker uses magnitude statistics, explanations, testimony, segment statistics, and examples.*

*(Continued)*

B.  Monitor mealtimes.
1.  To limit a high-density eating style, do not permit between-meal snacks.
2.  According to Dr. William Johnson and Dr. Peter Stalonas, teaching children to consume food at a slower pace is also helpful.
3.  It is easier on the child if the entire family switches to a low-fat diet.
C.  Substitute other activities for television viewing.
1.  Over fifty percent of obesity problems in children could be controlled more effectively if parents simply turned off the television set.
2.  Encourage activity in the child.
a. Enroll the child in athletic activities like swimming or soccer.
b. Encourage walking to and from school; just a half-hour of walking per day can correct a positive energy balance.
D.  Join a support group for the parents of obese children.
1.  Contact the World Service Office of Overeaters Anonymous.
2.  Speak to a representative of your local community service organization.

The conclusion to the speech offers segment statistics and testimony, plus a reference to the inroductory illustration.

VI.  Now that you understand the causes of childhood obesity and some of the solutions, it's time to act.
A.  Think about the consequences if you don't act now.
1.  Obesity in childhood predisposes a person to a lifetime of medical and psychological trouble.
2.  Obesity contributes to ninety percent of the cases of type II diabetes in later life; over half of the cases of cardiovascular disease; and immeasurable emotional distress.
B.  Remember Michelle? If her parents begin now, they can spare Michelle the bleak future faced by too many of our overweight American children.

## Assessing Your Progress

### Chapter Summary

1.  Your search for supporting materials should be purposeful. You should attempt to assemble materials that are relevant to your speech, your audience, and the occasion on which you're speaking.
2.  To plan your search, you should consider (a) the rational requirements of the topic, (b) the audience demands, (c) the power to prove that is generally associated with various kinds of supporting materials, and (d) the objectivity of your sources.
3.  In executing your searches, learn to use search engines, metasearch engines, directories, virtual libraries, and informational interviews.
4.  Supporting materials clarify, amplify, or strengthen the speaker's ideas.
5.  Comparisons and contrasts point out similarities and differences between things.
6.  Examples provide specific details about ideas or statements that you want listeners to accept. They can be hypothetical or factual.
7.  Statistics are numbers that show relationships between or among phenomena. Some emphasize size or magnitude, some describe subclasses or segments, and some establish trends or directions over time.

8. Testimony comes from the opinions or conclusions of credible persons.
9. Plagiarism is representing another's ideas or phrases as your own.

## Assessment Activities

Select a major problem, incident, or celebration that has appeared in the news recently. Examine a story or article written about it in several of the following publications: *New York Times, Christian Science Monitor, USA Today, Time, Newsweek, The New Republic,* and either the *Wall Street Journal* or *BusinessWeek.* In a column from each source, note specifically what major facts, people, incidents, and examples or illustrations are included and what conclusions are drawn. Evaluate the differences among the sources you consulted. How are their differences related to their readership? What does this exercise teach you about the biases or viewpoints of sources?

For additional chapter activities, log on to MySpeechLab at www.myspeech lab.com.

## Using the Web

The federal government compiles data on hundreds of topics. Check the variety of statistical information you can obtain from government sources. Use your search engine to locate the GAO (Government Accounting Office) reports or consult lib-www.ucr.edu/govpub/ for a database of federal, state, and local government resources that can be accessed by subject, key word, or title. Other archives for social science data are readily available online. Two excellent starting points are the Smithsonian Institution Research Information Web site and the Interuniversity Consortium for Political and Social Research at the University of Michigan.

## References

1. Find this and similar articles at www.lemmefind.com/about/reference_ resources.htm.

2. Jesse Ventura with Jay Waler, Jessica Allen, and Bill Adler, *The Wit and Wisdom of Jesse "the Body" ("the Mind") Ventura* (New York: Quill Books, 1999).

3. Mary Fisher, "A Whisper of AIDS." Reprinted in Victoria L. DeFrancisco and Marvin D. Jensen, eds., *Women's Voices in Our Time* (pp. 203–209). (Prospect Heights, IL: Waveland Press, 1994).

4. Brenda Theriault, "Fast Foods." Speech given at the University of Maine, Spring 1992.

5. "Ecommerce." Available at www.census.gov/compendia/statab.

6. Federal Trade Commission, *2007 Smokeless Tobacco Report.* Available at www.ftc .gov/bcp/reports/smokeless07.htm.

7. Carl Hall, "A Heap of Trouble," *Winning Orations* (Mankato, MN: Interstate Oratorical Association, 1977).

8. Janice Payan, "Opportunities for Hispanic Women: It's Up to Us," *Vital Speeches of the Day,* 56 (1 September 1990): 591.

9. Louisiana State University, "Academic Honesty and Dishonesty," adapted from LSU's Code of Student Conduct, 1981.

# WEB WORKSHOP

A few simple guidelines will help you get the most out of the Internet—some ideas for making your searches more efficient, some suggestions for critically evaluating Internet sites, and finally, a selection of sites that will get your Internet research started.

## Searching Efficiently

1. Determine whether you will get more productive results by using a key word/phrase, an author's name, or the title of a book/article.
2. Consider using a phrase (usually indicated by double quotation marks) rather than a string of words that might be sought individually and not together.
3. Think like a search engine. Many search engines use relationship terms (the Boolean principle) such as "and," "or," and "and not" to define what they will include and exclude as they seek matches. Some search engines also use "near" and "adjacent to" to find phrases in close proximity within texts.
4. If your first search doesn't yield useful hits, try again using a different phrase or search terms.
5. If your search generates too many hits, try again by refining your search terms.
6. You should also evaluate your search engine. Perhaps a virtual library search or academic site will avoid the purely popular treatments of your topic. Then, you can focus on a more limited number of hits that will probably be of higher quality.

## Evaluating Internet Sites

### Content and Evaluation

1. How complete and accurate are the information and the links provided by this source?
2. How good is this site vis-à-vis other sites or print sources? (A librarian can help you answer this question.)
3. What are the dates on the site and its materials?
4. How comprehensive is it? Is the site builder interested only in certain aspects of a topic (e.g., the Arab side of the Arab–Israeli conflict)? Does it attempt to cover everything available—and if so, how? Are evaluations of links to other sources provided?
5. What is the purpose of the sponsor of the site? Special interest groups often present information in a manner that slants it in one direction or another. The National Rifle Association, the Hemlock Society, the National Right to Life Organization, and AARP all have specific platforms endorsed on their Web sites. Some sites are intended to solicit funding, generate lists of contact information, or enlist volunteers.
6. Who does the site target? Another way to evaluate objectivity is to think about the intended audience. Can you draw a profile of a typical viewer? How is the

site developed to pull in that viewer? Once you have determined this, ask yourself why the site targets viewers of that profile.
7.  What does the domain name tell you? Use the URL to generally assess the quality of the information. You're likely to get more substantial information at an.edu
(education) or .gov (government) site than at a listserv posting or commercial/
private home page. Other common sites are .com (commercial), .net (network),
.org (nonprofit), and .mil (military).
8.  Is the information consistent with other sources? Always cross-check facts and
findings to assess their reliability. You may even consider whether the information agrees with what you already know to be true. Information that is inconsis-
tent should be scrutinized.

### Sources and Dates

1.  Who produced the site? Why? What authority or knowledge does the producer
have? Is there a sponsoring organization that has a vested interest in what
results from people using the site?
2.  Is there an evident bias in the materials that you find?
3.  Is the information current? Information in some disciplines changes rapidly. Be
sure to note when the information was last updated or when the data for surveys or other studies were collected.
4.  Is it easy to contact the producer with questions?

### Structure

1.  Does the site follow good graphics principles? Is the use of art purposive or just
decorative?
2.  Do the icons clearly represent what is intended?
3.  Does the text follow basic tenets of good grammar, spelling, and composition?
4.  Are links provided to Web subject-trees in directories—lists of Web sources
arranged by subject?
5.  How usable is the site? Can you get through it in a reasonable time?

## A Selection of Internet Sites

There are hundreds of excellent online (and print) sources for research materials. We
collected many Web sites that should get you started online. There, you will find the
links to virtual libraries, databases, and indexes by discipline, including the humanities,
cultural and ethnic studies, history, social sciences, business and technology, communication, and sciences. For additional resources, consult the *Guide to Reference Books*
used by librarians.

# 7 | Organizing and Outlining Your Speech

Think about the last time you shopped for groceries. Chances are good that you had a list of what you needed, either in your head or on paper. When you got to the store, you probably knew where to look for each item—canned goods and frozen foods in one section and fresh vegetables in another. When you think about it further, it's clear that much of your daily living is organized in patterns (or paradigms) that help you remember information and understand new concepts. In this chapter, we'll tell you how you can help your listeners with their management of information by utilizing these patterns.

Most patterns depend upon a relationship or an association of things or ideas. In a speech, an **association** is a connection asserted between two or more parts of an utterance or parts of the speech. If you were teaching someone how to serve a tennis ball, you might say, "So what happens when you hit the ball with sufficient force? *First* the ball starts spinning, *next* it slows down and curves in flight, and *then* when it hits the ground it bounces sideways." The words *first, next,* and *then* connect three events associatively to make a sequence. Words like *first, next,* and *then* keep the speech moving forward in ways that listeners can understand. When you hear a listener say, "I can follow that" or "I know what you mean," you know that you have created a clear association among your ideas.

We begin this chapter by helping you develop a general plan for laying out your speeches. Then, we examine two types of paradigms (speech-centered and audience-centered patterns). Finally, we look at some ways you can make your talks more coherent, including outlining. Taken together, this chapter helps you make sure you're in complete control of the shape of your speeches.

## Developing Your Speech Plan

Approaching your speech in an organized manner is important for several reasons. Just as you waste time wandering around a store if you don't have a shopping list, you appear confused if you give a disorganized speech. The result can be chaotic. There are five reasons to organize your speeches:

**1. Your listeners learn more from an organized speech, because there is an obvious pattern for categorizing the new material you present.** When you arrange the information, it's easier for listeners to learn it. Good organization leads to better comprehension.

**2. An organized speech is easier for you to present.** The ideas fit together more logically. And even if you forget a phrase or two, the speech will still flow naturally, because the ideas hold it together.

**3. You will appear more credible when you give an organized speech.** Your listeners will realize that you have prepared well and will be more likely to accept your expertise.

**4. Some evidence suggests that well-organized speeches are more persuasive.** You can see why—if listeners trust your preparation and don't have to strain to understand the ideas, they are more likely to be impressed by your message.

**5. Good organization lowers the frustration level for everyone—you and your listeners.** This is reason enough to practice developing clear and effective organization in your speaking.

### Developing Your Central Idea

The first step in planning the organization of your speech is determining your central idea. As you may recall from Chapter 2, your central idea is a statement of your speech goal, developed when you blend your general purpose to inform or to persuade with your topic.

Phrasing a central idea is especially critical, because the focus you select limits the scope of your speech and frames your relationship with your audience. Your central idea determines the way you develop your whole talk—your main points, the information you include, the organization you follow, and the ways you link your points. For example, each of the following central ideas expresses a different focus and relationship with listeners:

- "You can conserve energy on campus by recycling aluminum cans and plastic water bottles, riding the bus instead of driving, installing compact fluorescent light bulbs in your desk lamps, and adjusting your thermostat by a couple of degrees."

- "From its founding charter in 1912, this university has been dedicated to four educational objectives."

- "If our university decides to replace traditional grades with a pass-fail system, there will be several negative consequences for students."

These three central ideas establish very different parameters for developing a speech. The first offers three tangible actions every student can take to save energy. The scope of the speech is limited to practical, easy-to-implement solutions. The second suggests an historical perspective that provides information and less directly involves the audience. The speaker who proposes the third topic is preparing to develop an argument.

In each case, the phrasing of the central idea determines how the topic will be approached and the role of the listener. It also helps determine which organizational pattern is best for the speech.

## Choosing Your Organizational Plan

To help you further, here are some clear, general guidelines for organizing your speech. After you have identified your central idea, ask these questions to determine what you're looking for in an organizational pattern:

**1. What structure is best suited to the ideas in my speech?** Your speech topic may offer natural groupings among ideas that will be easy for your listeners to recognize. For example, if your speech traces the Battle of Gettysburg day by day, it is probably organized by time. If, on the other hand, you are detailing the causes, symptoms, and cures for Lyme disease, your ideas fall into a causal pattern. And a speech on the layout of your campus is clearly spatial. You should consider the natural pattern suggested by the ideas of your speech as you think about organizing it.

**2. What structure is best adapted to my audience's needs?** Keep your listeners in mind—what they know, expect, and need. If your listeners have never heard of bio-remediation, then you need to develop your speech on this topic in a very different way than if they are environmental scientists. You can't ignore your listeners' need to process information efficiently. That means beginning with what they already know.

**3. How can I make the speech move steadily forward toward a satisfying finish?** Listeners need a sense of forward motion—of moving through a series of main points toward a clear destination. Backtracking slows down the momentum of the speech, giving it a stop-and-start progression rather than a smooth, forward flow. You'll also enhance the sense of forward motion with forecasts and transitions to indicate progression.

Once you've developed your central idea and answered basic questions about the plan of your speech, you're ready to choose the type of arrangement. Often, your topic will determine the type of organization needed. Some topics require chronological order, while other topics can be organized in topical, spatial, or causal patterns. These are **speech-centered patterns**—that is, they are traditional organizational patterns based on the content of the speech. The needs of your audience, however, may require a special pattern of organization adapted to them. These are **audience-centered patterns**—that is, these patterns of organization are based on the ways that people think. First, we will discuss some speech-centered types of organization. Then we'll consider some audience-centered patterns of organization.

## Speech-Centered Patterns of Organization

As we use the term here, **organization** is the order or sequence of ideas in a pattern that suggests their relationship to each other. There are four general types of organization that arise from the demands of the topic: (1) chronological, (2) spatial, (3) causal, and (4) topical.

### Chronological Patterns

**Chronological patterns** order ideas in a time sequence—more or less as you naturally order your day or week. You begin at one point in time and move forward or backward to some other time. As a speaker, you pick a beginning by asking yourself, "How far do I have to go back for this thing or event to make sense to an audience?" The point you want to make ends the speech, but the beginning is chosen by what you want the audience to know—and, frankly, what you think that it needs to know—for your purpose.

Suppose you want to talk about twentieth-century efforts to fly. Should you drop back to the turn-of-the-century, reciprocating piston engines that were used in the time of the Wright Brothers? Or can you leave that out as a matter of common knowledge and start instead in the 1930s, when air-breathing turbine engines were successfully put into planes? It's easy enough to argue that serious commercial and military flight couldn't begin until the West had jets. But then, why not go all of the way into solid-fuel rockets—they were developed during World War II, caught the international imagination in 1957 when Russia launched *Sputnik,* demonstrated humanity's ability to explore other places via manned flight to the moon in 1969, and soon set off for the farthest reaches of the universe in unmanned flight? Again, what's your purpose? Extensive knowledge (all flight) or more recent, intensive knowledge (e.g., jet engines or rocketry)? Given your purpose, where does the audience need to start? From answers to those questions come decisions on how to start and finish chronologies.

Here's another example that traces the history of experts' advice to parents over the past century. Notice how time organizes the ideas in the speech:

I. Early in the twentieth century, experts began to focus on childhood as an important period of individual development.
   A. In 1914, books advised mothers to thwart bad habits like thumb sucking by pinning an infant's sleeves to the bed.
   B. During the Great Depression of the 1930s, the federal government developed welfare plans to aid children.

II. The baby boom years from 1940 to 1960 saw the rise of several models.
   A. Behaviorist models using stimulus-response training were popular.
   B. In 1946, pediatrician Dr. Benjamin Spock published one of the most popular manuals for raising children, offering an alternative to behaviorist models.

    C. In 1952, French psychologist Jean Piaget identified distinct stages in the intellectual maturation of children.

III. More recently, advice to parents has focused on nurturing children to strengthen their emotional development.

    A. In 1969, English psychiatrist Dr. John Bowlby proved that babies seek out specific adults for protection.

    B. In 1997, the Conference on Early Childhood Development and Learning drew attention to the crucial first years in a child's life.

## Spatial Patterns

In **spatial patterns**, the major points of the speech are organized by their position—that is, their location or direction from each other. A speech about the movement of weather systems from the north to the south across the United States would fit such a pattern. If you conduct a tour of your campus or describe the constellations in the Southern Hemisphere, you would probably use a spatial pattern. Spatial patterns can trace ideas from east to west, from top to bottom, from left to right, or even from inside to outside. Consider how this example circles the globe:

I. Around the world, active volcanoes continue to shape the face of the earth.

    A. Begin in Mexico with the famous Popocatépetl (2002 and 2007 eruptions) and Colima (2005 eruption).

    B. Then move up the American mountain chain to Mount St. Helens in the state of Washington (1991 and 2005 eruptions) and on to the Cleveland volcano in Alaska (2001 eruption).

    C. Take a left and cross the Pacific to the Japanese islands, which feature a number of active volcanoes, including. Miyakejima (2002 and 2005 eruptions) and Mount Asama (1991 eruption).

    D. Drop down south to Mount Kerinci in Sumatra (1987 and 2004 eruptions) and White Island in New Zealand (2000 eruption).

    E. Head west to the next continent, Africa, and the Congo's Mount Nyiragonogo (2002 and 2004 eruptions).

    F. Next travel north to Yemen's Jebel al-Tair volcano (2007 eruption).

    G. Then head to Europe to visit Italy's Mount Etna (2004 eruption) and Russia's Mount Sheveluch (2007 eruption), finishing with Iceland's Grimsvötn (2004 eruption).

    H. Return to the Northern Hemisphere where we started. We've arrived at the Appalachian Mountains in the eastern United States, thankful that their volcanic activity stopped eons ago.[1]

## Causal Patterns

**Causal patterns** of speech organization show a relationship between causes and effects. Causal patterns assume that one event results from or causes another. This pattern of organization gives listeners a sense of coherence, because ideas are developed in relationship to each other. Causal patterns may move in two directions: (1) from present causes to future effects, or (2) from present conditions to their apparent causes.

When using a *cause-effect pattern*, you might point to the increasing cost of attending college and then argue that one of the effects of these increased costs is reduced enrollments among students from less privileged socioeconomic backgrounds:

I. Colleges and universities across the United States are raising tuition.

II. The effect of these tuition hikes is to change the socioeconomic profile among students.
    A. Middle-income students are squeezed by tuition increases.
    B. Financially disadvantaged students often must drop out.

Or, using an *effect-cause pattern,* you could note that dropping college enrollments resulted, at least in part, from increasing costs, as in this outline:

I. The socioeconomic profile of American colleges and universities has changed.

II. Tuition increases have caused limited access to higher education.
    A. Middle-income students are not able to afford additional tuition increases.
    B. Financially disadvantaged students are forced to choose employment over education.

Notice that the first outline uses a cause-effect pattern and that the second uses an effect-cause pattern. Which should you choose? That depends on your listeners. Begin with the ideas that are better known to audience members, and then proceed to the lesser-known facets of the problem. Use the cause-effect pattern if listeners are better acquainted with the cause; use the effect-cause pattern if the opposite is true.

## Topical Patterns

Some speeches on familiar topics are best organized in terms of subject-matter divisions that are already well known to listeners. Sports strategy is divided into offense and defense; kinds of courts into municipal, county, state, and federal jurisdictions; and types of trees into deciduous and evergreen. When you use a **topical pattern** of organization, you list aspects of persons, places, things, or processes. Occasionally, a speaker tries to list all aspects of the topic. More often, however, a partial listing of the primary or most interesting aspects is sufficient. For example, suppose you wanted to give a speech to a general audience about stress. The following outline shows how you could organize the speech topically:

I. There are several easily recognized symptoms of stress.
    A. The physical symptoms of stress include insomnia, overeating, and even migraine headaches.
    B. The emotional symptoms of stress are more elusive but often include inability to concentrate and even depression.

II. There are two types of stress inducers—physical and emotional.
    A. Physical stress might result from overwork, lack of sleep, and even illness.
    B. Emotional stress can occur with financial problems, relationship difficulties, and the perception of personal failure.

**III.** Fortunately, there are several methods of stress reduction.

    **A.** Relaxation techniques that involve muscle relaxation and controlled breathing can be used immediately.

    **B.** Exercise also can be effective if you have the time and equipment to work out regularly.

    **C.** Mediation requires training but yields substantial results.

Topical patterns are among the most popular and easiest to use. If you plan to list only certain aspects of the topic, take care to explain your choices early in your speech. If you don't plan to talk about bio-feedback as a means of reducing stress, you should tell your listeners. You might say, "I will focus on the three most common approaches to stress reduction and will present simple techniques that anyone can use to reduce the stress in their life."

The patterns of speech organization discussed so far—chronological, spatial, causal, and topical—are determined principally by the subject matter. While these patterns do not ignore the audience, it's the subject that usually suggests the pattern of organization.

## Audience-Centered Patterns of Organization

At times, audience-oriented patterns of organization will more effectively arrange your material. These patterns often work well because they're based on the listeners' needs. You can ask several questions to determine whether an audience-oriented pattern of organization will work for you:

- Can I introduce a new idea by comparing it to something my listeners already know?
- How would a person approach this idea for the first time?
- What are common, recurring questions about this topic?
- Am I presenting a solution to a problem?
- Can I eliminate all but one alternative solution to a question or problem?

If you answer yes to any of these questions, you might consider organizing your speech based on your listeners' needs.

We'll examine five audience-centered patterns of organization: (1) familiarity-acceptance order, (2) inquiry order, (3) question-answer order, (4) problem-solution order, and (5) elimination order.

### Familiarity-Acceptance Order

**Familiarity-acceptance order** begins with what the audience knows or believes (the familiar) and moves on to new or challenging ideas (the unfamiliar). In an informative speech on the subatomic particles called quarks, you can begin with what the audience already knows about molecules and then introduce the new information on quarks.

Familiarity-acceptance order is very well suited to persuasive speeches, especially if your listeners are skeptical or hostile. You can begin your speech by acknowledging values or ideas that are accepted by your listeners and then proceed to more controversial issues. In this way, your listeners will have difficulty rejecting your claim without denying the underlying facts or values that they already accept.

*Even in seemingly informal settings, having a clear organizational pattern is a necessity for maximizing your impact on your listener.*

Here are the main points for a persuasive speech on a polarizing topic using familiarity-acceptance order:

I. How many in this room think it's possible that they'll get married sometime in the future?

    A. "Family values" is a phrase suggesting that stable relationships should be a goal of everyone in relationships.

    B. Spousal relationships frame the essence of family values.

II. And so, marriage is an important social institution in all societies.

    A. It sets up stable relationships between individuals, families, and even communities.

    B. It provides comparatively stable environments for raising children.

    C. It's a basic framework for social needs and services, such as retirement funding, medical plans, and government aid.

III. Same-sex marriages can provide the same benefits to individuals, families, and communities as heterosexual marriages do.

    A. They would help gay and lesbian partners deepen their commitments to each other in stable relationships.

    B. They would provide a long-term, supportive environment for any children brought to the relationship in the same way as heterosexual marriages do.

    C. Medical plans could be simplified, inheritance laws made applicable, and various sorts of family-oriented government aid extended to additional family units.

By starting with generally acceptable ideas like "family values" and "stable relationships" framing the argument, this speaker has a better chance of being heard by listeners who might otherwise reject the argument.

## Inquiry Order

**Inquiry order** provides a step-by-step explanation of how you acquired information or reached a conclusion. Often, scientists use this pattern as they carefully describe their research procedures in order to demonstrate the reliability of their findings. Similarly, if you want to persuade your neighbors to plant a new variety of elm tree, you could recount how you studied the varieties that seemed to be dying in your neighborhood, investigated possible choices, and searched to find the best variety.

Inquiry order has a double advantage. First, it displays relevant facts and alternatives for the audience. Second, it enables listeners to judge for themselves the worth of the information or policy being presented.

## Question-Answer Order

**Question-answer order** raises and answers listeners' questions. First, you must determine which questions are most likely to arise in your listeners' minds. Then, you need to develop your speech to answer each key question in a way that favors your conclusion. For example, when you buy a new car, you want to know about its principal features, available options, gas mileage, and cost. When first learning about a new bond issue, voters wonder how it will affect their taxes or government services. If fans hear about illegal drug use in professional sports, they'll wonder which players are affected and what kinds of drugs are being abused. By structuring your speech to address these questions, you can maintain audience interest and involvement.

## Problem-Solution Order

When you advocate changes in action or thought, your main points may fall naturally into a **problem-solution order.** First, you establish the existence of the problem. If your listeners are already aware of the problem, you can remind them of the primary issues. For example, if your listeners walk or ride bicycles to classes, they'll be unaware that there aren't enough parking spaces on campus; but if they drive automobiles, they'll be quite familiar with the parking shortage. You also need to depict the problem in a way that will help your listeners perceive it in the same way that you do. For example, your listeners may tolerate the parking shortage as a simple inconvenience of college life, so you will need to show them that there is no reason to accept a parking shortage.

Once you've established that a problem exists, you must propose a solution to it. Your solution should be workable and practical. It would be silly to suggest building a multimillion-dollar parking complex if financing isn't available or if the parking complex would be too small. However, a carpooling or busing system would be less expensive and might effectively solve the parking problem.

## Elimination Order

When your iPod doesn't work, you may systematically search for what's wrong: Are the batteries fresh? Is the lock switch on? Is it programmed correctly? Similarly, with **elimination order,** you first survey all the available solutions and courses of action that can reasonably be pursued. Then, proceeding systematically, you eliminate each of the possibilities until only one remains.

Elimination order is well suited to persuasive speeches. If you want student government to bring a special performer to campus, you might show that all other suggested entertainers are booked up, are too expensive, or lack widespread appeal. In this way, you lead the members of student government to agree with the choice you advocate.

To use elimination order effectively, you first must make an inclusive survey of options. If you overlook obvious choices, your listeners won't be convinced by your analysis. Second, you must make the options mutually exclusive; otherwise, your listeners may choose more than one. Consider this example in which the speaker makes only one alternative form of energy for propelling automobiles seem the best:

I. In today's automobile market, you have three engine choices, each with their own fuels.

   A. Gasoline or diesel engines power most cars on the planet today.

   B. Battery-powered cars store energy to drive not an engine but a motor.

   C. Hybrid cars combine a fuel-burning engine with a battery-driven motor.

II. Which form of road transportation is best overall?

   A. Gasoline and diesel engines are consuming fossil fuels at fantastic rates and creating most of the air pollution that troubles industrialized countries.

   B. Battery-powered cars currently do not store enough energy for serious travel and highway speeds.

III. This leaves us with the most exciting and encouraging development of today, the hybrid car.

   A. By combining a small gasoline engine, a battery system, and a generator, the hybrid car maximizes your road transportation–fueling dollar.

   B. Gasoline provides basic power, while the battery adds more power when accelerating or going uphill. The generator can recharge the battery system when you're driving and have little need for extra power.

   C. Dependence on fossil fuel therefore is significantly reduced, the act of driving (rather than an electrical outlet) recharges the batteries, and the gasoline engine sometimes even shuts down entirely (such as, when you're idling at a red light).

   D. Though hybrid cars are comparatively new, both Toyota and Honda models have won overwhelming consumer interest and demonstrated that hybrid automobiles are your best choice for a ground transportation vehicle until other energy sources, such as hydrogen, become available—and that's a long way off for now.

IV. So, go out and test drive an energy efficient hybrid engine.[2]

## Techniques for Creating Associative Coherence in Your Speech

Choosing a pattern of organization that suits your speech topic and listeners is important for communicating your ideas and achieving your speech goals. However, it's not enough by itself. You also need to guide your listeners as you move from point to point in your speech. Remember that they probably do not have a copy of your outline and might be unfamiliar with your ideas. So, it is your job to bring coherence to listeners' understanding of what you're talking about and how you're developing your speech.

Creating **associative coherence**, or the connections among parts of your speech, is not particularly difficult to do—but you do have to remember to do it. To create a sense of coherence as your speech unfolds, you should use forecasts or previews, summaries, and signposts or transitions to connect ideas.

**Forecasts**, or *previews,* precede the development of the body of the speech, usually forming part of the introduction. They provide an overview of the speech

*Set key elements from your outline firmly in your head so that you can keep your focus during your speech, especially in intimate settings, on you listener.*

structure. Previews are especially helpful in outlining the major topics of the speech. Consider the following examples:

> "Today I am going to talk about the causes of global warming and its three primary effects—rising temperatures, changes in sea levels, and increasingly violent weather patterns."
> "There are four major elements in developing a winning résumé. We'll look at establishing your strengths, forming a positive impression, including sufficient detail, and developing an edge."
> "The history of the Vietnam War can be divided into two periods: the French involvement, and the commitment of American troops."

Each of these forecasts links the introduction of the speech to the development of ideas in the body of the speech. The forecast shows the listener what to expect. In a sense, you are providing a road map when you signal your speech structure in a forecast, so your listeners can relax and enjoy the ride.

A **summary** provides coherence in your speech by recapping the ideas that you've covered. You can summarize ideas as you close a main topic before you move on to another topic—for example, "Worldwide dependence on fossil fuels is the primary contributor to global warming. Now, let's examine some effects of global warming."

It is especially important to summarize your main ideas at the end of your speech. This is your last chance to remind listeners of your main topics and leave them with a final impression of your speech. A final summary usually forms part of the conclusion and often parallels the forecast. For example, a final summary might look like this:

- "Today we've talked about what causes global warming. Experts agree that there are three primary effects that will result over the next few decades: an irreversible increase in temperatures, rising sea levels as the polar ice caps melt, and increasingly violent fluctuations in weather patterns."

- "When you sit down to apply for your first job, remember the four major elements in developing a winning résumé. Think about establishing your strengths, forming a positive impression, including sufficient detail, and developing an edge."

- "The history of the Vietnam War includes both the French involvement and the commitment of American troops."

Notice that all three examples of final summaries parallel the forecast for the speech. They are direct and clear, and they remind the listener of the primary structure of the speech.

In addition to forecasts and summaries, you must use **signposts**, or *transitions*, which are linking phrases that move an audience from one idea to another. Signposts or transitions are words or phrases, such as *first, next*, or *as a result*, that help listeners follow the movement of your ideas. Signposts such as "the history of this invention begins in" also provide clues to the overall message structure. The following are useful signposts:

- "In the first place . . . The second point is . . ."
- "In addition . . . to notice that . . ."
- "Now look at it from a different angle . . ."
- "You must keep these three things in mind in order to understand the importance of the fourth . . ."

- "What was the result?"
- "Turning now to . . ."

The preceding signposts are neutral. They tell an audience that another idea is coming, but they don't indicate whether it's similar, different, or more important. You can improve the coherence of your speeches by indicating the precise relationships among ideas. Those relationships include parallel/hierarchical, similar/different, and coordinate/subordinate relationships. Here are some examples:

- *Parallel:* "Not only . . . but also . . ."
- *Hierarchical:* "More important than these . . ."
- *Different:* "In contrast . . ."
- *Similar:* "Similar to this . . ."
- *Coordinated:* "One must consider X, Y, and Z . . ."
- *Subordinated:* "On the next level is . . ."

Forecasts, internal and final summaries, and signposts are important to your audience. Forecasts and summaries give listeners an overall sense of your entire message; if listeners can easily see the structure, they'll better understand and remember your speech. These signposts lead your listeners step by step through your speech, signaling specific relationships between and among ideas.

## Outlining Your Speech

Once you have determined the type of organization you will use to arrange your ideas, you should record the ideas in an outline. Outlining is an important tool for a speaker for two reasons:

**1. Testing.** A rough outline allows you to see your ideas. When you outline a speech, you can discover which ideas you've overemphasized and which you've excluded or underdeveloped. Your outline is a testing device.

**2. Guiding.** When you're actually delivering a speech, a speaking outline is the preferred form of notes for many—and perhaps even most—speaking occasions. A good speaking outline shows you where you've been, where you are, and where you want to get before you sit down. Your speaking outline also can include special directions to prompt your memory, such as "show map here" or "emphasize this idea."

You should develop your outline, as well as the speech it represents, gradually, through a series of stages. Your outline will become increasingly complex as the ideas in your speech evolve and as you move the speech closer to its final form. But then, once you're ready to speak, you must simplify the outline again so that your delivery can be conversational. For the purposes of the public speaker, the rough outline and the speaking outline are most important, because they govern the discovery of ideas and the presentation of them. So, we will concentrate on these.

## Developing a Rough Outline

A **rough outline** establishes the topic of your speech, clarifies your purpose, and identifies a reasonable number of subtopics. Suppose your instructor assigns an informative speech on a subject that interests you. You decide to talk about drunk driving, because a close friend was recently injured by an intoxicated driver. Your broad topic area, then, is drunk driving.

In the six to eight minutes you have to speak, you obviously can't cover such a broad topic adequately. After considering your audience and your time limit, you decide to focus your presentation on two organizations, Mothers Against Drunk Driving (MADD) and Students Against Driving Drunk (SADD).

As you think about narrowing your topic even further, you jot down some possible ideas. You continue to narrow your list until your final ideas include the following:

- Founders of MADD and SADD
- Accomplishments of the two organizations
- Reasons the organizations were deemed necessary
- Goals of MADD and SADD
- Action steps taken by MADD and SADD
- Ways in which your listeners can get involved

At this point, cluster similar ideas to help listeners follow your thinking. Experiment with several possible clusters before you decide on the best way to arrange your ideas.

Your next step is to consider the best pattern of organization for these topics. A chronological pattern would enable you to organize the history of MADD and SADD but would not allow you to discuss ways your listeners could help. Either a cause-effect or an effect-cause pattern would work well if your primary purpose is to persuade. This is an informative speech, however, and you want to talk about more than causes and effects of MADD and SADD.

In considering the audience-centered patterns, you decide that an inquiry order might work. You discard it, however, when you realize that you don't know enough about audience members' questions to use this organizational pattern effectively. After examining the alternatives, you finally settle on a topical pattern, which allows you to present three clusters of information:

1. **Background of MADD and SADD:** information about the founders, why the organizations came to be
2. **Description of MADD and SADD:** goals, steps in action plans, results
3. **Local work of MADD and SADD:** the ways in which parents work with their teenagers and with local media to accomplish MADD and SADD goals

As you subdivide your three clusters of information, you develop the following rough outline:

I. Background of MADD and SADD
   A. Information about the founders
   B. Reasons the organizations were founded

SPEAKING OF . . .
S K I L L S

## Memory and Organization

Research on organization and memory has shown that taking some specific outlining steps will help you and your listeners remember what you're talking about:

1. *The magic numbers.* In a classic study, psychologist George Miller concluded that there is a limit to the number of items a person can easily recall—seven, plus or minus two. More recent research has suggested that a more manageable number of items is five, plus or minus two. Limit the number of points you make (preferably to between three and five).

2. *Chunking.* What if you want to include a lot more information? The answer is: "Chunk it." Divide the information into chunks or groups. Listeners are much more likely to remember five chunks of information than seventeen separate points.

3. *Mnemonics.* Mnemonics help you remember ideas. When you learned "Thirty days hath September, April, June, and November . . .," you learned an easily recalled ditty that in turn helped you remember which months had thirty days and which had thirty-one. Speakers, too, can sometimes find a mnemonic to help listeners remember—for example, the three Rs of conserving resources ("recycle," "reduce," and "reuse") or the ABC sequence ("airway," "breathing," and "compression") for cardiopulmonary resuscitation taught in CPR classes.

*For further reading: see* G. Mandler, "Organization and Memory," in *Human Memory: Basic Principles,* edited by Gordon Bower (New York: Academic Press, 1977), 310–354. See also Mandler's articles in C.R. Puff, ed., *Memory Organization and Structure* (New York: Academic Press, 1979), 303–319, and G.A. Miller, "The Magic Number Seven, Plus or Minus Two: Some Limits on Our Capacity for Processing Information," *Psychological Review,* 63 (1956): 81–97.

II. Description of the organizations
   A. Their goals
   B. The action steps they take
   C. Their accomplishments so far
III. Applications of their work on a local level
   A. "Project Graduation"
   B. Parent-student contracts
   C. Local public service announcements

A rough outline identifies your topic, provides a reasonable number of subtopics, and reveals a method for organizing and developing your speech. Notice that you've arranged both the main points and the subpoints topically. You should make sure, however, that the speech doesn't turn into a "string of beads" that fails to differentiate between one topic and the next. With topical outlines, always figure out a way to make the topics cohere (hold together). Doing so will help you develop effective transitions as you practice your speech.

The next step in preparing an outline is phrasing your main headings as precisely as possible, usually in complete sentences, to capture your exact meaning. Then, you can begin to develop each heading by adding subordinate ideas. As you develop your outline, you'll begin to see what kinds of information and supporting materials you need to find.

## Developing a Speaking Outline

Your rough outline is too detailed to use when you're actually delivering a speech; you'd probably be tempted to read to your listeners. If you did that, however, you would lose your conversational tone. So, you need to compress your rough outline into a more useful form.

A **speaking outline** uses key words or phrases to jog your memory when you deliver your speech. It is a short, practical form to use while delivering your speech (see Figure 7.1). The actual speaking outline you use will depend on your personal preference; some people like to work with small pieces of paper and others with notecards. Whatever your choice, your speaking outline should be unobtrusive. Large notebook pages will distract your listeners from what you have to say.

**Figure 7.1** Sample Speaking Outline (on Notecards)

**FRIENDS DON'T LET FRIENDS DRIVE DRUNK**
I. Background
    A. MADD: 1980. Candy Lightner
    B. SADD: her other daughter for high school kids
II. Description
    A. Goals
        1. public agitation
        2. expose deficiencies in current legis. & control
        3. public education
    B. MADD's action steps
        1. goals
        2. educate organizers
        3. set research priorities
        4. formulate plans of action
        5. go public!

    C. Results
        1. 320 MADD chapters
        2. 600,000 volunteers
        3. state laws changing
        4. fatalities down (statistics)
        5. popularity of low-alc. beer, wines, coolers
III. Local projects
    A. contracts
    B. prom night (Operation Graduation)
    C. PSAs and publicity
        1. MADD TV ads
        2. SADD projects (SHOW POSTER)

There are five things to keep in mind as you prepare your speaking outline:

1. **Use key words or phrases.** A word or two should be enough to trigger your memory, especially if you've practiced the speech adequately.
2. **Fully write/type out the ideas that must be stated precisely.** You don't want to make mistakes with people's names, statistical information, or exact quotations.
3. **Include directions for delivery, such as "SHOW GRAPH."**
4. **Add emphasis to easily catch your eye, show the relationship of ideas, and jog your memory during your speech delivery.** You might use capital letters, white spaces, underlining, indentation, dashes, and highlighting with colored markers to emphasize important ideas.
5. **Use your speaking outline during your practice sessions so that you are familiar with it when you give your speech.**

## Guidelines for Preparing Outlines

The amount of detail that you include in an outline will depend on your subject, on the speaking situation, and on your previous experience in speech preparation. New subject matter, unique speaking contexts, and limited prior speaking experience all indicate the need for a detailed outline. Your instructor may even require a full-sentence outline to help you develop the content of your speech. Under any circumstances, a good outline should meet these basic requirements:

**1. Each unit in the outline should contain one main idea.** If two or three ideas merge under one subpoint, your audience will lose direction and become confused. Suppose you are outlining a speech advocating the use of U.S. military personnel to bolster airport security and you include the following subpoint: "Also, current airport security is lax, and placing military personnel in airports would cost less than hiring more civilians to screen passengers and baggage." Notice that this point combines two separate ideas about current security and costs. It would be more effective to separate the ideas and develop them as individual points, such as:

A. Current airport security is lax.

B. Placing armed military personnel in airports would cost less than hiring more civilians to screen passengers and baggage.

**2. Less important ideas in the outline should be subordinate to more important ones.** Subordinate ideas are indented in an outline, and they are marked with subordinate symbols. Doing a good job with subordination helps you know what to emphasize when you're speaking. Proper subordination emphasizes your main arguments and supporting materials. Consider the following example:

I. The cost of medical care has skyrocketed.

   A. Hospital charges are high.

      1. A private room may cost more than $2,000 a day.

      2. X-rays and laboratory tests are expensive.

   B. Doctors' charges constantly go up.

      1. Complicated operations cost thousands of dollars.

      2. Office calls usually cost between $55 and $100.

C. Drugs are expensive.

    1. Most new antibiotics cost $7 to $20 per dose.

    2. The cost of nonprescription drugs has mounted.

**3. Phrase your main points effectively.** You can help your listeners understand your message better if you are concise, choose vivid language, and use parallel structure. More specifically:

- *Be concise.* State your main points as briefly as you can without distorting their meaning. Crisp, clear, straightforward statements are easier to grasp than rambling, vague, complex declarations. Say "Get regular exercise," not "Regular and repetitive exertion, considering age and physical conditioning, lends itself to improved physiological functioning."

- *Use vivid language.* Whenever possible, state your main points in evocative words and phrases. Drab, colorless statements are easily forgotten; punchy lines grab attention. Phrase your main points so that they'll appeal directly to the concerns of your listeners. Instead of saying "We should take immediate action to reduce the costs of higher education," say "Cut tuition now!"

- *Use parallel structure.* In a speech, your listeners have only one chance to catch what you're saying; parallelism in sentence structure helps them do so. The repetition of key ideas aids the listener in remembering this series: "Cope with cold and flu season by washing your hands, getting enough sleep, and taking vitamin C. Wash your hands to destroy the viruses. Get enough sleep to reduce physical stress. Take vitamin C to fortify your body." Notice in this series that the three most important ideas are repeated. Such parallelism will help your listeners remember the major ideas in your speech.

## ▌ Assessing Your Progress

### Chapter Summary

1. Associations are connections between two or more parts of an utterance or a speech.
2. Some patterns of speech organization are speech-centered (based on ways people have been taught to understand ideas), and some are audience-centered (based on ways people habitually process new ideas psychologically).
3. Four speech-centered types of organization are chronological, spatial, causal (effect-cause and cause-effect), and topical organizational patterns.
4. The five audience-centered types of organization are familiarity-acceptance, inquiry, question answer, problem-solution, and elimination orders.
5. Associative coherence can be achieved through forecasts, summaries, and signposts.
6. Speakers can use outlines for testing their ideas and guiding their oral presentation of those ideas.

7. Rough outlines test ideas; speaking outlines guide the presentation of ideas.
8. Guidelines for outlining include: (a) Each unit should contain only one idea, (b) less important ideas should be subordinate to more important ones, and (c) main ideas should be phrased effectively.

## Assessment Activities

Bring a short magazine or newspaper article and a photocopy of it to class. Cut the photocopy into separate paragraphs or sentences. Ask a classmate to assemble the separated paragraphs or sentences into a coherent story. Compare your classmate's results to the original article. Go to MySpeechLab to sample outlines and outlining tutorials.

## Using the Web

Many online tutorials are available to help you develop your outlining skills. You might do a general search under the key word outlining. Or, check out sites maintained by colleges and universities, such as Purdue University (owl.english.purdue.edu).

## References

1. The data in this outline were taken from the University of North Dakota–Grand Forks Web site (volcano.und.edu/vwdocs/current_volcs/current.html).

2. Some of the descriptions used in this outline were paraphrased from the pages of www.howstuffworks.com, especially the sections on "Auto Stuff" and "Science Stuff." (This Web site is especially useful for descriptive and analytical speech assignments.)

# 8 | Beginning and Ending Your Speech

Just as people who run or jog begin with warm-ups and end with cool-downs, so must you systematically prepare your audience to encounter new ideas and then remember those ideas at the end of your speech. Your success in getting a listener's attention is partly due to how well you frame your speech ideas with a powerful introduction and a strong conclusion. Well-prepared introductions and conclusions also allow you to develop a relationship between you and your listeners.

Introductions and conclusions are not trivial aspects of public speaking. Introductions form first impressions that can affect your listeners' perceptions of the remainder of the speech. Conclusions give you one last opportunity to reinforce your main ideas, to leave a lasting impression, and to cement your relationship with your listeners. In fact, people most often remember what they first hear or see (the **primacy effect**) and what they most recently have seen or heard (the **recency effect**). That is why introductions and conclusions require special effort when you prepare your speeches.

In this chapter, we review ways to capture and sustain listeners' attention, examine the purposes of introductions and conclusions, and suggest various strategies for beginning and ending speeches.

## ▌ Capturing and Holding Attention

When you're on a favorite Web site, you can block out the rest of the world. Sometimes you can pay attention so completely that it seems like only minutes instead of hours have passed. **Attention** is the ability to focus on one element in a given perceptual field. When attention is secured, competing elements in the perceptual field fade and, for all practical purposes, cease to exist. That explains why everything else disappears when you are logged on to a Web site.

How can you capture and hold the attention of your listeners effectively when giving a speech? Your ideas can be framed by nine appeals that have high attention value. These factors of attention can be used anywhere in your speech. The **factors of attention** are (1) activity, (2) reality, (3) proximity, (4) familiarity, (5) novelty, (6) suspense, (7) conflict, (8) humor, and (9) the vital (see Figure 8.1).

### Activity

Suppose you've got two TV sets side by side. On one, you see two journalists seated at a table discuss U.S. foreign policy options in the Middle East, while on the other, you seeing fiery stump speakers getting crowds to go wild. Which set are you likely to watch? You, too, can create a sense of activity by doing the following:

- *Choose active verbs. Raced, tore, shot through, slammed, ripped, slashed, cata-pulted, flew, flashed*—most of these are simple verbs, but they depict activity.
- *Select dynamic stories.* Use illustrations that depict action, that tell fast-moving or emotionally involving stories. Propel your story forward, and your audience will stay with you.
- *Use short segments.* Keep your speech moving; it will seem to drag if you expand on one point but skim over others.

**Figure 8.1** The Factors of Attention

You can use the factors of attention to capture and hold the interest of your listeners.

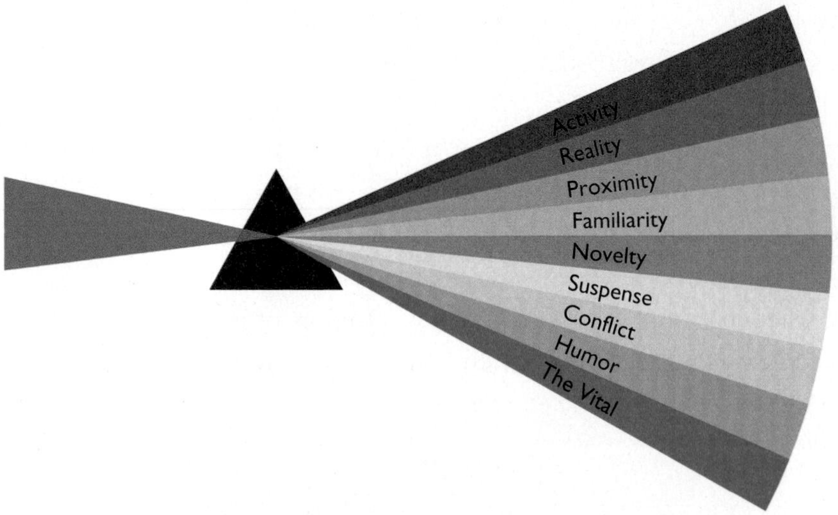

Activity
Reality
Proximity
Familiarity
Novelty
Suspense
Conflict
Humor
The Vital

## Reality

The earliest words you learned were names for tangible objects—like *mommy, cookie,* and *toy.* Such concrete concepts are the building blocks of our everyday worlds. When you need to abstract—to generalize—you don't want to lose your audience, so refer to specific events, people, and places. For example, when we used the abstract phrase "tangible objects" at the beginning of this paragraph, we gave you three concrete examples to clarify it. Words that refer to tangible items have more force than general references and abstractions.

## Proximity

*Proximity* means "nearness"; we usually notice things that closely surround us. A direct reference to a person in the audience, a nearby object or place, an incident that has just occurred, or the immediate occasion helps you to command attention. The following introduction uses proximity to engage the listeners:

> Within an easy drive of campus, you can stroll along the shores of Lake Superior or visit a marina. You can ski on the slopes of Spirit Mountain. And if you're adventurous, drive just a few more miles to thousands of acres of pristine forest in the Boundary Waters Canoe Area or see the sights of Canada. But all of these natural resources require our protection if we are to continue to enjoy them.

## Familiarity

References to the familiar are attention sustaining, especially in the face of new or strange ideas. The familiar is comfortable. People drive the same route to work, children sing the same songs over and over, and you've probably watched your favorite movie more than once. Stories about Cap Anson, Shoeless Joe Jackson, Babe Ruth, Dizzy Dean, and Joe DiMaggio get repeated on occasions when cultural memories of baseball, as America's great sport, are invoked. How many times have you heard speakers repeat Martin Luther King, Jr.'s famous phrase "I have a dream"? We like the reassurance that such familiarity provides.

## Novelty

Novel happenings, dramatic incidents, or unusual developments attract attention. Look at the tabloid newspaper headlines next time you're in the grocery store checkout line: "Grandmother Gives Birth to 80-lb. Baby," "Britney Spears to Marry Alien from Mars," and "Elvis Sighted at County Fair." These bizarre stories catch our attention. References to size and contrast work well to create novelty.

When using novelty, blending the familiar and the novel, the old and the new, often yields the best results. Otherwise, you risk stretching the credulity of your listeners—as do those supermarket tabloids. To stimulate interest in the evolving nature of the self-defense plea in criminal courts, you might cite recent, highly publicized trials in which alleged victims claim self-defense in response to years of physical or mental abuse. Citing specific cases, such as the Menendez brothers' murder of their parents, provokes interest through novelty.

## Suspense

Much of the appeal in mystery stories arises because we don't know how they will end. Films such as *Indiana Jones and the Kingdom of the Crystal Skull* or *The Illusionist* have enough unusual twists to hold audiences spellbound. You, too, can use uncertainty in your speeches by pointing to puzzling relationships or unpredictable forces. Introduce suspense into the stories you tell, building up to a surprising climax. Hint that you'll divulge valuable information later: "Stay with me through this speech, because by the end, you'll learn how to cut your book bill in half every semester."

## Conflict

Controversy grabs attention. Soap operas are fraught with love, hate, violence, passion, and power struggles. Conflict, like suspense, suggests uncertainty; like activity, it's dynamic. The next time you hear the news, listen for conflict. Newscasters often portray shipwreck survivors as "battling nature." Sportscasters describe athletes as "overcoming adversity." Talk show hosts like Jerry Springer pit guests against each other. And even weather forecasters talk about "fighting off Arctic blasts of frigid air." The concept of struggle brings a sense of urgency to the day's events.

In your speeches, you can create conflict among ideas, such as the competing theories about the aggressiveness of young boys: Are males genetically programmed to be aggressive, or are they made that way by environmental influences, such as media violence? Put these competing theories in conflict with each other to reveal their differences. When your ideas are cast as pugilists, they become dramatic and engaging.

## Humor

Listeners usually pay attention when they're enjoying themselves. Humor can unite you and your audience by relaxing everyone and providing a change of pace. When using humor to capture and hold attention, remember to stick close to your central idea by choosing humor that is relevant. Be sure to use only humorous stories that are in good taste and so avoid offending members of your audience. Comedian Bill Cosby met both of these requirements when he poked fun at a University of South Carolina graduating class. In his commencement speech, Cosby reminded his listeners:

> All across the United States of America, people are graduating. And they are hearing so many guest speakers tell them that they are going forth. As a parent I am concerned as to whether or not you know where "Forth" is. Let me put it to you this way: We have paved a road—the one to the house was already paved. "Forth" is not back home.[1]

## The Vital

The phrase "the vital" was coined by Alan Monroe, the original author of this textbook, to reflect our tendency to be concerned with things that immediately benefit us. We pay attention to matters that affect our health, reputation, property, or employment. When a speaker says, "Students who take internships while in college find jobs after graduation three times as fast as those who don't," you're likely to pay attention, because getting a job is vital to you. Appealing to the vital, therefore, is a matter of personalizing the speech for a particular audience—making it as relevant to their concrete circumstances as possible.

In summary, there are nine different ways to stimulate attention: (1) activity, (2) reality, (3) proximity, (4) familiarity, (5) novelty, (6) suspense, (7) conflict, (8) humor, and (9) the vital. Use these attention-getters to grab and maintain your listeners' attention throughout your speech. They give your speech sparkle and spunk, reach out to your listeners, and help your listeners follow and remember your speech.

# Beginning Your Speech

You can use the factors of attention to engage your listeners during the beginning moments of your speech, but attention is not enough. You must also secure good will and respect as well as prepare your listeners for the main ideas that follow your introduction. In many situations, your own reputation or the chairperson's introduction will help generate good will. You can also share your experience with the topic and background research to boost your credibility.

You gain additional respect from your listeners when you are well prepared to speak.

You can prepare your listeners for your speech by stating your purpose early. Let them engage the subject matter clearly and openly. Audiences that are forced to guess the purpose of a speech soon lose interest. A preview of your ideas and speech structure will help your audience follow along.

There may be times when your audience is opposed to you or your topic. In these instances, it's important to deal with the opposition openly so that you will receive a fair hearing. By commenting on the differences between your views and those of your listeners, you can let them know that you're aware of disagreements but are seeking areas of consensus. And when confronted by indifference, distrust, or skepticism, you must take steps early in the speech to acknowledge these attitudes. Even if your listeners don't agree, you can often secure their respect for your honesty and integrity by dealing directly with them.

An introduction that secures your audience's attention and good will and that prepares them to listen lays a solid foundation for acceptance of the central idea of your speech. You can establish attention by presenting your ideas in ways that create interest. We will examine a number of established means for tailoring your introduction to achieve the best results (see Figure 8.2).

## Referring to the Subject or Occasion

If your audience already has a vital interest in your subject, you need only to state that subject before presenting your first main point:

> "I'm glad to see how many of you came to learn more about finding summer internships. As the poster around campus indicated, I'm here tonight to talk about how you can get a head start on finding the perfect summer internship. My experiences as an intern last summer and my current job with the university placement office have taught me three things about the internship process—start early, be patient, and write a winning resume."

This speaker wastes no time in addressing the topic, because listeners have selected to attend the talk. The speaker still must establish expertise, however, and provide a brief preview of the main ideas in the speech.

**Figure 8.2** Types of Introductions and Conclusions

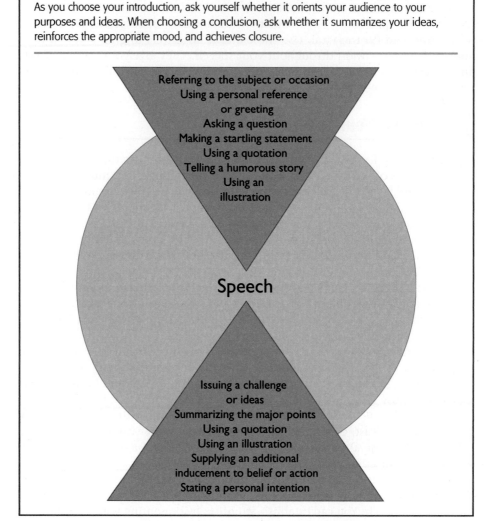

You can choose among different types of introductions and conclusions for your speeches. As you choose your introduction, ask yourself whether it orients your audience to your purposes and ideas. When choosing a conclusion, ask whether it summarizes your ideas, reinforces the appropriate mood, and achieves closure.

Referring to the subject or occasion
Using a personal reference
or greeting
Asking a question
Making a startling statement
Using a quotation
Telling a humorous story
Using an
illustration

**Speech**

Issuing a challenge
or ideas
Summarizing the major points
Using a quotation
Using an illustration
Supplying an additional
inducement to belief or action
Stating a personal intention

President George W. Bush began his statement to the nation after the September 11, 2001, attacks on the World Trade Center and Pentagon by referring directly to the occasion:

> Today, our fellow citizens, our way of life, our very freedom came under attack in a series of deliberate and deadly terrorist acts. The victims were in airplanes, or in their offices; secretaries, businessmen and women, military and federal workers; moms and dads, friends and neighbors. Thousands of lives were suddenly ended by evil, despicable acts of terror. The pictures of airplanes flying into buildings, fires burning, huge structures collapsing, have filled us with disbelief, terrible sadness, and a quiet, unyielding anger. These acts of mass murder were intended to frighten our nation into chaos and retreat. But they have failed; our country is strong.[2]

Notice how President Bush moved from recognition of the events, the victims, and the media images to the American reaction in just a few sentences.

## Using a Personal Reference or Greeting

At times, a warm, personal greeting from a speaker or the remembrance of a previous visit can quickly establish positive rapport between a speaker and the audience. This is especially important if the speaker is representing an organization. Official ties are one thing, but if they can be personalized, the audience may be even more open to developing a relationship with the speaker. When Halle Berry accepted an Oscar for Best Actress in 2002, she connected her personal feelings with her predecessors: "This moment is so much bigger than me. This moment is for Dorothy Dandridge, Lena Horne, Diahann Carroll. It's for the women that stand beside me, Jada Pinkett, Angela Bassett, Vivica Fox. And it's for every nameless, faceless woman of color that now has a chance because this door tonight has been opened."[3]

Berry reminded her listeners of their common connection to the past and responsibility for the future. The brevity and forthrightness of her introduction struck exactly the right note on this occasion. If you and your listeners don't have a previous relationship, you'll need to discuss what brought you together to establish this connection.

The way that a personal reference introduction can be used to gain the attention of a hostile or skeptical audience is illustrated by a speech presented by Anson Mount, manager of public affairs for *Playboy*, to the Christian Life Commission of the Southern Baptist Convention:

> I am sure we are all aware of the seeming incongruity of a representative of *Playboy* magazine speaking to an assemblage of representatives of the Southern Baptist Convention. I was intrigued by the invitation when it came last fall, though I was not surprised. I am grateful for your genuine and warm hospitality, and I am flattered (though again not surprised) by the implication that I would have something to say that could have meaning to you people. Both *Playboy* and the Baptists have indeed been considering many of the same issues and ethical problems; and even if we have not arrived at the same conclusions, I am impressed and gratified by your openness and willingness to listen to our views.[4]

If a personal reference is sincere and appropriate, it will establish good will as well as gain attention. Avoid extravagant, emotional statements, however, because listeners are quick to sense a lack of genuineness. At the other extreme, avoid apologizing. Don't say, "I don't know why I was picked to talk when others could have done it so much better" or "Unaccustomed as I am to public speaking . . ." Apologetic beginnings suggest that your audience needn't waste their time listening. Be cordial, sincere, and modest, but establish your authority and maintain control of the situation.

## Asking a Question

Another way to open a speech is to ask a question or series of questions to spark thinking about your subject. For example, Nicholas Fynn of Ohio University opened a speech about free-burning of timberland by saying, "How many of you in this room have visited a national park at one point in your life? Well, the majority of you are in good company."[5] Such a question introduces a topic gently and, with its direct reference to the audience, tends to engage the listeners.

**Rhetorical questions**—that is, those for which you do not expect direct audience response—are often used to forecast the development of the speech. One speaker used rhetorical questions to capture her listener's interest and then used rhetorical questions again to forecast her major speech topics: "Can you imagine losing everything—your house, your car, your savings accounts? All because you used your credit card to purchase something online? This could happen to you. It's called identity theft, and last year alone, there were hundreds of cases. You don't have to be the next victim. What is identity theft, and how can you prevent it?" Rhetorical questions are most often used with topical organizations, when other types of forecasts are more difficult to use.

## Making a Startling Statement

On certain occasions, you may choose to open a speech by making a startling statement of fact or opinion. This approach is especially useful when listeners are distracted, apathetic, or smug. It rivets their attention on your topic. For example, the executive director of AARP, after asking some rhetorical questions about health care, caught his listeners' attention with a series or startling statements:

> Given what we're spending on health care, we should have the best system in the world. But the reality is that we don't. Thirty-seven million Americans have no health insurance protection whatsoever, and millions more are underinsured. We are twentieth—that's right, twentieth—among the nations of the world in infant mortality. The death rate for our black newborn children rivals that of Third World countries. And poor children in America, like their brothers and sisters in Third World nations, receive neither immunizations nor basic dental care.
>
> Those statistics give us a sense of the scope of the problem. What they don't adequately portray is the human factor—the pain and the suffering. While terminally ill patients may have their lives extended in intensive care units—at tremendous cost—middle-age minority women die of preventable and treatable cancer, hypertension, and diabetes. [6]

There's a fine line between startling your listeners and scandalizing them. The technique can backfire if your listeners become angry when you threaten or disgust them. Keep in mind that what you tell your listeners should be directly tied to your speech and not simply there for shock value alone. You should present facts or ideas that are verifiable. Your goal is to startle your listeners by giving them something new to think about or by providing a new perspective on known facts and ideas.

## Using a Quotation

A quotation may be an excellent means of introducing a speech. It can prod listeners to think about something important and it often captures an appropriate emotional tone. A student in a public speaking class opened her informative speech by saying:

> One of my favorite movies is *Braveheart*. I've seen it so many times, I think I have it memorized. Maybe you remember one point in the movie where Mel Gibson's character, William Wallace, says, "Every man dies. Not every man truly lives." The historical William Wallace has lived, in myth and legend, for hundreds of years. In my speech today, I'd like to investigate his life as history records it. Who was William Wallace the man? What are the facts about his life and death? Let's begin with the historical record.

Quotations also can be used to capture the theme of a speech. Marlan Cleveland, president of the World Academy of Art and Science, established the central idea for his speech to a group of business leaders by quoting from his favorite author, Mary Parker Follett: "All polishing is done by friction . . . The music of the violin we get by friction. We left the savage style when we discovered fire by friction. So we talk of the friction of mind on mind as a good thing."[7] Using this thought as his theme, the speaker argued that "friction," or disagreement in business organizations, contributed to progress and that good managers ought to encourage such friction.

There are many places for you to find quotations. You can quote from your favorite author, actor, politician, or even your favorite movie. *Bartlett's Familiar Quotations* online or in print offers a good selection of quotations on various subjects. As you choose a quotation, ask yourself several questions: Is it relevant to my speech topic? Is it succinct? Is it memorable? Your quotation should be more than decoration; it should capture the mood and central idea of your speech. And don't forget to give credit to your source with an oral citation.

## Telling a Humorous Story

You can begin a speech by telling a funny story or relating a humorous experience. When doing so, however, observe the following three rules of communication:

**1. Be sure that the story is at least amusing, if not funny.** Test it out on others before you actually deliver the speech. Be sure that you practice sufficiently so that you can present the story naturally. And use the story to make a point instead of making it the center of your remarks. In other words, brevity is crucial.

**2. Be sure that the story is relevant to your speech.** If its subject matter or punch line is not directly related to you, your topic, or at least your next couple of sentences, the story will appear to be a gimmick.

*Engaging an audience, getting them attuned to you and your message early on, greatly enhances your chances for rhetorical success.*

**3. Be sure that your story is in good taste.** In a public gathering, an off-color or doubtful story violates accepted standards of social behavior and can undermine an audience's respect for you. You should avoid sexual, racist, antireligious, ageist, homophobic, and sexist humor.

The late actor Christopher Reeve used this humorous observation as the introduction to his 2003 Ohio State University commencement address:

> "Before I begin, you should know that I have enjoyed watching Ohio State football on television for many years, but I never knew what a buckeye was. I always assumed it was a common name for a species of a little-known but dangerous wild animal. I recently learned that it's just a tree. At first glance, it appears to be useless: The wood doesn't burn well, the bark smells, and the meat of the nut is bitter and mildly toxic. Yet it grows where others cannot, it's difficult to kill, and it adapts to its circumstances. So much for first impressions."[8]

Reeve went on to discuss the challenges that his listeners would face in the future.

## Using an Illustration

A real-life incident, a passage from a novel or short story, or a hypothetical illustration can also get a speech off to a good start. An illustration should be not only interesting to the audience but also relevant to your central idea. Deanna Sellnow, then a student at North Dakota State University, used this technique to introduce a speech on private credit-reporting bureaus:

> John Pontier, of Boise, Idaho, was turned down for insurance because a reporting agency informed the company that he and his wife were addicted to narcotics, and his Taco Bell franchise had been closed down by the health board when dog food had been found mixed in with the tacos. There was only one small problem. The information was made up. His wife was a practicing Mormon who didn't touch a drink, much less drugs, and the restaurant had never been cited for a health violation.[9]

The existence of a problem with private credit-reporting bureaus is clear from this introduction. If the illustration is humorous instead of serious, the effect may be different but equally useful. Illustrations can come from your own personal experience or from the experiences of others you know. You can also adapt the experiences of famous people gleaned from biographies, news accounts, and other sources. Be sure to cite the source of the story in your speech.

## Completing Your Introduction

You can use one of the approaches that we've discussed alone, or you can combine two or more. You might open with a startling illustration or a humorous reference to the occasion, for example. No matter what type of introduction you use, however, you should have three purposes in mind: (1) gaining the attention of your listeners, (2) winning their good will and respect, and (3) setting the direction for the substance of your talk. Your introduction should be relevant to the purpose of your speech and should lead smoothly into the first of the major ideas that you wish to present—that is, your introduction should be an integral part of the speech.

Your introduction should also forecast the speech's development by means of a preview. The preview establishes your listeners' confidence in the organization of your speech, thus enhancing your credibility. It creates listener receptivity by

---

## SPEAKING OF...
## S K I L L S

### How Long Should It Be?

According to a classic study, the average speaker spends about ten percent of the total speech on the introduction and five percent on the conclusion. The introduction may increase to thirteen percent in speeches that are designed to stimulate or inspire, such as sermons, dedications, or memorials. In practical terms, this means that you will probably take one minute to introduce a ten-minute speech—and thirty seconds to conclude it.

Can you think of circumstances in which you would spend more time introducing or concluding your remarks? Less time?

For the original study, see N. Edd Miller, "Speech Introductions and Conclusions," *Quarterly Journal of Speech*, 32 (1946): 181–183.

---

providing a structure for you and your listeners to follow during the speech. Here are some examples of types of previews:

**1. Announce the organizational pattern.** You might say, "I'll develop the effects of the problem of spousal abuse and then examine its causes" (causal pattern) or "In demonstrating how to check basic problems with your computer, I'll consider three topics. I'll be talking about the hard drive, the ancillary drive systems, and the word-processing program" (topical order).

**2. Use mnemonic devices.** Acronyms aid memory—for example, "I'm going to discuss the ABCs of jogging: Always wear good shoes. Baby your feet. Call a podiatrist if problems develop."

**3. Employ alliteration.** Rely on sound similarities to create interest—for example, "My advice for finding someone to marry? Use the three As—availability, attitude, and *amour.*"

**4. Use repetition.** Reinforce your message by repeating the main phrases. You can say, "We need to examine how a lack of street lights creates a problem on campus, a problem on nearby streets, a problem on downtown streets, and ultimately, even a problem on the seemingly quiet, wooded streets of suburbia."

When effective, your introductory remarks will both establish a common ground of interest and understanding and provide a structure to guide your audience toward the conclusion that you intend to reach.

## Ending Your Speech

Just as the introduction to your speech accomplishes specific purposes, so, too, does the conclusion. An effective conclusion does three things: (1) It reinforces the message of the speech, letting listeners understand one more time the importance and significance of what you're saying; (2) it completes the emotional relationship you've constructed with your listeners; and (3) it creates a sense of completeness or closure.

If your speech has one dominant idea, you should restate it in a clear and forceful manner. If your speech is more complex, you may summarize the key points, or you may spell out the action or belief that these points suggest. Take advantage of the recency effect—that your listeners are more likely to remember the most recent ideas in your speech, your conclusion.

In addition to reinforcing the central idea, your conclusion should leave the audience in the proper mood. If you want your listeners to express vigorous enthusiasm, stimulate that feeling with your closing words. Decide whether the response you seek is a mood of seriousness or good humor, of warm sympathy or utter disgust, of thoughtfulness or action. Then, end your speech in a way that will create that mood.

Finally, a good ending should convey a sense of completeness and finality. Listeners grow restless and annoyed when they think the speech is finished, only to hear the speaker ramble on. Tie the threads of thought together so that the pattern of your speech is brought clearly to completion.

A number of conclusion techniques are used regularly by speakers. Let's examine several of them.

## Issuing a Challenge

You may conclude your speech by issuing a challenge to your listeners, requesting support or action, or reminding them of their responsibilities. That challenge can be as direct as the one used in this student speech:

Imagine the satisfaction you'll feel when you return to classes after spring break. You'll have contributed to the well-being of others instead of squandering your days lying on a beach. You'll have

*UN Secretary-General Kofi Annan was a master of speech conclusions—especially issuing challenges to neutral nations in times of crisis.*

improved the lives of people for years to come instead of getting a tan that will just fade within the month. By volunteering to build a house for Habitat for Humanity, you will have changed our society.

Notice the use of parallel structure in this conclusion—to contribute instead of squander, to improve instead of tan. Such attention to style elevates the challenge, giving it a seriousness that inspires listeners.

In his remarks following receipt of the 2007 Nobel Peace Prize for his work on global warming, former Vice President Al Gore framed a challenge to his listeners as a series of questions posed by future generations:

> The future is knocking at our door right now. Make no mistake, the next generation will ask us one of two questions. Either they will ask, "What were you thinking; why didn't you act?" Or they will ask instead, "How did you find the moral courage to rise and successfully resolve a crisis that so many said was impossible to solve?"[10]

To motivate his listeners to act to stop global warming, Gore envisioned the future and made his listeners accountable for their current choices. Because he placed the decision with them, Gore made his listeners responsible for the future.

## Summarizing the Major Points or Ideas

In an informative speech, a summary allows the audience to pull together the main strands of information and to evaluate the significance of the speech. In a persuasive speech, a summary gives you a final opportunity to present, in brief form, the major points of your argument. For example, a student presented this summary of an informative speech on tornadoes:

> You've seen the swirling funnel clouds on the six o'clock news. They hit sometimes without much warning, leaving in their paths death and destruction. Now you should understand the formation of funnel clouds, the classification of tornadoes on the Fujita scale, and the high cost of tornadoes worldwide in lives and property. Once you understand the savage fury of tornadoes, you can better appreciate them. Tornadoes are one of nature's temper tantrums.

If the student's purpose had been to persuade listeners to take safety precautions during a tornado alert, the summary of the speech might have sounded like this:

> The devastation left in the path of a tornado can be tremendous. To prevent you and your loved ones from becoming statistics on the six o'clock news, remember what I told you this afternoon. Seek shelter in basements, ditches, or other low areas. Stay away from glass and electric lines. And remember the lesson of the Xenia, Ohio, disaster. Tornadoes often hit in clusters. Be sure the coast is clear before you leave your shelter. Don't be a statistic.

In each case, summarizing the main ideas of the speech gives the speaker another opportunity to reinforce the message. Information can be reiterated in the summary of an informative speech, or the major arguments or actions can be strengthened in the summary of a persuasive speech.

## Using a Quotation

You can cite others' words to capture the spirit of your ideas in the conclusion of your speech. Quotations are often used to end speeches. Quoted prose, if the author is credible, may gather additional support for your central idea. So, in a speech on the need to reformulate this country's system of managed care,

Howard Veit said, "I believe all the dynamics are in place for this transformation [of care systems] to take place. Dwight Eisenhower once said, 'Neither a wise man nor a brave man lies down on the tracks of history to wait for the train of the future to run over him.' Well, the train is coming. Fortunately, you have a choice about how you'll react."[11]

Poetry, too, may distill the essence of your message in uplifting language. Bishop Leontine Kelly concluded her speech celebrating the diversity of human talents with the words of a well-known Christian hymn: "How firm a foundation ye saints of the Lord, Is laid for your faith in God's excellent word."[12] The recognition of these familiar words probably inspired members of her audience.

## Using an Illustration

Illustrations engage your listeners emotionally. If you use a concluding illustration, it can set the tone and direction of your final words. Your illustration should be both inclusive of the main focus or thrust of your speech and conclusive in tone and impact. Capturing the message and the way a speaker wanted an audience to feel about the message is nicely illustrated in this description by Nancy Dickey, president of the American Medical Association, of that organization's new plan for health reform:

> There is an old painting that hangs in many medical museums that depicts this relationship [between patient and doctor] better than any words I can offer here. Perhaps some of you have even seen it. It shows a physician at a child's bedside. The physician is pensive, maybe even a bit prayerful. The child's parents are all but faded into the background. And there sits the physician—with none of today's tools or technologies to call upon—but nonetheless clearly connected to his patient.
>
> I want to be sure, that as we craft this new health system, that I am again allowed—even encouraged—to connect in that way to my patients . . . to listen, to hear, and to respond to their concerns.[13]

## Supplying an Additional Inducement to Belief or Action

Sometimes you may conclude a speech by quickly reviewing the principal ideas presented in the body and then supplying one or more additional reasons for endorsing the belief or taking the proposed action. So, in a student speech, Michael Twitchell spoke at length about the devastating effects of depression. After proposing numerous reasons for people to get involved in the battle, he offered in the conclusion to his speech an additional inducement:

> Why should you really care? Why is it important? The depressed person may be someone you know—it could be you. If you know what is happening, you can always help. I wish I had known what depression was in March of 1978. You see, when I said David Twitchell could be my father, I was making a statement of fact. David is my father. I am his son. My family wasn't saved; perhaps now yours can be.[14]

## Stating a Personal Intention

Stating your own intention to adopt the action or attitude you recommend in your speech is particularly effective when your prestige with the audience is high or when you have presented a concrete proposal requiring immediate action. By professing your intention to take immediate action, you and your ideas gain credibility. During a news conference in April 2005, six-time Tour de France cycling champion Lance Armstrong announced that he would retire after trying for his seventh straight Tour de France victory. Armstrong, a high-profile survivor of testicular cancer, personalized his comments and challenged himself by saying, "I was fortunate to win six times. Can I win again this year? I'm not sure, but I'm going to try."[15] Armstrong won.

Regardless of the means you choose for closing your speech, remember that your conclusion should focus the attention of your listeners on the central theme you've developed. In addition, a good conclusion should be consistent with the mood or tenor of your speech and should convey a sense of completeness and finality.

## Sample Outline for an Introduction and Conclusion

An introduction and conclusion to a persuasive speech on spaying and neutering pets might take the following form. Notice that the speaker uses an illustration and a startling statement of statistics to lead the audience into the subject. The conclusion combines a summary with a final illustration and a statement of personal intention.

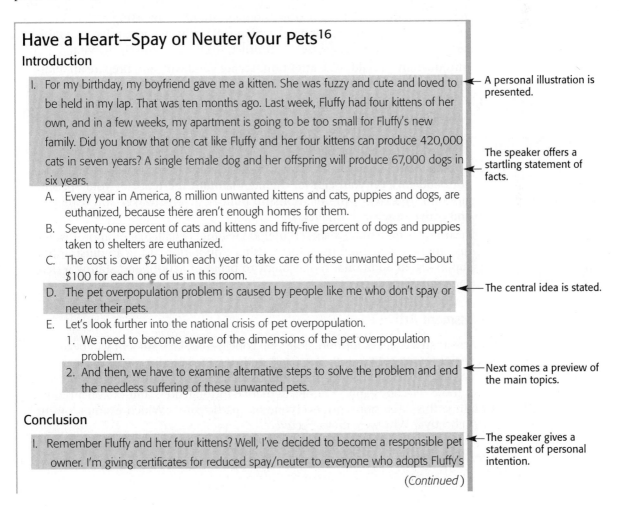

### Have a Heart—Spay or Neuter Your Pets[16]

**Introduction**

I. For my birthday, my boyfriend gave me a kitten. She was fuzzy and cute and loved to be held in my lap. That was ten months ago. Last week, Fluffy had four kittens of her own, and in a few weeks, my apartment is going to be too small for Fluffy's new family. Did you know that one cat like Fluffy and her four kittens can produce 420,000 cats in seven years? A single female dog and her offspring will produce 67,000 dogs in six years. ← *A personal illustration is presented.* / *The speaker offers a startling statement of facts.*

   A. Every year in America, 8 million unwanted kittens and cats, puppies and dogs, are euthanized, because there aren't enough homes for them.

   B. Seventy-one percent of cats and kittens and fifty-five percent of dogs and puppies taken to shelters are euthanized.

   C. The cost is over $2 billion each year to take care of these unwanted pets—about $100 for each one of us in this room.

   D. The pet overpopulation problem is caused by people like me who don't spay or neuter their pets. ← *The central idea is stated.*

   E. Let's look further into the national crisis of pet overpopulation.

      1. We need to become aware of the dimensions of the pet overpopulation problem.

      2. And then, we have to examine alternative steps to solve the problem and end the needless suffering of these unwanted pets. ← *Next comes a preview of the main topics.*

**Conclusion**

I. Remember Fluffy and her four kittens? Well, I've decided to become a responsible pet owner. I'm giving certificates for reduced spay/neuter to everyone who adopts Fluffy's ← *The speaker gives a statement of personal intention.*

*(Continued)*

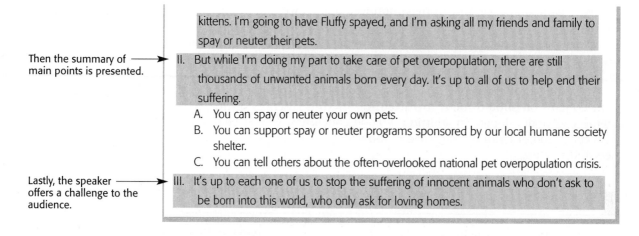

Then the summary of main points is presented.

kittens. I'm going to have Fluffy spayed, and I'm asking all my friends and family to spay or neuter their pets.

II. But while I'm doing my part to take care of pet overpopulation, there are still thousands of unwanted animals born every day. It's up to all of us to help end their suffering.
   A. You can spay or neuter your own pets.
   B. You can support spay or neuter programs sponsored by our local humane society shelter.
   C. You can tell others about the often-overlooked national pet overpopulation crisis.

Lastly, the speaker offers a challenge to the audience.

III. It's up to each one of us to stop the suffering of innocent animals who don't ask to be born into this world, who only ask for loving homes.

## Assessing Your Progress

### Chapter Summary

1. You can capture and sustain your listeners' attention by using one or more of the nine factors of attention: (a) activity, (b) reality, (c) proximity, (d) familiarity, (e) novelty, (f) suspense, (g) conflict, (h) humor, and (i) the vital.

2. Introductions should seize attention, secure good will, and prepare an audience for what you will be saying.

3. Types of introductions include referring to the subject or occasion, using a personal reference or greeting, asking a rhetorical question, making a startling statement of fact or opinion, using a quotation, telling a humorous story, and using an illustration.

4. In concluding your speech, you should attempt to focus the thoughts of your audience on your central theme, maintain the tenor of your speech, close off (or extend) the relationship built between speaker and listeners, and convey a sense of finality.

5. Techniques for ending a speech include issuing a challenge or appeal, summarizing the major points or ideas, using a quotation, using an illustration, supplying an additional inducement to belief or action, and stating a personal intention.

### Assessment Activities

Participate in a chain of introductions and conclusions. One student will begin by suggesting a topic for a speech. A second student will suggest an appropriate introduction and conclusion and then justify those choices. A third student will challenge those selections and propose alternative introductions and/or conclusions. Continue this discussion until everyone has participated. Which examples were most effective? Why were they effective?

For additional suggestions and activities, log on to MySpeechLab at www.my speechlab.com.

## Using the Web

Go to MySpeechLab for sample speeches, or locate a database that includes a collection of speeches, such as the Top 100 American Speeches of the 20th Century (www.americanrhetoric.com/top100speeches.htm). Identify the types of introductory and concluding strategies used by each speaker, and evaluate the effectiveness of these strategies.

## References

1. Bill Cosby, "University of South Carolina Commencement Address," 1990, unpublished manuscript available from the author.
2. President Bush's statement can be found at www.yale.edu/lawweb/avalon/sept11/presstate001.htm.
3. For a complete text of Halle Berry's speech, see www.americanrhetoric.com/speeches/halleberryoscarspeech.htm.
4. Anson Mount, Manager of Public Affairs for *Playboy* magazine, from a speech presented to the Christian Life Commission, in *Contemporary American Speeches*, 5th ed., edited by Wil A. Linkugel et al. (Dubuque, IA: Kendall/Hunt, 1982).
5. Nicholas Fynn, "The Free Burn Fallacy," *Winning Orations 1989*. Reprinted by permission of Larry Schnoor, Executive Secretary, Interstate Oratorical Association, Mankato, MN.
6. Horace B. Deets, "Health Care for a Caring America: We Must Develop a Better System," *Vital Speeches of the Day*, 55 (1 August 1989).
7. Harlan Cleveland, "Imagination and Creativity," *Vital Speeches of the Day*, 65 (1 February 1999).
8. See the entire text of Christopher Reeve's commencement address at www.chrisreevehomepage.com/sp-ohio_uni_address2003.html.
9. Deanna Sellnow, "Have You Checked Lately?" *Winning Orations 1982*. Reprinted by permission of Larry Schnoor, Executive Secretary, Interstate Oratorical Association, Mankato, MN.
10. You can read Al Gore's entire Nobel Prize acceptance speech at www.huffingtonpost.com/2007/12/10/read-al-gores-nobel-priz_n_76054.html.
11. Howard Veit, "The Next Generation of Managed Care: The Age of Consumerism," *Vital Speeches of the Day*, 65 (15 April 1999).
12. Bishop Leontine Kelly, "Celebrating the Diversity of Our Gifts," in *Women's Voices in Our Time*, edited by Victoria L. DeFrancisco and Marvin D. Jensen (Prospect Heights, IL: Waveland Press, 1994), 115.
13. Nancy W. Dickey, "Health Care for the New Millennium: The AMA Plan for Health System Reform," *Vital Speeches of the Day*, 65 (15 April 1999).
14. Michael A. Twitchell, "The Flood Gates of the Mind," *Winning Orations 1996*. Reprinted by permission of Larry Schnoor, Executive Secretary, Interstate Oratorical Association, Mankato, MN.
15. For more on Lance Armstrong's news conference, see sportsillustrated.cnn.com/2005/more/04/18/lance.retire.ap.
16. Information for this example was taken from humanesocietyofamerica.org, americanhumane.org, www.allforanimals.com, and www.adoptapet.com.

# 9 | Wording Your Speech

"Heck, speaking isn't so hard—you've been doing it all of your life!" Well, you probably didn't start using **written language** for a while, but you were likely talking merrily before you were potty-trained. **Oral language** has been integral to your self-understanding and relationships with others for longer than you can remember, but that doesn't mean it's not complicated.

Language functions on multiple levels. It is a referential, relational, and symbolic medium of communication. Because language refers to things, it is *referential* When you label or name things such as *dog*, *tree*, or *bagel*, you are employing the referential nature of language. Young children learn the power of language as a referential tool early.

Language also has *relational powers;* it suggests associations between people. "Give me that bagel!" not only points to the circular bread, it also indicates that one person has the power or authority to command another person. Some groups even use their own special languages that exclude. Technical language is used most often by professionals, and slang doesn't sound right when spoken by an outsider. It might sound odd, for example, to hear your grandmother say, "Rad!"

Language is also *symbolic;* it can be disconnected from the concrete world. We can talk about unreal things, such as unicorns and gremlins, or abstract constructs, such as democracy and love. Whole empires of thought can be constructed out of language. When

## CHAPTER OUTLINE

Using Oral Style

*Speaking of . . . Skills: Oral Versus Written Style*

Using Language Strategically

Creating an Atmosphere

*Speaking of . . . Ethics: Doublespeak*

Sample Speech: "On Accepting the Nobel Prize for Literature," by William Faulkner

Assessing Your Progress

## KEY TERMS

you speak, it's not enough to know the words. You must also understand how language reflects human relationships, shared senses of reality, and human abstractions—your culture and thinking.

In essence, we've been talking about the fundamental quality of *orality* that exists in our use of language. When you put ideas into words or actions, **encoding** occurs. Encoding includes your choice of oral language, use of visual aids, and even bodily and vocal behaviors. In this chapter, we'll focus on using an oral speaking style, using language strategically, and creating a speaking atmosphere.

## Using Oral Style

Generally, spoken language is uncomplicated. It has to be, because we use it every day—at the grocery store, over the back fence, around the supper table, and in our classes. Usually, public speakers adopt the conversational quality of everyday language; listeners prefer it. Most of the time when you speak, you will choose this oral style.

**Oral style** is informal, similar to conversation. Occasionally, spoken language assumes a more complicated and formal style that more closely resembles written work; this is referred to as **written style**. It usually indicates a formal occasion or weighty topic. Good oral style handles referentiality by making perfectly clear what's being talked about, it is made up of language that's appropriate to the

SPEAKING OF...
S K I L L S

### Oral Versus Written Style

How do you instantly recognize that a speaker has written out a speech? It inherently sounds as though its been written. The speaker uses written rather than oral style. Here are some ways in which oral style differs from written style:

1.   The average sentence is shorter in oral communication.

2.   You use fewer different words when you speak.

3.   You use a large number of short words, such as *it* and *the,* when you speak. In fact, fifty simple words constitute almost half of your speaking vocabulary.

4.   You refer to people more often with words like *I, you, me, our,* and *us* when you speak.

5.   You use more qualifying words, such as *much, many, a lot,* and *most,* when you speak.

6.   Your language choices are more informal when you speak, and you use more contractions.

relationships you have with your listeners, and it symbolically handles imaginary matters, such as unicorns, or abstractions, such as "just war," in concrete ways. Consider the following examples of written and oral style:

| Written Style | Oral Style |
| --- | --- |
| Remit the requested amount forthwith. | Pay your bill. |
| Will you be having anything else? | Whutkinahgitcha? |
| To avoid injury, keep hands away from the cutting surface. | Don't touch the blade! |
| Contact a service representative to register your dissatisfaction with the product. | Call to complain. |

If you write out your whole speech before giving it, the result is likely to be stilted and stiff. It might sound more like an essay than a speech. For example, consider the following introduction:

> I am most pleased that you could come this morning. I would like to use this opportunity to discuss with you a subject of inestimable importance to us all: the impact of inflationary spirals and shrinking government-insured loans on students enrolled in institutions of higher education.

Translated into an oral style, a speaker would say:

> Thanks for coming. I'd like to talk today about a problem for all of us: the rising cost of going to college.

Notice how much more natural the second version sounds. The first example is wordy—filled with prepositional phrases, complex words, and formal sentences. It's probably okay for a university president who will publish it in an alumni magazine or school Web site, but the second example contains shorter sentences and simpler vocabulary. It also addresses an audience of students more directly.

For most speech occasions, you should cultivate an oral style. On rare, highly ceremonial occasions, you may decide to read from a prepared text. Even then, however, you should strive for an oral style. Three fundamental qualities will help you develop a clear and effective oral style: (1) accuracy, (2) simplicity, and (3) restatement.

## Accuracy

Careful word choice is an essential ingredient to effectively transmitting your meaning to an audience. Oral language is usually concrete and specific. If you tell a hardware store clerk, "I broke the doohickey on my whachamicallit, and I need a thingamajig to fix it," you'd better have the whachamicallit in your hand, or the clerk won't understand you. When you speak, your goal is precision. You should leave no doubt about your meaning.

Because words are symbols that represent not only objects but also ideas about those objects, your listeners may attach a meaning to your words that's quite different from the one you intended. Say the word *cow*, and we'll likely all envision the same beast. However, for kids from a farm in western Iowa, that animal was central to the family's livelihood and their 4-H experiences; from an inner-city asphalt neighborhood, a kid saw a cute calf only in a petting zoo; and for some Buddhist households in India, the animal was possibly the reincarnation of a relative.

Referentiality includes not only the object being recalled but also people's experiences with it—and so different (mis)interpretations can come to mind. Such misinterpretation becomes more likely as your words become more abstract, such as *democracy* or *capitalism*, or as you use phrases like "the American way of life."

To avoid vagueness or misinterpretation, choose words that express the exact shade of meaning you wish to communicate in language that listeners are likely to know. You might say that an object shines, but the object might also *glow, glitter, glisten, flare, gleam, glare, blaze, shimmer, glimmer, flicker, sparkle, flash,* and *beam*. Each word allows you to describe the experience more precisely. And remember to consider people's backgrounds: Don't assume that non-Jews (or non-Persians) know what "purim" celebrates. **Accuracy** includes the pursuit of both exactness and comprehensible information.

## Simplicity

"Speak," said Abraham Lincoln, "so that the most lowly can understand you, and the rest will have no difficulty." Because electronic media reach audiences and cultures more varied than Lincoln could have imagined, you have even more reason to follow his advice today. Say *learn* rather than *ascertain, try* rather than *endeavor, use* rather than *utilize, help* rather than *facilitate*. Don't use a longer or less familiar word when a simple one is just as clear. Evangelist Billy Sunday illustrated the effectiveness of familiar words in this example:

> If a man were to take a piece of meat and smell it and look disgusted, and his little boy were to say, "What's the matter with it, Pop?" and he were to say, "It is undergoing a process of decomposition in the formation of new chemical compounds," the boy would be all in. But if the father were to say, "It's rotten," then the boy would understand and hold his nose. "Rotten" is a good Anglo-Saxon word, and you do not have to go to the dictionary to find out what it means.[1]

**Simplicity** doesn't mean *simplistic*. If you talk down to your audience, they will be insulted. Instead, speak directly and use words that convey precise, concrete meanings.

## Restatement

If accuracy and simplicity were your only criteria as a speaker, your messages might resemble a famous World War II bulletin: "Sighted sub, sank same." Because words literally disappear into the atmosphere as soon as they're spoken, however, you don't have the writer's advantage when transmitting ideas to others. They can't be re-read. Instead, you must rely on restatement.

**Restatement** is the repetition of words, phrases, and ideas so as to clarify and reinforce them. The key here is not simply to repeat yourself but to rephrase in order to advance listeners' understanding or acceptance of an idea—to reach each listener with at least one of the phrasings. Advertisers frequently depend on restatement to reinforce their point. For example, an ad for an energy bar might make its point this way: "BimBam kicks your body into gear! It awakens your muscles by boosting them with high-octane fuel! They're ready for the challenge of running, swimming, wrestling, peddling, crunching, or rowing! BimBam gives you peak performance!" Notice a couple of metaphors, an enumerated list of activities, and a summary claim; yet each statement is making the same point.

Restating an idea from a number of perspectives usually involves listing its components or redefining the basic concept. You can see the principle of reiteration at work in this speech that a student gave on the topic of recycling:

> If you're like most Americans, you pass by an almost unseen mass mess of recyclable garbage every day. You jog by drink containers along the path, fast-food wrappers and cups beside the interstate. Garbage? No—stuff for the recycling center's bins. The lawnmower that quit working two years ago is rusting in your neighbor's backyard. Garbage? No—recyclable metal and motor oil. He's got two sets of tires in his garage, too. Garbage? No—recyclable as a versatile material for highway construction or even power plant fuel. A mass mess along sidewalks, highways, and backyard fences? You bet. But that mass mess also can be turned back into new products without consuming new natural resources.

This student speaker realized that her audience probably was tired of being berated for not recycling. So, she sought out examples of recyclable materials not usually thought about, and she built a refrain—"Garbage? No"—that attempted to pierce that feeling of "same-old, same-old" stuff. Reiteration allowed her to attack complacency again and again.

Restatement can help your listeners remember your ideas more readily and better understand the significance of various aspects of them.

## Using Language Strategically

Developing an effective oral speaking style is important. You will also, however, want to think more about the powers of language—the powers to alter people's thinking and to move them to action. To accomplish those goals, you need to use oral language strategically. We will focus on three of the most common language strategies: (1) definitions, (2) imagery, and (3) metaphor.

Getting someone to see your point of view often depends on strategic rhetorical decisions.

### Definitions

Audience members need to understand the fundamental concepts of your speech. As a speaker, you have several options when working to define unfamiliar or difficult concepts.

You're most familiar with a **dictionary definition**, which categorizes an object or concept and specifies its characteristics: "An *orange* is a fruit (category) that is round, orange in color, and a member of the citrus family (characteristics)." If you do use dictionary definitions, go to specialized dictionaries. You certainly wouldn't depend on *Webster's Third International Dictionary* to define foreclosure or subprime mortgages for a presentation on real estate woes. For this technical application, sources such as *Black's Law Dictionary* and *Guide to American Law* are more highly respected.

Occasionally, a word has so many meanings that you have to choose one. If that's the case, use a stipulative definition to orient your listeners to your subject matter. A **stipulative definition** designates how a word will be used in a certain context. You might say, "By *rich* I mean a household earning enough annually to be classified in the top five percent of American households," or you might use an expert's stipulative definition, such as "The American Kennel Club identifies three kinds of miniature dachshunds: the smooth, . . ."

You can further clarify a term or a concept by telling your audience how you are *not* going to use the concept—that is, by using a **negative definition.** Someone teaching this course might say the following after assigning Chapter 1:

> For many of you, the word *rhetoric* has only been talked about in negative, even pejorative, ways. Talk show hosts will refer to "mere rhetoric" that is empty of meaning and force. That's not good enough for a real definition. Or, some say that a person who uses rhetoric is a liar and a cheat. Maybe, but that's hardly a useful understanding of rhetoric in general. Or you can call someone who is a blowhard and only likes to hear him- or herself talk a rhetorician. That's another badly defined idea. Empty, dishonest, and self-inflated people may use rhetoric, but I'm not going to let them define it. By *rhetoric* I mean . . .

Defining negatively can clear away possible misconceptions. Using a negative definition along with a stipulative definition, as that teacher of rhetoric was about to do, allows you to treat a commonplace phenomenon in a different (and more positive) way.

Sometimes you can reinforce an idea by telling your listeners where a word came from. One way to do this is by using an etymological definition. An **etymological definition** is the derivation of a single word. An example of this would be tracing the word *communication* back to its Latin origins, *cum-* and *munis,* meaning with + working, so that *communication* represents working-with-others in public ways.

One of the best ways to define is by an exemplar definition, especially if the concept is unfamiliar or technical. An **exemplar definition** is a familiar example. You might tell your listeners, "Each day, most of you stroll past the Old Capitol on your way to classes. That building is a perfect example of what I want to talk about today: Georgian architecture." Be careful, however, to use in your definition only those examples that are familiar to your audience members.

A **contextual definition** tells listeners how a word is used in a specific situation. For example, a speech instructor tells her students:

> The word *schemes* to you likely means open or secret plans to do something. That definition doesn't work well when talking about oral style. In traditional rhetoric, a *scheme* was a particular kind of manipulation of sentence structure used to achieve a particular effect. So, Julius Caesar's "I came, I saw, I conquered" (*veni, vidi, vici* to you Latin students) cut out the connective *and.* Why? Probably because the rhythm of "I came, I saw, I conquered"—even better rhythm in Latin!—gave that scheme a nice feeling of flow and regular beat. Ease and pleasantness of listening made that scheme a popular classical manipulation of sentences. In this class, then, that's how we'll use the word *scheme.*

Still another means of making technical or abstract notions easier to understand is the **analogical definition.** An *analogy* compares a process or event that is unknown with ones that are known, as in "Hospitals and labs use cryogenic tanks, which work much like large thermos bottles, to freeze tissue samples, blood, and other organic matter." By referring to what is familiar, the analogical definition can make the unfamiliar much easier to grasp. The speaker must be sure, however, that the analogy fits.

The points here are simple but important:

1. There are many different kinds of definitions to choose from when working with unfamiliar or difficult concepts.
2. Select definitional strategies that make sense for your subject matter, your audience, and your purposes.
3. Use definitions strategically to make your style more accurate and simple and to encode ideas in ways that can give them more popular appeal.

## Imagery

People grasp their worlds through the senses of sight, smell, hearing, taste, and touch. To intensify listeners' experiences, you can appeal to these senses. You can stimulate your listeners' sensory recall by using language to stimulate images that they have previously experienced. **Imagery** consists of sets of sensory impressions evoked in the imagination and memory through language. The language of imagery is rooted in the particular sensation that it seeks to evoke:[2]

- *Visual imagery* describes optical stimuli, such as size, shape, color, and movement. You might use contrasts of light and dark, brilliant hues of paint, and foreground action to help your listeners appreciate your favorite artists.

- *Auditory imagery* creates impressions of sounds through description. You can help your listeners hear the patterned chaos of punk rock or the soft stillness of a fall Maine lake experience by choosing your language carefully.

- *Gustatory imagery* depicts sensations of taste. Mention the saltiness, sweetness, sourness, or spiciness of various foods. Remember textures as well. While demonstrating how to make popcorn, you might mention the crispness of the kernels, the oily sweetness of the melted butter, and the grittiness of the salt.

- *Olfactory imagery* helps your audience smell the odors connected with the situation you describe. Smell is a powerful sense, because it normally triggers a flood of associated images. Think about a state fair. Blended with the press of people is a swirl of smells—Polish sausages with fried onions, diesel fumes, rancid grease, barn fumes, cotton candy, and freshly mown grass.

- *Tactile imagery* comes to us through physical contact with external objects. In particular, tactile imagery gives sensations of texture and shape, pressure, and heat or cold. Let your listeners feel the smooth, slimy, stickiness of modeling clay. Let them sense the weight of a yard–waste bag, the pinch of high heels, the bite of sea mist while jet-skiing.

- *Kinesthetic imagery* describes the sensations associated with muscle strain and neuromuscular movement. You can share the triumph of marathon racing by letting your listeners feel the muscle cramps, the constricted chest, the struggle for air, and the magical serenity of getting a second wind before running relaxed toward the finish line.

- *Organic imagery* focuses on internal feelings or sensations, such as hunger, dizziness, and nausea. There are times when an experience is incomplete without the description of inner feelings. The sensation of light-headed giddiness as a parasailor catches an upward thermal running behind a power boat is one example. Another is the way the bottom seems to drop out of your stomach on a roller coaster.

Different people respond to different kinds of imagery, so you should insert several types of imagery in your speeches. In the following example, note how the speaker combines various sensory appeals to arouse listener interest and reaction:

> The strangler struck in Donora, Pennsylvania, in October of 1948. A thick fog billowed through the streets enveloping everything in thick sheets of dirty moisture and a greasy black coating. As Tuesday faded into Saturday, the fumes from the big steel mills shrouded the outlines of the landscape. One could barely see across the narrow streets. Traffic stopped. Men lost their way returning from the mills. Walking through the streets, even for a few moments, caused eyes to water and burn. The thick fumes grabbed at the throat and created a choking sensation. The air acquired a sickening bittersweet smell, nearly a taste. Death was in the air.[3]

In this example, college student Charles Schaillol uses vivid, descriptive phrases to affect the senses of his listeners—visual: "thick sheets of dirty moisture"; organic: "eyes to water and burn"; and olfactory, gustatory: "sickening bittersweet smell, nearly a taste." He offers a plausible account of the event in a fashion that arouses feelings. His listeners wouldn't have been able to share the experience if he had simply said, "Air pollution was the cause of death in Donora."

## Metaphor

A **metaphor** is the comparison of two dissimilar things. Scholar Michael Osborn notes that the metaphor should "result in an intuitive flash of recognition that surprises or fascinates the hearer."[4] In addressing the complex issue of race in politics during his successful 2008 run for the presidency, Barack Obama described his mixed-race background in a metaphor that defines the country, *e pluribus unum* ("out of many, one"). He said: "[My story] is a story that has seared into my genetic makeup the idea that this nation is more than the sum of its parts—that out of many, we are truly one."[5] His own body became a metaphor for the country as a whole. And the very place where he was standing—Constitutional Center, Philadelphia—itself was a symbol of political unity.

Metaphors drawn from everyday experiences provide wide audience appeal. In the following speech, Martin Luther King, Jr., relied on our experiences of light and darkness:

> With this faith in the future, with this determined struggle, we will be able to emerge from the bleak and desolate midnight of man's inhumanity to man, into the bright and glittering daybreak of freedom and justice.[6]

This basic light-dark metaphor allowed King to suggest (1) sharp contrasts between inhumanity and freedom and (2) the inevitability of social progress as "daybreak" follows "midnight." The metaphor communicated King's beliefs about justice and injustice, and if urged others to action.

Words are not neutral pipelines for thought. Words not only reflect the world outside your mind but also, as critic Kenneth Burke suggests, help shape our perceptions—and your listeners' perceptions—of people, events, and social contexts. Language has a potent effect on audiences' willingness to believe, to feel, and to act.

## Creating an Atmosphere

You cultivate the atmosphere of the speaking occasion largely through your speaking style. Sometimes the atmosphere of the occasion dictates what speaking style should be used. You don't expect howling humor during a funeral. Even so, sometimes a friend or relative will tell a funny or amusing story about the deceased. Yet the overall tone of a speech at a funeral should be respectful, even solemn. In contrast, a speech after a football victory, an election win, or a successful fund drive is seldom somber. Victory speeches are times for celebration and unity.

SPEAKING OF . . .
E T H I C S

### Doublespeak

You can probably identify hundreds of words or phrases that are used to disguise facts. The Reagan and Clinton administrations didn't want to raise taxes but pursued *revenue enhancement* through *user fees*. People below the poverty line are *fiscal underachievers.* Nuclear weapons are labeled *radiation enhancement devices* and *peacekeepers.* And the 1984 invasion of Grenada was officially a *predawn vertical insertion.* Some language usage makes the unpleasant seem good and the positive appear negative. Language can shield us from the reality it represents.

Such name-calling is by no means limited to politicians. Advertisers market *new and improved* products. We're tantalized with *real faux pearls* and *genuine imitation leather.* Advertisers exploit our health consciousness with *low-cholesterol* and *high-fiber* ingredients. Take a few moments to think about the following uses of language:

1. Suppose that you notice biased language in an article you're reading to research a speech topic. Should you cite the article as supporting material in your speech?

2. You genuinely believe in your recommendations for solving the problems you outline in a speech, and you want to convince your listeners to sign a petition for change. Is it fair to use scare tactics or tell them they have only one day left to act when in fact there's more time?

3. Should you ever use racy, obscene, or questionable language during a speech? Does it affect the relationship you establish with your listeners?

4. Is it ever fair to call people who aren't present *crooks* or attach similar labels to them?

5. Do you think language can obscure our understanding of reality? Under what circumstances do you think this happens? Should anything be done to make language more honest? What can you do to accomplish this?

The speaking **atmosphere** is the mind-set or mental attitude that you attempt to create in your audience. When former President George H. W. Bush eulogized former President Gerald R. Ford in 2007, he worked hard both to praise a president and to humanize an associate and friend:

> When we served together in the House of Representatives years ago, I watched, from the back bench, I watched this good man. And even from way back there, I could see the sterling leadership qualities of Jerry Ford.
>
> And later, after I followed his footsteps into the Oval Office, he was always supportive.
>
> On the lighter side, Jerry and I shared a common love of golf and also a reputation for suspect play before large crowds. [laughter]
>
> "I know I'm playing better golf," President Ford once reported to friends, "because I'm hitting fewer spectators." [laughter][7]

Bush thus broke up his lines of praise for Ford's political virtues, showing a light-hearted piece of Ford's humanity before recovering the serious atmosphere.

How do you generate an atmosphere or mood in your listeners? You can adjust the intensity of feelings by managing the tone and appropriateness of your language and by adapting to diverse listeners, your relationship to the subject, and the cultural rules governing the occasion.

## Intensity

**Intensity**—the emotional force of words-in-contexts—tells your listener how deeply you feel about your talk and how you hope the listeners will react as well. In a sense, you are trying to recreate your feelings through language choices. For example, consider these attitudinally weighted terms:

| Highly Positive | Relatively Neutral | Highly Negative |
|---|---|---|
| companion animal | dog | cur |
| defender of the innocent | lawyer | bloodsucker |
| wedded bliss | marriage | entrapment |
| holy warrior | soldier | terrorist |

These terms are organized by their intensity, ranging from highly positive terms, such as *defender of the innocent* and *holy warrior,* to highly negative terms, such as *bloodsucker* and *terrorist.* Such terms gain their potency by tapping audiences' attitudes and, when used in combinations during an actual speech, become even more powerful, especially when employed metaphorically. To talk about one's political opponent as "a cur on the streets of his district, a bloodsucker who extorts from his constituents, a veritable terrorist in congressional committees," the negative associations pile up on each other—and on the person you've made a target.

How intense should your language be? Communication scholar John Waite Bowers suggested a useful rule of thumb: Let your language be, roughly, one step more intense than the position or attitude held by your audience.[8] For example, if your audience is already committed to your negative position on tax reform, then you can choose intensely negative words, such as *regressive* and *stifling.* If your audience is uncommitted, you should opt for comparatively neutral words, such as *burdensome.* And if your listeners are in favor of tax changes, you can use still less negative words, such as *unfair,* to encourage them to keep an open mind and avoid having them tune you out. Intense language can generate intense reactions—but only if you match your word choices to your listeners' attitudes.

## Appropriateness

Your oral language should be appropriate not only to your listeners but also to the speech topic and situation. Solemn occasions call for restrained and dignified language; joyful occasions call for informal and lively word choices. The language used for a marriage ceremony wouldn't work at a rock concert, and vice versa. Fit your oral language to cultural expectations.

**Informal Language** Make sure that your language is appropriate to your audience. Before you use informal language, check to see who's listening. Informal language, including slang, quickly goes out of style. *Gee whiz, wow, good grief, hip, cool, far out, homeboy, awesome, radical, gnarly,* and *hottie* became popular at different times. *Far out* would sound silly in a speech to your peers, and *rad* would sound ridiculous to an audience of senior citizens. As you work through your speech, consider your language choices as inherent elements in developing the tone of your speech.

**Gender-Neutral Language** Words can communicate values or attitudes to your listeners. As we suggested in the introduction to this chapter,

*By using gender-neutral pronouns, you can avoid excluding many people when you speak about members of a profession.*

they also suggest relationships between you and your audience. Gender-linked words, particularly nouns and pronouns, require special attention. **Gender-linked words** are those that directly or indirectly identify males or females—*policeman, washerwoman,* or *poet* and *poetess.* Pronouns such as *he* and *she* as well as adjectives such as *his* and *her* are gender-linked words. **Gender-neutral words** do not directly or indirectly denote males or females—*chairperson* or *chair, police officer,* or *firefighter.*

The question of whether language use affects culture and socialization is debated. As a speaker, however, you must be careful not to alienate your audience or to propagate stereotypes unconsciously through your use of language. For example, some uses of gendered pronouns inaccurately reflect social-occupational conditions in the world: "A nurse sees her patients eight hours a day, but a doctor sees his for only ten minutes." Many women are doctors, just as many men are nurses. Most audience members are aware of this and may be displeased if they feel that you're stereotyping roles in the medical profession.

A speaker who habitually uses sexist language is guilty of ignoring important speaking conventions that have taken shape over the past several decades. How can you avoid sexist language? Here are four easy ways:

1. **Speak in the plural.** Say "Soldiers are often . . . They face . . ." This tactic is often sufficient to make your language gender-neutral.

2. **Say "he or she" when you must use a singular subject.** Say "A student majoring in business is required to sign up for an internship. He or she can . . ." This

strategy works well as long as you don't overdo it. If you find yourself cluttering sentences with "he or she," switch to the plural.

3. **Remove gender inflections.** It's painless to use *firefighter* instead of *fireman*, *chair* instead of *chairman*, and *tailor* instead of *seamstress*. Gender inflections can usually be removed without affecting your speech.

4. **Use gender-specific pronouns for gender-specific processes, people, or activities.** It is acceptable to talk about a mother as *her* or a former president of the United States as *him*. Men do not naturally bear children, and a woman has not yet completed a presidential term.

Ultimately, the search for gender-neutral expressions is an affirmation of mutual respect and a recognition of equal worth and the essential dignity of individuals. Gender differences are important in many aspects of life, but when they dominate public talk, they're ideologically oppressive. Be gender neutral in public talk to remove barriers to effective communications.[9]

## Adapting to Diverse Listeners

While the atmosphere created by the occasion sometimes affects which speaking style you should use, there are times when the audience influences your speaking style. Imagine that you are a white, male business owner who is running for political office in a small southwestern city. You are invited to speak to a group of Hispanic working women. How do you negotiate the clear differences between you and your listeners in gender, socioeconomic class, and culture? As the cultural diversity of our nation increases, adapting to listeners becomes increasingly complex.

As a speaker, your goal is to establish a relationship with your listeners even though they haven't had the same life experiences and probably don't share your perspectives. So, what do you say? In part, the answer is to cultivate a speaking style that surmounts the barriers of gender, class, and culture. Shane Miller has referred to this as a "bicultural" speaking style.[10] In essence, choose language strategies that allow you to connect with your listeners regardless of their backgrounds.

As we've already discussed, your speaking style arises from your word choices, your language intensity, and your rhetorical strategies. It also arises from your economic, social, and ethnic experiences, because these experiences are reflected in the ways that you speak—what you choose to talk about and how you construct your messages. A white, male business owner running for political office may have interests and experiences very different from a majority of his listeners. After all, he is seeking political office, they are not; he owns a business, they do not; and so on. Without considering ways to bridge the gaps—that is, without a bicultural speaking style—he is less likely to get his listeners' votes.

To negotiate the differences between yourself, as speaker, and your listeners, we suggest that you adapt some of the language strategies suggested by Jane Blankenship and Deborah Robson for women working in politics.[11] We've tailored these language strategies for speakers who must adapt to listeners who are very different from themselves.

First, allow your listeners to understand your perspective by casting issues in terms of your life experience. This allows your listeners to observe the issue as you have lived it. In 2007, when Mitt Romney decided that he had to address the issue of his Mormonism during the presidential primary, he phrased his religious beliefs in ways he hoped would reflect his own thoughts but also reach out to non-Mormons:

> There is one fundamental question about which I often am asked. What do I believe about Jesus Christ? I believe that Jesus Christ is the Son of God and the Savior of mankind. My church's beliefs about Christ may not all be the same as those of other faiths. Each religion has its own unique doctrines and history. These are not bases for criticism but rather a test of our tolerance. Religious tolerance would be a shallow principle indeed if it were reserved only for faiths with which we agree.[12]

By sharing his own belief and then relating it to the general value of tolerance, Romney was able to be true to himself yet attach his beliefs to a broad American religious principle.

Second, speakers should appreciate inclusivity and the relational nature of being. This includes recognizing the worth of others, acknowledging their relationships to us, and valuing their contributions to our lives. And so Romney continued:

> I believe that every faith I have encountered draws its adherents closer to God. And in every faith I have come to know, there are features I wish were in my own: I love the profound ceremony of the Catholic Mass, the approachability of God in the prayers of the Evangelicals, the tenderness of spirit among the Pentecostals, the confident independence of the Lutherans, the ancient traditions of the Jews, unchanged through the ages, and the commitment to frequent prayer of the Muslims. As I travel across the country and see our towns and cities, I am always moved by the many houses of worship with their steeples, all pointing to heaven, reminding us of the source of life's blessing.[13]

Third, empower others. To empower others is to share the risks and responsibilities of common goals with them. This is what Romney did near the end of his speech, when he said, "And you can be certain of this: Any believer in religious freedom, any person who has knelt in prayer to the Almighty, has a friend and ally in me."[14] This sort of rhetorical move binds you together with your listeners through action and gives them a stake in the issues that you value.

Fourth, conceptualize issues holistically. You might ask the question, "How does my message affect all of us?" In this way, you are shifting the focus of your message to include others, and this reorientation of your thinking reveals that you care about your listeners. Romney's transcendent move was to remind Americans that while the authors of the Constitution separated church and state, they did not eliminate religion, so religious diversity in fact becomes a national strength:

> We should acknowledge the Creator as did the Founders—in ceremony and word. He should remain on our currency, in our pledge, in the teaching of our history, and during the holiday season, nativity scenes and menorahs should be welcome in our public places. Our greatness would not long endure without judges who respect the foundation of faith upon which our Constitution rests. I will take care to separate the affairs of government from any religion, but I will not separate us from "the God who gave us liberty".[15]

Even though your listeners may differ from you in terms of gender, culture, ethnicity, or even religious conviction, you can transcend those differences by making strategic rhetorical choices. You can adapt to your listeners by cultivating a bicultural speaking style that recognizes and promotes community in spite of diversity.

## ▮ Sample Speech

William Faulkner (1897–1962) presented the following speech on December 10, 1950, as he accepted the Nobel Prize for literature. His listeners might have expected a speech filled with the kind of pessimism so characteristic of his novels. Instead, he greeted them with a stirring challenge to improve humankind.

## "On Accepting the Nobel Prize for Literature" by William Faulkner[16]

Faulkner establishes a series of contrasts built around a "not this . . . but this" construction to deflect attention from himself to his work.

He frames his whole speech as an address to young writers.

When he addresses the issue of the bomb and our fear of it, he attacks that fear immediately. First he suggests the presence of the fear and then, via restatement, comes back to it in the next three sentences. Second, he continues the linguistic contrasts between fear and spirit, human heart in conflict, and the agony and the sweat.

Faulkner expands this central idea via a series of literal and metaphorical contrasts. Read these sentences aloud to capture the pounding rhythm that guides them. Body metaphors complete the paragraph.

Faulkner concludes with a flood of imagery: Images are auditory, visual, tactile, and organic "lifting his heart".

The restatement of vocabulary, the images, the affirmation of life, and of course, the sheer person of Faulkner himself combine to make this one of the two or three greatest Nobel Prize speeches ever given.

I feel that this award was not made to me as a man, but to my work—a life's work in the agony and sweat of the human spirit, not for glory and least of all for profit, but to create out of the materials of the human spirit something which did not exist before. So this award is only mine in trust. It will not be difficult to find a dedication for the money part of it commensurate with the purpose and significance of its origin. But I would like to do the same with the acclaim, too, by using this moment as a pinnacle from which I might be listened to by the young men and women already dedicated to the same anguish and travail, among whom is already that one who will some day stand here where I am standing.

Our tragedy today is a general and universal physical fear so long sustained by now that we can even bear it. There are no longer problems of the spirit. There is only the question: When will I be blown up? Because of this, the young man or woman writing today has forgotten the problems of the human heart in conflict with itself which alone can make good writing because only that is worth writing about, worth the agony and the sweat.

He must learn them again. He must teach himself that the basest of all things is to be afraid; and, teaching himself that, forget it forever, leaving no room in his workshop for anything but the old verities and truths of the heart, the old universal truths lacking which any story is ephemeral and doomed—love and honor and pity and pride and compassion and sacrifice. Until he does so, he labors under a curse. He writes not of love but of lust, of defeats in which nobody loses anything of value, of victories without hope and, worst of all, without pity or compassion. His griefs grieve on no universal bones, leaving no scars. He writes not of the heart but of the glands.

Until he relearns these things, he will write as though he stood among and watched the end of man. I decline to accept the end of man. It is easy enough to say that man is immortal simply because he will endure: that when the last ding-dong of doom has clanged and faded from the last worthless rock hanging tideless in the last red and drying evening, that even then there will still be one more sound: that of his puny inexhaustible voice, still talking. I refuse to accept this. I believe that man will not merely endure: he will prevail. He is immortal, not because he alone among creatures has an inexhaustible voice, but because he has a soul, a spirit capable of compassion and sacrifice and endurance. The poet's, the writer's, duty is to write about these things. It is his privilege to help man endure by lifting his heart, by reminding him of the courage and honor and hope and pride and compassion and pity and sacrifice which have been the glory of his past. The poet's voice need not merely be the record of man, it can be one of the props, the pillars to help him endure and prevail.

Notice in particular Faulkner's use of language. Although known for the tortured sentences in his novels, he expresses his ideas clearly and simply in his speech. His style suggests a written speech, yet his use of organic imagery and powerful metaphors keeps the speech alive. The atmosphere is generally serious, befitting the occasion. You might expect a Nobel Prize winner to talk about himself, but Faulkner did just the opposite. He stressed his craft—writing—and the commitment necessary to practice that craft; this material emphasis led naturally to an essentially propositional rather than narrative form. William Faulkner offered a speech that is as relevant today as it was in 1950.

## Assessing Your Progress

### Chapter Summary

1. Language functions on referential, relational, and symbolic levels.
2. Encoding occurs when you put ideas into words and actions.
3. Successful speeches generally follow the oral style that is typical of conversations.
4. You can cultivate oral style through accurate word choice, simple phrasing, and restatement.
5. Rhetorical strategies are word and phrase choices intended to control the impact of the speech. Three of the most common rhetorical strategies are definition, imagery, and metaphor.
6. Speakers can define unfamiliar or difficult concepts in many ways, including dictionary, stipulative, negative, etymological, contextual, and analogical definitions.
7. Imagery consists of word pictures that intensify listeners' experiences by engaging their senses. There are seven types of images: (a) visual, (b) auditory, (c) gustatory, (d) olfactory, (e) tactile, (f) kinesthetic, and (g) organic sensations.
8. Metaphor is the comparison of two dissimilar things.
9. The intensity and appropriateness of language can be altered to contribute to the atmosphere created for your audience.
10. To develop a bicultural speaking style, share your life experiences with your listeners, value inclusivity, empower others, and conceptualize ideas holistically.

### Assessment Activities

Choose one of the items listed below, and describe it using at least two different types of imagery to create an involving portrait for your listeners. Aim at making the images feel "natural" and not "poetic"—that is, make them feel like oral language that a speaker might actually use. Your instructor will assess your skill at using images in orally sensitive ways.

A scene from your favorite movie
A tropical plant
A breakfast food

A roller coaster ride
A complicated machine
The oldest building on campus
A walk through a nature park

For additional suggestions and activities, log on to MySpeechLab at www.my speechlab.com.

## Using the Web

Some people seem, rather naturally, to use metaphors appropriately and effectively, probably because of how they were raised. Others need to work on themselves to develop metaphor-making as a speech habit. A Web site that will help you develop both practical metaphor-making skills and better conceptual understandings of metaphors is fictionwriting.about.com/od/writingexercises/qt/metaphorex.htm.

## References

1. Quoted in John R. Pelsma, *Essentials of Speech* (New York: Crowell, Collier, and Macmillan, 1934), 193.

2. For a handbook on the creative and therapeutic uses of sensory recall through language, see Penny Tompkins and James Lawley, *Metaphors in Mind: Transformations Through Symbolic Modelling* (London: The Developing Co., 2000).

3. From Charles Schaillol, "The Strangler," *Winning Orations 1986* (pp. 42–46). Reprinted by permission of Larry Schnoor, Executive Secretary, Interstate Oratorical Association, Mankato, MN. Published by the Interstate Oratorical Association.

4. Michael Osborn, *Orientations to Rhetorical Style* (Chicago: Science Research Associates, 1976), 10.

5. Given March 18, 2008. Text taken from www.huffingtonpost.com/2008/03/18/obama-race-speech-read-t_n_92077.html.

6. From Martin Luther King, Jr., "Love, Law and Civil Disobedience" (Martin Luther King Jr., 1963). Reprinted by permission of Joan Daves.

7. Former President George H. W. Bush's address at former President Gerald R. Ford's funeral, Grand Rapids, MI, January 2, 2007. Text taken from www.washingtonpost.com/wp-dyn/content/article/2007/01/02/ AR2007010200418.html.

8. John Waite Bowers, "Language and Argument," in *Perspectives on Argumentation*, edited by G. R. Miller and T. R. Nilsen (Glenview, IL: Scott Foresman, 1966), 168–172.

9. A variety of positions on gendered talk and on ways of analyzing it can be found in Pamela J. Kalbfleisch and Michael J. Cody, eds., *Gender, Power, and Communication in Human Relationships* (Hillsdale, NJ: Lawrence Erlbaum Assoc., 1995); Julia T. Wood, *Gendered Lives: Communication, Gender, and Culture* (Belmont, CA: Thomson/Wadsworth, 2004); and Bonnie J. Dow and Julia T. Wood, eds., *The Sage Handbook of Gender and Communication* (Thousand Oaks, CA: Sage, 2006).

10. Shane Miller, "The Woven Gender: Made for a Woman, but Stronger for a Man," *Southern Communication Journal*, 62 (1997); 217–228.

11. Jane Blankenship and Deborah C. Robson, "A 'Feminine Style' in Women's Political Discourse: An Exploratory Essay," *Communication Quarterly*, 43 (1995); 252–366.

12. "Romney's Religious Speech" (December 6, 2007). Available at www.observer.com/2007/romneys-religion-speech.

13. Ibid.

14. Ibid.

15. Ibid. The quoted line, from Thomas Jefferson, is slightly paraphrased on the Jefferson Memorial in Washington, D.C.

16. © The Nobel Foundation 1950.

# 10 | Delivering Your Speech

Consider some of the famous people you know about: Abraham Lincoln suffered from extreme stage fright. Eleanor Roosevelt was awkward and clumsy, as was blind and deaf Helen Keller. John F. Kennedy had a strong Yankee dialect and repetitive gestures, and George W. Bush sometimes wears a smirk that puts off many people. And you? You worry sometimes about what to do with your hands, where to look, how to stand, and whether you should scratch the little itch on the end of your nose.

## CHAPTER OUTLINE

Working Within Oral Relationships

Selecting the Method of Delivery

*Speaking of . . . Apprehension: Impromptu Speaking*

Using Your Voice to Communicate

*Speaking of . . . Skills: Vocal Exercises*

Using Your Body to Communicate

*Speaking of . . . Apprehension: Breath Control*

Assessing Your Progress

## KEY TERMS

## Working Within Oral Relationships

Most of the important relationships in your life are constructed, maintained, repaired, deepened, and even ended through talk. Your most personal—and we think important—connections with others happen as you interact through communication. You've made and lost friends through conversation, used cell phones to stay in touch, shouted encouragement to your favorite teams, negotiated orally with teachers for better grades, survived oral reports, and participated in church groups or club meetings.

*Public speaking is simply a special form of oral relationship.* There will always be times in your life when communication gets a bit more formal, when one person does all or most of the talking. These times call for special forms of speaking and listening. That's what is happening more systematically in this course: You're being taught about more formal oral relationships.

Specifically, in this chapter, we will focus on **delivery**—a word suggesting the transfer of information and understanding from one person to others. First, we will examine your options for delivering speeches, and then, we will discuss the use of your voice and your body to enhance your speech delivery. More specifically, we're dealing with how sound is shaped into meaning and how your body can add intelligibility, emphasis, and even emotion to your words—what Walter Ong calls the *verbomotor delivery* of thoughts and ideas from one person to others.[1]

## Selecting the Method of Delivery

How should you deliver your speech to others? Your choice will be based on several criteria, including the type of speaking occasion (audience expectations), the purpose of your speech, your audience analysis, and your own strengths and weaknesses as a speaker. Usually, you have four choices: You can deliver a speech in an extempore mode, as an impromptu speech, read from a manuscript, or memorized.

### The Extemporaneous Speech

Most speeches that you'll deliver will be extemporaneous. An **extemporaneous speech** is one that is prepared in advance and presented from abbreviated notes. Most of the advice in this textbook pertains to extemporaneous speaking. Extemporaneous speeches are nearly as polished as memorized ones, but they are more vigorous, flexible, and spontaneous.

Before giving an extemporaneous speech, you must plan and prepare a detailed outline and speaking notecards. Then, working from the notecards, you practice the speech aloud, using your own words to communicate the ideas. Your words may differ somewhat each time you deliver the speech. That's fine, because your notes regulate the order of ideas. With this approach, you gain control of the material and also preserve your spontaneity of expression. Good preparation is the key to extemporaneous speaking. Otherwise, your speech may resemble an impromptu speech; in fact, the terms *impromptu* and *extemporaneous* are often confused.

While you may use all four types of speech delivery for different occasions during your lifetime, extemporaneous speaking is the most important. Extemporaneous speaking displays your enthusiasm for speaking and the sincerity of your ideas. To develop your skills as an extemporaneous speaker, you will need to learn to use both your voice and your body to communicate with your listeners.

*By speaking extemporaneously, this speaker can control her message yet maintain spontaneity of expression.*

## The Impromptu Speech

An **impromptu speech** is delivered on the spur of the moment, with minimal preparation—the way you do most of your speaking with other people. Somebody says something about a person or a news event, and you just jump in, telling others what you feel or what you know.

In an impromptu speech, you are relying entirely on previous knowledge, your skills in talking with others, and if they respond, their questions as ways to push your thinking even further. So, your friends might be discussing the American presence in Iraq; you might know a soldier who has just returned and so give an impromptu speech on what that person saw and felt. Or, you might tell your classmates why you think the author of your reading assignment was absolutely wrong. Or, you might respond to questions in a survey interview.

For best results, try to focus your impromptu remarks on a single idea, tying in details to explain or reinforce your point. That will keep you from wandering aimlessly through disconnected images and reactions, which will only make you seem confused and maybe even ditzy. (See "Speaking of . . . Apprehension: Impromptu Speaking" for more advice.)

## The Manuscript Speech

A **manuscript speech** is written out beforehand and then read from a manuscript or teleprompter. By using teleprompters, speakers can appear to be looking at their listeners while they're really reading their manuscripts projected onto clear sheets of Plexiglas. When extremely careful wording is required, the manuscript speech is appropriate. When the president addresses Congress, for example, a slip of the tongue could misdirect domestic or foreign policies. Many radio and television speeches are read from manuscripts because of the strict time limits imposed by broadcasting schedules.

## The Memorized Speech

On rare occasions, you might write out your speech and commit it to memory. When notecards or a teleprompter cannot be used, it may be acceptable for you to give a **memorized speech.** When making a toast at your parents' twenty-fifth

SPEAKING OF...
# APPREHENSION

## Impromptu Speaking

You'll probably be called on many times during your life to express your opinion, volunteer information, or contribute to a discussion. In these speaking situations, you can hone your impromptu speaking skills. As general preparation, consider these suggestions:

- Pay close attention to the discussion or the question being asked.

- Jot down a few notes to remind yourself of the key points being made.

- Relax by taking a few deep breaths and by making a conscious effort to think about the ideas rather than your feelings of apprehension.

- Channel your emotional energy into enthusiasm for your ideas.

The most critical part of an impromptu speech is its organization. Your listeners will be impressed by organized thoughts, because it will appear to them that you have prepared your comments. Organization increases your credibility. It also provides cues for you as you present your ideas. Most impromptu speeches can be organized using the following pattern:

1. *Point step.* Tell your listeners your main point.

2. *Reason step.* State a reason why your point is worth considering.

3. *Support step.* Provide an example, comparison, quotation, statistic, or story to support your reason.

4. *Restatement step.* Summarize by restating your main point.

To practice this plan for impromptu speaking, have someone ask you a question. Repeat the question, and then answer it using the four steps. As with many other skills, you will respond more effectively in an impromptu manner if you practice—so get started!

wedding anniversary, for example, you probably wouldn't want to speak from notecards. Some speakers, such as comedians, deliver their remarks from memory in order to free their hands to mimic the movements of the character they are playing.

Speakers who use memorized presentations are usually most effective when they write their speeches to sound like informal, conversational speech rather than formal, written essays. Remember that with a memorized speech, you'll have difficulty responding to audience feedback. Because the words of the speech are predetermined, you can't easily adjust them as the speech progresses.

## ▌ Using Your Voice to Communicate

Your voice is an instrument that helps convey the meaning of language. Since preliterate times, when all cultures were oral, voice has been the primary connector between people. Sounds flow among people, integrating them and creating a sense of identification, of community.[2] Although you have been speaking for years, you have probably not tapped the full potential of your voice—its power to connect you with others. You'll need to take time to practice in order to achieve your vocal potential, just as you would to master any instrument. The suggestions in this section will help you to get started.

You communicate your enthusiasm to your listeners through your voice. By learning about the characteristics of vocal quality, you can make your ideas more interesting. Listen to a stock market reporter rattle off the daily industrial averages. Every word might be intelligible, but the reporter's vocal expression may be so repetitive and monotonous that the ideas seem unexciting. Then, listen to your favorite sportscaster doing a play-by-play of a football game or covering a basketball game. The excitement of their broadcasts depends largely on their voices.

Our society prizes one essential vocal quality above all others—a sense of **conversationality**.[3] The conversational speaker creates a sense of a two-way, interpersonal relationship even when behind a lectern. The best hosts of afternoon talk shows or evening newscasts speak as though they're engaging each listener in a personal conversation. Speakers who have developed a conversational quality—Oprah Winfrey, Jon Stewart, Barbara Walters, and Jay Leno, for example—have recognized that they're talking with, not at, an audience.

Don't assume that you'll be able to master all of the vocal skills we have described in one day. Take your time to review and digest the ideas presented. Above all, practice aloud. Record yourself, and then listen to the way you're conveying ideas. Ask your instructor to provide exercises designed to make your vocal instrument more flexible.

## The Effective Speaking Voice

Successful speakers use their voices to shape their ideas and emotionally color their messages. A flexible speaking voice possesses intelligibility, variety, and understandable stress patterns.

**Intelligibility** Intelligibility refers to the ease with which a listener can understand what you're saying. It depends on volume, rate, enunciation, and pronunciation. Most of the time, slurred enunciation, a rapid speaking rate, or soft volume is acceptable, both because you know the people you're talking with and because you're probably only three to five feet from them. In public speaking, however, you may be addressing people you don't know, often from twenty-five feet or more away. When speaking in public, you have to work on making yourself intelligible:

**1. Adjust your volume.** Probably the most important single factor in intelligibility is how loudly you speak. **Volume**—how loudly or softly you talk—is related to the distance between you and your listeners and the amount of noise that is present. You must realize that your own voice sounds louder to you than it does to your listeners. Obviously, if you're speaking in an auditorium filled with several hundred people, you need to project your voice by increasing your volume. The amount of surrounding noise with which you must compete also has an effect on your volume. So, unless you have a microphone, you'll need to adjust your volume to suit your situation (see Figure 10.1).

**2. Control your rate. Rate** is the number of words spoken per minute. In animated conversation, you may jabber along at 200 to 250 words per minute. This rate is typical of people raised in the northern, midwestern, or western United States. As words tumble out of your mouth during informal conversations, they're usually intelligible, because they don't have to travel far. In large auditoriums or outdoors, though, rapid delivery can impede intelligibility.

**Figure 10.1** Loudness Levels

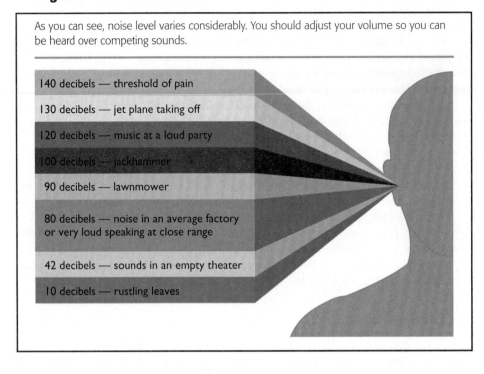

As you can see, noise level varies considerably. You should adjust your volume so you can be heard over competing sounds.

140 decibels — threshold of pain

130 decibels — jet plane taking off

120 decibels — music at a loud party

100 decibels — jackhammer

90 decibels — lawnmower

80 decibels — noise in an average factory or very loud speaking at close range

42 decibels — sounds in an empty theater

10 decibels — rustling leaves

Echoes sometimes distort or destroy sounds in rooms; ventilation fans interfere with sound. Outdoors, lots of sounds compete with your voice. When addressing larger audiences, cut your rate by a third or more. Get feedback from your instructors and classmates regarding your speaking rate.

**3. Enunciate clearly. Enunciation** refers to the crispness and precision with which you form words. Good enunciation is the clear and distinct utterance of syllables and words. Most of us are "lip lazy" in normal conversation. We slur sounds, drop syllables, and skip over the beginnings and endings of words. This laziness might not inhibit communication between friends, but it can seriously undermine a speaker's intelligibility.

If you're having trouble enunciating clearly, ask your instructor for some exercises to improve your performance (see "Speaking of . . . Skills: Vocal Exercises").

**4. Meet standards of pronunciation.** To be intelligible, you must meet audience expectations regarding acceptable pronunciation. Any peculiarity of pronunciation is sure to be noticed by some listeners. For example, the "t" in *often* is silent, but some speakers pronounce it. Your different pronunciation can distract your listeners and undermine your credibility as a speaker.

A **dialect** is language use—including vocabulary, grammar, and pronunciation—that is unique to a particular group or region. Your pronunciation and grammatical or syntactical arrangement of words determine your dialect. You may have a foreign accent, a southern or a northern dialect, a Vietnamese pitch pattern, a New England twang, or an Hispanic trill. A clash of dialects can result in confusion and frustration for both speaker and listener. Audiences can make

SPEAKING OF . . .
S K I L L S

### Vocal Exercises

If you are concerned about improving your vocal control, these exercises can be helpful:

1. *Breath control.* Say the entire alphabet using only one breath. As you practice, try saying it more and more slowly to improve your control of exhalation.

2. *Control of pitch.* Sing "low, low, low, low," dropping one note of the musical scale each time you sing the word until you reach the lowest tone you can produce. Then, sing your way back up the scale. Now, sing "high, high, high, high," going up the scale to the highest note you can reach. Then, sing your way back down. Go up and down, trying to sense the notes you're most comfortable with–your so-called optimum pitch. Give most of your speeches around your optimum pitch.

3. *Articulatory control.* Pronounce each of the following word groups, making sure that each word can be distinguished from the others. Have someone check your accuracy: jest, gist, just; thin, think, thing; roost, roosts, ghost, ghosts; began, begun, begin; wish, which, witch; affect, effect; twin, twain, twine. Or, try the following tongue twisters:

   The sixth sick sheik's sixth sheep's sick.
   Three gray geese in the green grass grazing; gray were the geese and green was the grazing.
   Barry, the baby bunny's born by the blue box beating rubber baby buggy bumpers.

● ● ● ● ● ● ● ● ● ● ● ● ● ● ● ● ● ●

negative judgments about the speaker's credibility—that is, the speaker's education, reliability, responsibility, and capacity for leadership—based solely on dialect.[4] Researchers call these judgments *vocal stereotypes*.[5] Wary of vocal stereotypes, many news anchors have adopted a midwestern American dialect, a manner of speaking that is widely accepted across the country.

**Variety** As you move from conversations with friends to speaking before larger groups of listeners, you should compensate for the greater distance that sounds have to travel by varying certain characteristics of your voice. Variety is produced by changes in rate, pitch, stress, and pauses.

   **1. Vary your rate.** Earlier, we discussed the rate at which we normally speak. Alter your speaking rate to match your ideas. Slow down to emphasize your own thoughtfulness, or quicken the pace when your ideas are emotionally charged. Observe, for example, how Larry King varies his speaking rate from caller to caller or how an evangelist regularly changes pace. A varied speaking rate keeps an audience's attention riveted to the speech.

   **2. Change your pitch. Pitch** is the frequency of sound waves in a particular sound. Three aspects of pitch—level, range, and variation—are relevant to effective vocal communication. Your everyday pitch level—whether it is habitually in the soprano, alto, tenor, baritone, or bass range—is adequate for most of your daily communication needs.

**3. Use stress effectively.** A third aspect of vocal behavior is stress. **Stress** is the way in which sounds, syllables, and words are accented. Without vocal stress, you would sound like a computer. Vocal stress is achieved in two ways: through vocal emphasis, and through the judicious use of pauses.

*Use Vocal Emphasis*   **Emphasis** is the way in which you accent or attack words. You create emphasis principally through increased volume, changes in pitch, or variations in rate. Emphasis can affect the meanings of your sentences. Notice how the meaning of "Jane's taking Tom out for pizza tonight" varies with changes in word emphasis:

- "JANE's taking Tom out for pizza tonight." (Jane, not Alyshia or Shani, is taking Tom out.)
- "Jane's taking TOM out for pizza tonight." (She's not taking out Olan or Christopher.)
- "Jane's taking Tom OUT for pizza tonight." (They're not staying home as usual.)
- "Jane's taking Tom out for PIZZA tonight." (They're not having hamburgers or tacos.)
- "Jane's taking Tom out for pizza TONIGHT." (They're going out tonight, not tomorrow or next weekend.)

A lack of vocal stress not only gives the impression that you are bored but also causes misunderstandings about your meaning. Changes in rate can also be used to add emphasis. Relatively simple changes can emphasize where you are in an outline: "My s-e-c-o-n-d point is . . . " Several changes in rate can indicate the relationship among ideas. Consider the following example:

> We are a country faced with [moderate rate] . . . financial deficits, racial tensions, an energy crunch, a crisis of morality, environmental depletion, government waste [fast rate], . . . and - a - stif - ling - na - tion - al - debt [slow rate].

The ideas pick up speed through the accelerating list of problems but then come to an emphatic halt with the speaker's main concern, the national debt. Such variations in rate emphasize for an audience what is and what is not especially important to the speech. If you want to emphasize the many demands on their time faced by parents, you could relate a list of daily activities at an increasingly rapid rate. By the end of the list, your listeners would probably feel some of the stress facing parents.

*Use Helpful Pauses*   Pauses are the intervals of silence between or within words, phrases, or sentences. When placed immediately before a key idea or the climax of a story, they can create suspense: "And the winner is [pause]!" When placed after a major point, pauses can add emphasis, "And who on this campus earns more than the president of the university? The football coach [pause]!" Inserted at the proper moment, a dramatic pause can express feelings more forcefully than words. Clearly, silence can be a highly effective communicative tool if used sparingly and if not embarrassingly prolonged. Too many pauses—and those that seem artificial—will make you appear manipulative or over rehearsed.

Sometimes speakers fill silences in their discourse with sounds: *um, ah, er, well-uh, you know,* and other meaningless fillers. Undoubtedly, you've heard speakers say, "Today, ah, er, I would like, you know, to speak to you, um, about a pressing, well-uh, like, a pressing problem facing this, uh, campus." Such vocal intrusions convey feelings of hesitancy and a lack of confidence. Practice your speech until the sentences flow naturally, with as few of these fillers as possible.

## Using Your Body to Communicate

Just as your voice can add dimension to your message, your physical behavior carries messages through the visual channel. You can use both your voice and your body to create a better understanding of your presentation. To help you explore ways of enhancing your use of the visual channel, we'll examine the speaker's physical behavior.

### Dimensions of Nonverbal Communication

While some use the phrase *nonverbal communication* to refer to all aspects of interpersonal interaction that are nonlinguistic, we'll focus the discussion here on physical behavior in communication settings. In recent years, research has re-emphasized the important role of physical behavior in effective oral communication.[6] Basically, three generalizations about nonverbal communication should guide your speechmaking:

**1. Speakers disclose their emotional states through their nonverbal behaviors.** Your listeners read your feelings toward yourself, your topic, and your audience from your facial expressions. Consider the contrast between a speaker who walks briskly to the front of the room, head held high, and one who shuffles, head bowed and arms hanging limply. Communication scholar Dale G. Leathers summarized a good deal of research on nonverbal communication processes when suggesting that feelings and emotions are more accurately communicated via nonverbal rather than verbal means.[7]

**2. The speaker's nonverbal cues enrich the message that comes through words.** You can use physical movement to reinforce the ideas of your speech. The phrase "We must do either this or that" can be illustrated with appropriate arm-and-hand gestures. Taking a few steps to one side tells an audience that you're moving from one argument to another. A smile enhances your comment on how happy you are to be there, just as a solemn face reinforces the dignity of a wedding.

**3. Nonverbal messages form a reciprocal interaction between speaker and listener.** Listeners frown, smile, shift nervously in their seats, and engage in many types of nonverbal behavior. The physical presence of listeners and the natural tendency of human beings to mirror each other when they're close together mean that nonverbal behavior is a social bonding mechanism.

For this chapter, we'll concentrate on the speaker's control of physical behavior in four areas: (1) proxemics, (2) movement and stance, (3) facial expressions, and (4) gestures.

**Proxemics** **Proxemics** is the use of space by human beings. Two components of proxemics, physical arrangement and distance, are especially relevant to public speakers. Physical arrangements include the layout of the room in which you're speaking, the presence or absence of a lectern, the seating plan, the location of chalkboards or whiteboards and similar aids, and any physical barriers between you and your audience. Distance refers to the extent or degree of separation between you and your audience.[8]

Both of these components affect the message you communicate publicly. Typical speaking situations involve a speaker facing a seated audience. Objects in the physical space—the lectern, a table, several flags—tend to set the speaker apart from the listeners. This setting apart is both physical and psychological. Literally as well as figuratively, objects can stand in the way of open communication. If you're trying to create a more informal atmosphere, you should reduce the number of physical barriers in the setting. You might stand beside or in front of the lectern instead of behind it. In very informal settings, you might even sit on the front edge of a table while talking.

So, what influences your use of physical space?

1. **The formality of the occasion.** The more solemn or formal the occasion, the more barriers will be used; on highly formal occasions, speakers may speak from an elevated platform or stage and use a microphone.

2. **The nature of the material.** Extensive quoted material or statistical evidence may require use of a lectern; the use of visual aids often demands such equipment as an easel, computer-aided projection equipment, a DVD player, or an overhead projector.

3. **Your personal preference.** You may feel more at ease speaking from behind rather than in front of the lectern.

Elizabeth Dole used physical space in an unusual way during her speech to the 1996 Republican National Convention. Normally, convention-goers are separated from speakers by the raised stage, but Dole chose to move down among her listeners, captivating them and television audiences. Dole told her audience, "Tradition is that speakers at National Republican Conventions remain at this imposing podium. I'd like to break with tradition for two reasons. I'm going to be speaking to friends and secondly I am going to be speaking about the man I love. Just a lot more comfortable for me to do that down here with you."[9] Her explanation for her use of physical space addresses the three factors we've just discussed.

**Movement and Stance** The ways you move and stand provide a second set of bodily cues for your audience. **Movement** includes physical shifts from place to place; **posture** refers to the relative relaxation or rigidity and vertical position of the body. Movement and posture can communicate ideas about yourself to an audience. The speaker who stands stiffly and erectly may, without uttering a word, be saying "This is a formal occasion" or "I'm tense, even afraid, of this audience." The speaker who leans forward, physically reaching out to the audience, often is saying silently "I'm interested in you. I want you to understand and accept my ideas." The speaker who sits casually on the front edge of a table and assumes a relaxed posture may suggest informality and readiness to engage in a dialogue with listeners.

Movements and postural adjustments regulate communication. As a public speaker, you can, for instance, move from one end of a table to the other to indicate a change in topic, or you can accomplish the same purpose by changing your posture. At other times, you can move toward your audience when making an especially important point. In each case, you're using your body to reinforce transitions in your subject or emphasize a matter of special concern.

Keep in mind, however, that your posture and movements can also work against you. Aimless and continuous pacing is distracting. Nervous bouncing or swaying makes listeners seasick, and an excessively erect stance increases tension in listeners. Your movements should be purposeful and enhance the meaning of your words. Stance and movement can help your communicative effort and produce the impressions of self-assurance and control that you want to exhibit.

**Facial Expressions** When you speak, your facial expressions function in a number of ways. First, they express your feelings. What researchers Paul Ekman and Wallace V. Friesen call "affect displays" are communicated to an audience through the face. **Affect displays** are facial signals of emotion that an audience perceives when scanning your face to see how you feel about yourself and about them.[10]

Second, facial changes provide listeners with cues that help them interpret the contents of your message. Are you being ironic or satirical? Are you sure of your conclusions? Is this a harsh or a pleasant message? Researchers tell us that a high percentage of the information conveyed in a typical message is communicated nonverbally. Psychologist Albert Mehrabian has devised a formula to account for the emotional impact of the different components of a speaker's message. Words, he says, contribute seven percent, vocal elements thirty-eight percent, and facial expression fifty-five percent.[11] This formula suggests how important the dimensions of delivery, particularly your voice and facial expressions, are in communication.

Third, the "display" elements of your face—your eyes, especially—establish a visual bond between you and your listeners. Mainstream U.S. culture values eye contact. The speaker who looks people square in the eye is likely to be perceived as earnest, sincere, forthright, and self-assured. In other words, regular eye contact with your listeners helps establish your credibility. Speakers who look at the floor, who read from notes, or who deliver speeches to the back wall sever the visual bond with their audiences and lose credibility.

Of course, you can't control your face completely—but that's all right. You do want your listeners to know how you feel: happy, angry, frustrated. You must learn to let your feelings show through as clearly in public speaking as they do in private conversation. As you know from your own experience, when conversers are engaged with their topic, their argument, and their audience through words, facial display, and bodily action, they're much more communicative and influential. The same is true when you're working from a lectern.

**Gestures** Gestures are purposeful and expressive movements of the head, shoulders, arms, hands, and other areas of the body that give performative shape to ideas and add emotional intensity to human expressiveness. Pulling on your clothing, picking lint out of your pocket, or sticking a finger in your ear is not a purposive gesture. There are just distracting behaviors. To be gestures, movements must work with the verbal symbolic meanings that make up human communication. Three types of gestures are especially useful:

1. **Conventional gestures** are physical movements that are symbols with specific meanings assigned by custom or convention, such as the circle formed by placing the thumb on the index finger to signal "Okay." These gestures condense ideas; they are shorthand expressions of things or ideas that would require many words to describe fully. A speaker can use the raised-hand "stop" gesture to interrupt listeners who are drawing premature conclusions or the "thumbs up" sign when congratulating them for jobs well done. Because culture determines the meanings of conventional gestures, you should understand how your audience views the gestures you'll use. Misunderstandings can be embarrassing—or even disastrous.

*Many of the gestures we use can have culturally defined meanings. These are called conventional gestures.*

2. **Descriptive gestures** are physical movements that describe the idea to be communicated. Speakers often depict the size, shape, or location of an object by movements of the hands and arms—that is, they draw pictures for listeners. You might demonstrate the size of a box by drawing it in the air with a finger, or you might raise an arm to show someone's height.

3. **Indicators** are movements of the hands, arms, or other parts of the body that express feelings. Speakers throw up their arms when disgusted, pound the lectern when angry, shrug their shoulders when puzzled, or point a threatening finger when issuing a warning. Such gestures communicate emotions to your listeners and encourage similar responses in them. Your facial expressions and other body cues usually reinforce such gestures.[12]

You can improve your gestures through practice. As you practice, you'll obtain better results by keeping in mind that relaxation, vigor, definiteness, and proper timing affect the effectiveness of gestures.

1. **If your muscles are tense, your movements will be stiff and your gestures awkward.** You should make a conscious effort to relax your muscles before you start to speak. You might warm up by taking a few steps, shrugging your shoulders, flexing your muscles, or breathing deeply.

**2. Good gestures are natural and animated.** They communicate the dynamism associated with speaker credibility. You should put enough force into your gestures to show your conviction and enthusiasm. However, avoid exaggerated or repetitive gestures, such as pounding the table or chopping the air, to emphasize minor ideas in your speech. Vary the nature of your gestures as the ideas in your speech demand.

**3. Timing is crucial to effective gestures.** The *stroke* of a gesture—that is, the shake of a fist or the movement of a finger—should fall on or slightly before the point the gesture emphasizes. Just try making a gesture after the word or phrase it was intended to reinforce has already been spoken; it appears ridiculous. Practice making gestures until they're habitual, and then use them spontaneously as the impulse arises.

## Adapting Nonverbal Behavior to Your Presentations

You can gain more effective control of your physical behavior by learning how to orchestrate your gestures and other movements. You can make some conscious decisions about how you will use your body together with the other channels of communication to communicate effectively.

**1. Signal your relationship with your audience through proxemics.** If you're comfortable behind a lectern, use it; however, keep in mind that it's a potential barrier between you and your listeners. If you want your whole body to be visible to the audience but feel the need to have your notes at eye level, stand beside the lectern, and arrange your notecards on it. If you want to relax your body, sit behind a table or desk, but compensate for the resulting loss of action by increasing your volume. If you feel relaxed and want to be open to your audience, stand in front of a table or desk. Learn to use the space around you while speaking publicly.

Consider your listeners' needs as well. The farther they are from you, the more important it is for them to have a clear view of you, the harder you must work to project your words, and the broader your physical movements must be. The speaker who crouches behind a lectern in an auditorium of 300 people soon loses their interest. Think of large lecture classes you've attended or

---

SPEAKING OF . . .
# APPREHENSION

### Breath Control

You can adapt some of the breathing techniques from yoga and meditation to help you control the physical stress that inhibits movement and vocal quality. Here's a simple but effective exercise to try:

1. Breathe in slowly, counting to six (one one thousand, two one thousand, etc.).

2. Hold your breath for a count of three.

3. Exhale slowly, counting to six.

Repeat this exercise before you practice your speech. Then use it again to prepare for the delivery of your speech.

outdoor rallies you've witnessed. Recall the delivery patterns that worked effectively in such situations, and put these to work for you.

**2. Adapt the physical setting to your communicative needs.** If you're going to use visual aids—chalkboards or whiteboards, a flipchart, or a working model—remove the tables, chairs, and other objects that might obstruct your audience's view. Increase intimacy by arranging chairs in a small circle, or stress formality by using a lectern.

**3. Adapt your gestures and movement to the size of the audience.** Remember that subtle changes of facial expression or small hand movements can't be seen clearly in large rooms or auditoriums. Although many auditoriums have a raised platform and a slanted floor to make you more visible, you should adjust to the distance between yourself and your audience by making your movements and gestures larger.

**4. Establish eye contact with your audience, looking specific individuals in the eye.** Your head should not be in constant motion, scanning the audience with rhythmic, nonstop movement. Rather, take all of your listeners into your field of vision periodically, and establish firm visual bonds with individuals occasionally. Such bonds enhance your credibility and keep your auditors' attention riveted to you.

Some speakers identify three audience members—one to the left, one in the middle, and one to the right—and make sure they regularly move from one to the other of them. Another technique is to do the same thing from front to back. Making sure that you are achieving even momentary eye contact with specific listeners in different parts of the audience can create powerful visual bonding.

**5. Use your body to communicate your feelings.** When you're angry, don't be afraid to gesture vigorously. When you're expressing tenderness, let that message come across your relaxed face. In other words, when you communicate publicly, use the same emotional indicators as you do when you talk to individuals on a one-to-one basis.

**6. Regulate the pace of your presentation with bodily movement.** Shift your weight as your speech moves from one idea to another. Move more when you're speaking more rapidly. Reduce bodily action and gestures accordingly when you're slowing down to emphasize particular ideas.

**7. Finally, use your full repertoire of gestures.** You probably do this in everyday conversation without even thinking about it; re-create that behavior when addressing an audience. Physical readiness is the key. Keep your hands and arms free and loose so that you can call them into action easily, quickly, and naturally. Let your hands rest comfortably at your sides, relaxed but ready. Then, as you unfold the ideas of your speech, use descriptive gestures to indicate size, shape, or relationships, making sure the movements are large enough to be seen in the back row. Also use conventional gestures to give visual dimension to your spoken ideas.

Selecting the appropriate method of delivery and using your voice and body productively will enhance your chances of gaining support for your ideas. Practice is the key to effective use of these nonverbal elements. Through practice, you'll have an opportunity to see how your voice and body complement or detract from your ideas. The more you prepare and practice, the more confident you'll feel about presenting the speech and the more comfortable you'll be. Remember that the nonverbal channel of communication creates meaning for your audience.

## Assessing Your Progress

### Chapter Summary

1. Public speaking is an event in the oral lives of cultures, and most of the important relationships in life are constructed, maintained, repaired, deepened, and even ended through talk.
2. Public speaking is simply a special form of oral relationship.
3. Speech delivery includes the transfer of information and understanding from one person through sounds reinforced by the body.
4. Choose an appropriate method of delivery—extemporaneous, impromptu, manuscript, or memorized.
5. Your method of delivery is determined by the type of speaking occasion (audience expectations), the purpose of your speech, your audience analysis, and your own strengths and weaknesses as a speaker.
6. A flexible speaking voice has intelligibility, variety, and understandable stress patterns.
7. Volume, rate, enunciation, and pronunciation interact to affect intelligibility.
8. Different standards of pronunciation create regional differences known as dialects.
9. Changes in rate, pitch, and stress as well as the use of pauses create variety in delivery and help rid speeches of monotony.
10. Three generalizations about nonverbal communication are important: (a) Speakers reveal and reflect their emotional states through their nonverbal behaviors; (b) nonverbal cues enrich or elaborate the speaker's message; and (c) nonverbal messages form an interaction between speaker and listener.
11. Speakers can use proxemics or space to create physical and psychological intimacy or distance. A speaker's movement and posture regulate communication.
12. Facial expressions communicate feelings, provide important cues to meaning, establish a visual bond with listeners, and establish speaker credibility.
13. Relaxed, definite, and properly timed gestures can enhance the meaning of a message.
14. Speakers commonly use conventional gestures, descriptive gestures, and indicators.

## Assessment Activities

Divide the class into teams, and play charades. A game of charades will help you focus on the nonverbal elements of communication. Identify conventional gestures, facial expressions, and movements that clarify messages during the game.

For additional suggestions and activities, log on to MySpeechLab at www.myspeechlab.com.

## Using the Web

Many Web sites as well as encyclopedias and other resources now accompany speech texts with segments of audio and video. Locate a famous speech, such as Martin Luther King, Jr.'s "I Have a Dream" speech or John F. Kennedy's inaugural address. View the video and listen to the words of these speakers. Start with douglassarchives.org.

## References

1. Walter J. Ong, *Orality and Literacy: The Technologizing of the World* (New York: Methuen, 1982), 68.

2. For a fascinating discussion of oral speech's communal powers—of its "psychodynamics"—see ch. 3 of Ong.

3. Thomas Frentz, "Rhetorical Conversation, Time, and Moral Action," *Quarterly Journal of Speech,* 71 (1985): 1–18.

4. Mark Knapp, *Essentials of Nonverbal Communication* (New York: Holt, Rinehart and Winston, 1980).

5. Klaus R. Scherer, H. London, and Garret Wolf, "The Voice of Competence: Paralinguistic Cues and Audience Evaluation," *Journal of Research in Personality,* 7 (1973): 31–44; Jitendra Thakerer and Howard Giles, "They Are—So They Spoke: Noncontent Speech Stereotypes," *Language and Communication,* 1 (1981): 255–261; and Peter A. Andersen, Myron W. Lustig, and Janis F. Andersen, "Regional Patterns of Communication in the United States: A Theoretical Perspective," *Communication Monographs,* 54 (1987): 128–144.

6. Much of the foundational research is summarized in Mark L. Knapp and Judith Hall, *Nonverbal Communication in Human Interaction,* 5th ed. (New York: Holt, Rinehart and Winston, 2002).

7. Dale G. Leathers, *Successful Nonverbal Communication: Principles and Applications,* 3rd ed. (Boston: Allyn & Bacon, 1997).

8. For further discussion, see Leathers.

9. Elizabeth Dole, "This Is a Defining Moment in Our Nation's History: Speech to the 1996 Republican National Convention," Available of gos.sbc.edu/d/dole.html.

10. Paul Ekman, *Emotion in the Human Face,* 2nd ed. (Cambridge UK: Cambridge University Press, 1982).

11. Albert Mehrabian, *Silent Messages* (Belmont, CA: Wadsworth, 1972); and Robert Rivlin and Karen Gravelle, *Deciphering the Senses: The Expanding World of*

*Human Perception* (New York: Simon and Schuster, 1984), 98. Such numbers, of course, are only formulaic estimates and are important only as proportions of each other; meaningfulness, after all, differs from listener to listener.

12. For a complete system of gestures, see David B. Givens, *The Nonverbal Dictionary of Gestures, Signs, & Body Language Cues* (Spokane, WA: Center for Nonverbal Studies Press, 2005); members.aol.com/nonverbal2/diction1.htm.

PART THREE

# Using Visual Media

Television monitors and large-screen projections, films, DVDs, streaming video and related digital technologies, SMS and photographic capabilities on cell phones, PDAs, overhead and data projectors, billboards, sidewalk posters—images from an amazing range of sources dominate our everyday world.[1] From the time that you participated in "show-and-tell" in elementary school, you've used visual objects and technologies in your communication efforts. As you develop additional skills for speaking in front of an audience, you'll continue to make use of visual channels as essential parts of the speech transaction. For these reasons, you need to learn more about visual media.

Research on visual media, learning, and attitude change has given us a lot of information about the impact of visual aids on audiences.[2] In this chapter, we'll combine what we've learned from social-scientific research with your needs as a speaker. First, we'll focus on the functions of visual media; then, we'll examine the various types of visual aids and explore ways to use them effectively. The bottom line when thinking about visual matters is this: *Public speaking is a multimedia event, where oral language, vocal characteristics, use of face and body, and employment of various other visual media all combine to create multifaceted messages for audiences.* It's your job to integrate all these channels together into a coherent, informative, and powerful message for your audience.

## The Functions of Visual Media

**Visual media** are illustrative and persuasive materials that rely primarily on sight. Visual materials enhance your presentation in two ways: (1) They aid listener comprehension and memory, and (2) they add persuasive impact to your message.

### Comprehension and Memory

Remember the old saying "A picture is worth a thousand words"? This saying contains a great deal of truth. We understand ideas better, and we remember them longer, if we see as well as hear them. Research has demonstrated that bar graphs are especially effective at making statistical information more accessible to listeners. Charts and human interest visuals, such as photographs, help listeners process and retain data.[3] Even simple pictures have significant effects on children's recall and comprehension during storytelling.[4] Visuals can be immensely valuable if your purpose is to inform or teach an audience. Visuals make information easier to understand, retain, and recall.

### Persuasion

In addition to enhancing comprehension and memory, visuals can heighten the persuasive impact of your ideas, because they actively engage listeners in the communicative exchange. Aware of the dramatic persuasive effects of visuals, lawyers often include photographs of injuries or diagrams of crime scenes in their cases to sway the opinions of juries. Some lawyers even have experimented with the use of video technology to create dramatic portrayals of events to influence jury decisions—by showing the dangerous traffic flow of an intersection in a vehicular homicide case, for instance. Legal presentations, business presentations, the ways in which architects offer a building design to clients, medical reports—almost every profession has its own **scopic regime**, rule-like prescriptions for how one is expected in particular times and places to display information and ideas orally, in written forms, and visually. Today, lawyers almost must use photographic representations of evidence; business leaders, PowerPoint; architects, physical and computer-generated models; and so on.[5] Different times and different places have different sccopic regimes. Undeniably, good visuals, adapted to cultural expectations, enhance both your credibility and your persuasiveness.[6]

## Types of Visual Media

There are many different types of visual materials. Depending on your speech topic and purpose, you may choose one or several types of visual media. We will discuss each type and examine specific approaches for using it to supplement your oral presentations.

### Actual Objects or Props

You can often bring to a presentation the **actual objects,** or props, illustrating something you're discussing. Under some circumstances, live animals or plants can be used to make arguments and ideas concrete. If your speech explores the care and feeding of iguanas, for example, you can literally point to the iguana's features by bringing one (in a properly equipped cage) to your presentation. (Be sure to check your university's regulations regarding live animals in classrooms!) Describing the differences between two varieties of soybeans also may be easier if you demonstrate the differences with real plants.

Using the actual object or a prop should focus audience attention on your ideas, not serve as a distraction. To make sure of this, prepare your prop ahead of time, and practice talking with it in your hands and beside your body.

## Your Own Body

Your own **body** can add concreteness and vitality to your presentation. You might, for example, demonstrate warm-up exercises, swing-dance steps, sign language, or tennis strokes during your speech; in each case, your body is a medium of communication. Remember to control the experience. Make sure that everyone, even people in the back rows, can see you. Slow the tempo of a tennis stroke so that the audience can see any intricate action and subtle movements. One advantage of properly controlled visual action is that with it, you can control the audience's attention to your demonstration. You also should dress appropriately. A physical therapy major might add credibility by wearing a white coat when demonstrating CPR, and a yoga instructor could wear workout clothing. Such apparently minor pieces of visual appeal add to your credibility.

If you decide to ask another person to demonstrate a technique while you describe it, plan ahead. Instead of hoping for someone to volunteer from the audience, contact one of your classmates, and practice the demonstration before you give your speech. Practice will help you create an engaging, dynamic speech event.

## Photographs

**Photographs** can often be a good substitute for the real thing, providing the audience with a visual sense of your topic. For example, photographs can illustrate the damage to fire-ravaged homes or show the beauty of a wooded park that is threatened by a new shopping mall. Such pictures provide information and intensify listeners' emotional reactions—all to the good. Make sure that your audience can see details from a distance. You can enlarge photos or use projection technology so that people can see your illustrations more easily. Avoid passing small photos through the audience, however, because such activity is disruptive and disengages your audience.

Photographs allow you to depict color, shape, texture, and relationships. Such dimensions of the visual help rivet listeners' attentions on you and your ideas. If you're describing the Padre Islands as a good place to vacation, you might show your audience photographs of the buildings and landscape of both islands. If you're giving a speech on the history of locomotives, you can use pictures to show various types. If you're speaking against the construction of a river reservoir, you can enhance your persuasiveness by showing the whitewater that will be disrupted by the dam.

You can project photographs in several ways, including computer-projection systems such as **PowerPoint** (see the special workshop section on using

*Representations convey information in various ways. For instance, an illustration of the parts of an inline skate (top) gives an audience a realistic but complicated view of the object. An action shot (bottom) provides a feeling of excitement and stimulates listeners' Interest.*

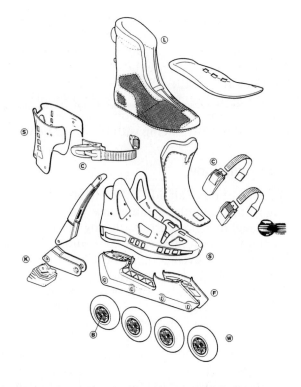

Power-Point™) or, in most classrooms today, by uploading them to a Web site. If such technology isn't available, you can also consider other projection devices, such as slides and overhead projectors. Transfer your print images to a suitable format. Whichever technology you choose for projecting your photographs, there are several things to remember as you prepare for your presentation: Have you remembered to give credit to the photographers whose work you're using? Will the correct equipment be available and in working order? Do you know how to connect the equipment, which so often varies from classroom to classroom? Can you practice with the equipment before your speech? Will you speak from the front of the room or next to the projection equipment? What will you do if the equipment fails? Attention to small, seemingly inconsequential details ensures that you and the pictures become complementary presentational media.

## Videotapes, DVDs, Films, and Video Streaming

Computer technology offers almost unlimited possibilities for speakers who wish to use moving images, from movie clips to newscasts to taped performances. Keep in mind, however, that your visual media should not overpower your message. This is always a threat with moving images, because they will draw your listeners' immediate interest. If computer projection is available, you can load Flash graphics or other

### SPEAKING OF . . .
### SKILLS

#### Using Visual Media in Business

It's wise to use visuals when developing a professional presentation for a client or business meeting. Research has shown that visual media are effective tools for three reasons. First, visuals make your presentation more persuasive. Second, they enhance your audience's estimate of your credibility and appearance of professionalism. Third, presenters using visuals require less meeting time to achieve their results.

Overall, it makes good sense to incorporate visual media in your presentations. Observe some simple rules:

1. *Prepare a professional look.* The business world expects professional-looking visuals: desktop computer-generated overheads, high-quality slides, folders with eye-catching paper, PowerPoint computer projections with clickable URLs, and so on.

2. *Always make something to take away.* Large businesses especially run on team meetings and project presentation sessions—often more than one a day. Give your listeners something to take away so that they can remember your work. Summarize the main dimensions of the problem and your proposed solutions, and hand out your business card with e-mail and phone and fax numbers. Better still, give them a CD with images and important materials on it.

3. *Know the equipment before you start.* Know how to run the particular VCR, DVD player, computer, or slide projector in the room you're using. Make sure you know where the switch for the power screen is. Fumbling will make you look less than professional.

forms of **video streaming**, or if you're hooked up to the Internet, you can find online streaming images. There's always a danger in trying to go online for materials during a speech, because just about the time you want to head to some URL, the system can go down or a key link on the site will be broken. You can protect yourself by downloading the material onto a DVD and then playing the video/film from that. Be sure to check on the legality of downloading protected material, however. For the Federal Trade Commission's views on the legality and other dangers of downloading, go to www.ftc.gov/bcp/edu/pubs/consumer/alerts/alt128.shtm.

And of course you can play **videotapes, DVDs**, and even **films.** Video clips from several current news shows can dramatically reinforce your claim that news outlets are biased. Two or three political ads from YouTube or www .livingroomcandidate.movingimage.us can help you illustrate methods for questioning opponents. Make sure that you can operate the equipment properly and quickly. Cue up the segment on the tape, film, or DVD that you wish to use before you speak. Delays increase your nervousness and detract from your presentation. Smooth integration of video clips into the stream of your words enhances audiences' experiences with your speech.

## Whiteboard Drawings

**Whiteboard drawings** (or chalkboard drawings) are especially valuable when you need a quick illustration or want to show something step by step. By drawing each step as you discuss it, you can center the audience's attention on your major points. Coaches often use this approach when showing players how to execute particular plays. Time sequences also can be sketched on a whiteboard. To visually represent the history of the civil rights movement in the United States, you can create a timeline that illustrates key events, such as the arrival of the first slaves in Jamestown, the signing of the Emancipation Proclamation, the passage of the 1965 Voting Rights Act, and the 2001 Patriot Act (which many have argued curtails civil rights).

Whether or not you use drawings will depend on the formality of the situation. If you're brainstorming ideas for a building renovation with a prospective client, quick sketches might suffice. If you're meeting with the client's board of directors, however, the same rough drawings will be inadequate. The board will expect a polished presentation, complete with a professionally prepared proposal or prospectus. Similarly, whiteboard drawings might be sufficient to explain the photovoltaics of solar power to a group of classmates, but when presenting such data as part of a science fair project, you need refined illustrative materials. Consider whiteboard drawings for informal presentations.

## Overhead Projections

You can use **overhead projectors** just as you would use whiteboards—to illustrate points as you talk. An overhead projector offers some advantages, however. You can turn it off when you've made your point, thus removing a competing image that might distract listeners. You can also uncover one part of the overhead screen at a time, keeping the remainder covered to control the flow of information. Finally, you can prepare overheads, including computer-generated graphics, before the speech, giving them a more professional appearance than whiteboard drawings.

When you're using an overhead projector, be aware of your technique. First, make your illustrations large enough that the audience can see them. If you are using computer-generated visual materials, you should probably enlarge them. Second, talk to the audience rather than to the screen or the light source; otherwise, your listeners' attention might drift away from you and your message. Third, stand so that you don't block the audience's view of your visuals. Fourth, when you're through talking about the illustration, turn off the projector to eliminate the competing message channel. Fifth, make sure that your graphics aren't "tired"—that is, the kinds of items that have been used too many times by too many speakers.[7]

Even with large-screen displays, limit the amount of information you put on any single screen, because you don't want to overwhelm listener-viewers by making them scan back and forth across ten feet of numbers and words. If you're in a room with desktop imaging screens at each seat, make sure that you don't push information too fast. Only a small amount can be seen and understood at a time.

## Graphs

**Graphs** show relationships among various parts of a whole or between variables across time. Graphs are especially effective for representing numerical data. There are several types of graphs:

**1. Bar graphs** show the relationships between two or more sets of figures (see Figure 11.1 on page 190). Research has demonstrated that plain bar graphs are the most effective method for displaying statistical comparisons, perhaps because bar graphs represent numbers in a visual form. If you were illustrating the difference between male and female incomes in various fields, you would probably use a bar graph.

**2. Line graphs** show relationships between two or more variables, usually over time (see Figure 11.2 on page 191). If you were interested in showing popular support for GOP presidential hopefuls from July through December 2007, you would use a line graph, which would allow you to show the dramatic entrance of Mike Huckabee into the race in late fall.

**3. Pie graphs** show percentages by dividing a circle into the proportions being represented (see Figure 11.3 on page 192). A speaker who is raising funds for a local hospice could use a pie graph to show how much of its income is spent on administration, nursing care, drugs, and equipment for terminally ill patients. City managers use pie graphs to show citizens what proportion of their tax dollars go to municipal services, administration, education, recreation, and law enforcement.

**4. Pictographs** function like bar graphs but use symbols instead of bars to represent size and numbers (see Figure 11.4 on page 193). A representation of U.S., Canadian, and Russian grain exports might use a miniature drawing of a wheat shock or an ear of corn to represent 100,000 bushels; this representation would allow a viewer to see at a glance the disparity among the exports of the three countries. You can easily create pictographs with computer clip art.

Your choice of bar, line, pie, or pictorial graphs will depend on the subject and the nature of the relationship you wish to convey. A pie graph, for example, cannot easily illustrate discrepancies between two groups, nor can it show change over time. Bar and line graphs don't easily show the total amount being represented.

**Figure 11.1** Sample Bar Graph

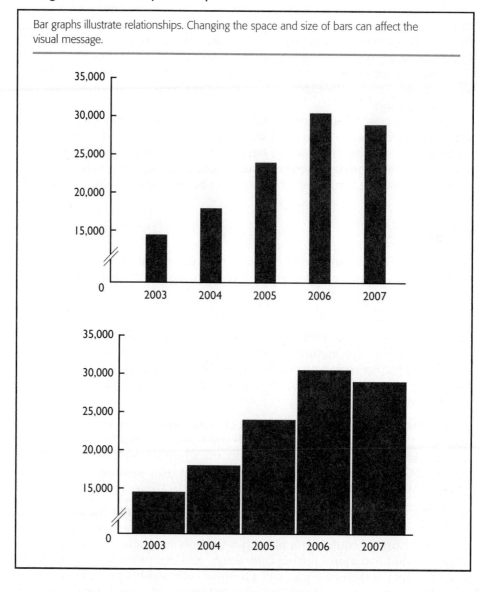

Bar graphs illustrate relationships. Changing the space and size of bars can affect the visual message.

Regardless of the type of graph you choose, you must be very careful not to distort your information when using these visual media. A bar graph can create a misleading impression of the difference between two items if one bar is short and wide while the other is long and narrow. Line graphs can portray very different trends if the units of measurement are not the same for each time period. You can avoid misrepresenting information by using consistent measurements in your graphs and by generating your graphs with a computer.

## Charts and Tables

Charts and tables condense large blocks of information into a single picture. **Tables** present information in parallel columns, as in the tax tables of the U.S. 1040 tax

**Figure 11.2** Sample Line Graph

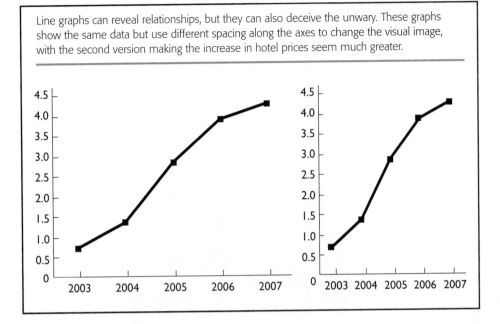

Line graphs can reveal relationships, but they can also deceive the unwary. These graphs show the same data but use different spacing along the axes to change the visual image, with the second version making the increase in hotel prices seem much greater.

form. **Charts** can present data in a variety of forms. The periodic table of elements is a common chart that you've probably seen. If they are not too complicated,[8] charts and tables work well in technical speeches. So, if you discuss various contributions to the operation of the United Nations, you can break down the contributions of, say, 10 countries to five of the major agencies. If you want to compare how the Republicans or Democrats actually select delegates to their national conventions, an organizational chart showing how convention delegates from the two parties are selected in the county, district, and state conventions is very, very useful.

There are two special types of charts. **Flipcharts** unveil ideas one at a time on separate sheets; **flowcharts** show relationships among ideas or facts on a single sheet. Both flipcharts and flowcharts may include drawings or photographs. If you present successive ideas with a flipchart, you'll focus audience attention on specific parts of your speech. In a speech on the invasion of and fighting in Iraq during the spring, summer, and fall of 2003, you could use a separate chart for each month of the engagement. If you presented the entire seven months on one chart, the chart would become cluttered, and your audience might stray from your explanation to read the entire chart. You could also use separate charts to focus on specific military units.

You can use a flowchart to indicate the chronological stages of a process; for example, a flowchart will allow audiences to visualize the process of making cheese. You can also use a flowchart to show the relationships among ideas, such as the differences between theories about the flow of bird species across the earth. And of course, you're familiar with the organizational flowcharts used by groups to show the relationships among members of the group. As long as the information is not too complex or lengthy, tables and charts may be used to indicate changes over time and to rank or list items and their costs, frequency of use, or relative importance.

**Figure 11.3** Sample Pie Graph

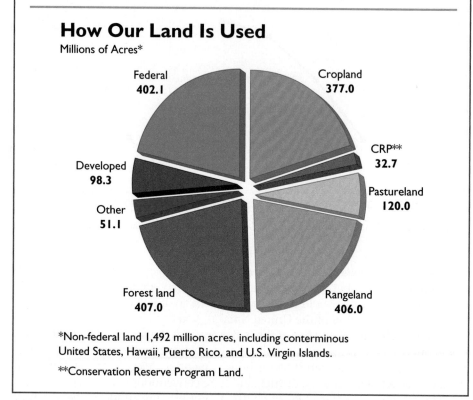

Pie graphs dramatize relationships among a limited number of segments. Ideally, a pie graph should have from two to five (and never more than eight) segments. This one compares types of land use in the United States and its territories.

Based on information from the USDA National Resources Conservation Service, 1997 National Resources Inventory, revised December 2000.

## How Our Land Is Used
Millions of Acres*

Federal 402.1

Cropland 377.0

CRP** 32.7

Pastureland 120.0

Developed 98.3

Other 51.1

Forest land 407.0

Rangeland 406.0

*Non-federal land 1,492 million acres, including conterminous United States, Hawaii, Puerto Rico, and U.S. Virgin Islands.

**Conservation Reserve Program Land.

Tables and charts should be designed so that they can be seen and so that they convey data both simply and clearly. Too much information will force the audience to concentrate more on the visual material than on your oral explanation. For example, a dense chart showing all the major and minor offices of your college might overwhelm listeners as they try to follow your explanation. Don't junk up your charts! If the organization is too complex, you might want to develop several charts, each one focusing on a smaller unit of information.

## Models

Like props, **models** are reduced- or enlarged-scale replicas of real objects. Architects construct models of new projects to show clients. You can use models of genes to accompany your explanation of the Human Genome Project. As with other visual media, models need to be manageable, visible to the audience, and integrated smoothly into your speech. You can increase listener interest if you use a model that comes apart so that different pieces can be examined. Be sure to practice removing and replacing the parts before your speech.

**Figure 11.4** Sample pictograph

Speakers with artistic or computer skills can create interesting visual aids, such as this graphic representation of the percentage of male players in five sports who graduate from college. The pictures really are only horizontal bar graphs, but turning them into a pictograph creates a stronger sense of dynamism and competition.

Based on information from the NCAA, www.ncaa.org. © National Collegiate Athletic Association, 2006.

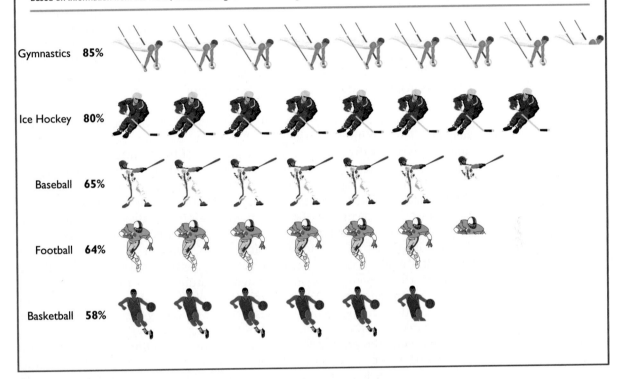

## Strategies for Selecting and Using Visual Media

Your decision about which visual aids will work best for you should be based on three considerations: (1) the characteristics of the audience and occasion, (2) your ability to integrate verbal and visual materials effectively, and (3) the potential of computer-generated visual materials.

### Consider the Audience and Occasion

Think about the people you're talking to when you decide on visuals. Do you need to bring a map of the United States to an audience of college students when discussing the spread of contagious diseases in this country? If you're going to discuss a field hockey team's offensive and defensive formations, should you provide diagrams for your listeners? Can you expect an audience to understand the administrative structure of the Department of Homeland Security without providing an organizational chart? Can you really go into a boardroom of a serious corporation without a PowerPoint presentation in hand?

How can you answer those questions? It might be quite difficult, for example, to decide what your classmates know about governmental structures or what

Rotary Club members know about rugby plays. Probably the best thing you can do is conduct a little firsthand interviewing by speaking with several of your potential listeners ahead of time. In other words, before making any final decisions about visual supporting materials, do as much audience research as you can.

You should also consider the response you'd like to achieve with your visual materials. In general, pictorial or photographic visuals can make an audience feel the way you do, intensifying their emotional responses to your words. For example, you can use slides, movies, sketches, or photographs of your travels in western Colorado to accompany your speech on high plateaus. Such visual media stimulate your audience to share in the awe and beauty that you experienced. If you show slides of civilian victims of the conflict in Darfur, you're likely to heighten your listeners' sense of horror and anger, maximizing your persuasive effect.

Visuals containing descriptive or written materials, on the other hand, can help an audience think the way you do. For example, models, diagrams, charts, and graphs about the population and economy of the Mediterranean area may persuade your listeners to conclude that the United States should help Turkey deal with Kurdish populations both inside its own borders and inside Iraq. A timeline representing ethnic conflicts in Sri Lanka can help your listeners understand the historical context of contemporary fighting on that island. Such visual media encourage understanding and thought rather than emotional responses.

As part of your preparation for using visuals, take into account the speaking occasion. Certain occasions demand certain types of visual media. The district manager who presents a report of projected future profits to the central office without a printed handout or diagram will probably find his or her credibility being questioned. The military adviser who proposes governmental expenditures for new refueling airplanes without offering pictures or videos of the proposed weapons and printed technical data on their operation is not likely to be a convincing advocate. A basketball coach without a whiteboard on the sidelines may succeed only in confusing players when setting a defense at the last minute.

Plan ahead to be sure you supply the visual media demanded by the situation. Use your imagination. Be innovative. Don't overlook opportunities to make your speech more meaningful, more exciting, and more interesting for your listeners.

## Integrate Verbal and Visual Materials Effectively

To be effective, your visual aids should complement your spoken message. Visuals should save time, enhance the impact of your speech, clarify complex relationships, and generally enliven your presentation. Consider the following suggestions for getting the maximum benefit from your visuals:

1. **Use color to create interest.** Use contrasting colors (red on white, black on yellow) to highlight information in an organizational chart or differentiate the segments of a pie graph or bars of a bar graph. As a rule, color commands attention better than black and white.

2. **Keep visual aids clear and simple.** This advice is especially important for charts and other graphic devices. By ensuring that essential information stand out clearly from the background, you make it easier to work the verbal and visual channels in harmony with each other.

**3. Make your visuals large enough to be seen easily.** Listeners get frustrated when they must lean forward and squint in order to see detail in a visual aid. Make your figures and lettering large enough so that everyone can see them. Follow the example of John Hancock, who, when signing the Declaration of Independence in 1776, wrote his name large enough to "be seen by the King of England without his glasses."

**4. Make your visuals neat.** Spell words correctly, and make sure diagrams, charts, graphs, and any digital images look good. Such advice might seem unnecessary, but too often, beginning speakers throw together visual materials at the last minute or just type a string of words onto a PowerPoint slide. They forget that their visual media contribute to the audience's assessment of their credibility and their message. Misspelled words and sloppy graphs will lower listeners' estimation of your competence.

**5. Decide in advance how to handle your visual media.** Prepare and practice with your visuals well in advance, especially for demonstration speeches. Suppose you want to show your listeners that anyone can change a tube, even on the rear wheel of a bicycle without screwing up the chain. Do you bring in a whole bike? (Probably.) Do you actually change a tube on that bike? (Probably not. It would take too long.) So do you bring another wheel and change a tube on that? (Yes.) Do you demonstrate how to put the wheel back on the bike? (In part. Then show them a chart recording the process step by step.) In thinking through how much of the process you can demonstrate in the available time, you can figure out how to handle actual objects and other visuals.

**6. Hand your listeners a copy of the materials you wish them to reflect on after your speech.** If you're making recommendations to your college's disciplinary review committee, provide copies of your proposal for their subsequent action. Or, if you're reporting the results of a survey on campus-wide alcohol consumption, your listeners will better digest the key statistics if you give each audience member a copy of them. Few people can recall the seven warning signs of cancer, but they might keep a wallet-sized list handy if you order enough for all your listeners from the American Cancer Society. Of course, don't duplicate your entire speech—and don't just read the handout to your listeners! You and your handouts have complementary yet different roles in public speaking. For handouts, select only those items that have lasting value or the ability to clarify your message.

**7. Coordinate visual, verbal, and electronic messages.** Mechanical or electronic messages from slides, films, overhead projections, and videos can easily distract your listeners. You need to talk louder and move vigorously when using a machine to communicate, or you need to show the film or slides either before or after you comment on their content or draw something on a whiteboard. Whatever strategy you choose, make sure that your visuals are well integrated into your oral presentation. That is, use transitions that integrate your visuals with the speech. If you are using a chart, you might say, "This chart shows you what I've been saying about the growing season for different varieties of tomatoes." Also, make sure to indicate where you obtained the information represented on the chart, and summarize the information before you go on to your next idea.

**8. Above all, remember that your message is more important than your visual media.** The visual channel should reinforce, not overpower, your central idea or claim. Listeners might find the visuals so intriguing that they miss part of your message. You can partially compensate for any potential distraction by building repetition into your speech. By repeating your main ideas, you give listeners several chances to follow your thoughts. As added insurance, you also might keep your visuals out of sight until you need them. Control each channel—voice, language choice, face and body, and, yes, visual media.

## Evaluate Computer-Generated Visual Materials

You might not be able to produce visuals that are similar to the action shots that accompany a televised football game, but you can still use readily available, computer-generated visuals. Computers are very effective for processing numerical data and converting them into bar, line, and pie graphs. You can scan in images and, with Photoshop, even morph them for humorous effects. As with other types of visual media, choose the computer graphics that fit your purpose, physical setting, and audience needs. Here are some suggestions for ways to use such materials:

1. **Use computer graphics to create an atmosphere.** It's easy to make computer banners with block lettering and pictures. Hang a banner in the front of the room to set a mood or establish a theme. For example, a student who wanted to urge her classmates to get involved in a United Way fund-raising drive created a banner with the campaign slogan "Thanks to you, it works for all of us." Initially, the banner captured attention; during the speech, the banner reinforced the theme.

2. **Enlarge small computer-generated diagrams.** Most computer diagrams are too small to be seen easily by an audience. If a computer-projector is not available, you can shoot a digital slide right from your screen so that you can project it. Or, if you have access to a computer-projection table, images you've stored on a DVD can be projected directly.

3. **Enhance the computer-generated image in other ways.** Suppose you printed some images or tables in black and white and don't have

---

### Can Pictures Lie?

Can pictures lie? Aren't they each worth a thousand words? Isn't seeing believing? Isn't showing better than telling? Not necessarily, especially in today's visually centered world. Consider the following:

- Hopes of finding American soldiers missing in action (MIAs) in Vietnam were briefly inspired by photos that seemed to show the Americans holding signs that displayed current dates. Those pictures turned out to have been faked.

- During the 2004 presidential campaign, a high-circulation picture showed Vietnam War–protestor Jane Fonda standing beside John Kerry in Hanoi. He'd been Photoshopped

into the picture; the fact that he'd been a "winter soldier," testifying against the war even after receiving medals for his bravery, made the picture seem accurate.

- Thanks to digital editing, you now can easily add to or subtract from pictures, printing the altered photos so cleanly that the forgery is almost impossible to detect. Or, images that transform the meanings of words can be added. The visual dimension can be helpful to both speaker and audience when it is used in morally defensible ways; it can be destructive of the truth when it is not.

SPEAKING OF . . .
S K I L L S

## Using Visual Aids Effectively

Here are some tips and reminders to assist you in preparing and using visual aids in your presentation:

1. *Good visuals reinforce the spoken message.* They do not convey the entire message.

2. *Have a presentation plan.* Begin with an introduction, and end with a summary or set of conclusions. Identify several major points you want to cover; supporting points reinforce the main points but can be sacrificed if you're running out of time.

3. *Words and graphics should not be complex.* Remember KISS (Keep It Simple Stupid).
   - Complex ideas belong in a handout or paper.
   - Tables generally are not effective. Schematic drawings often are too detailed unless you modify them, leaving out unnecessary details.
   - Simplify organizational charts to show only the segments you are discussing.
   - Equations, by themselves, are not an effective visual aid. You can make an equation more visually appealing, however, by adding pictorial elements.
   - Bar, pie, and line charts that are too busy can confuse the audience.

4. *Design visuals to maximize their effectiveness.*
   - The type size of text or characters should be 18 to 24 points.
   - Use bullets and dash lines, but avoid too many subtopics.
   - Use a ragged right margin.
   - Bold text is preferable to underlined text.
   - Avoid overcrowding.

5. *Use—but don't abuse—available technology to produce visuals.*
   - Use your spill check (spell), and then proofread.
   - TEXT IN ALL CAPITALS IS HARD TO READ.
   - Use color carefully: Black backgrounds cause problems. Dark blue works best, but red and blue appear to "jump" when used together.

Adapted from omar.llnl.gov/EFCOG/tips.html

computer-projectors available in a room. In that case, just work it up by hand. Use markers to color the slices of a pie graph or darken the lines of a line graph. Use press-on letters to make headings for your graphs. Mixing media in such ways can give your presentations a professional look even if you're not working with a color printer or computer-projector.

The world of electrified sight and sound offers exciting possibilities for the public speaker. If you learn to integrate personal talk, bodily action, and audiovisual presentation, you'll find that your ability to reach audiences will be enhanced. Working an audience across channels—verbal, visual, and acoustic—allows you to give your messages a powerful presence that informs and persuades.

## ▌ Assessing Your Progress

### Chapter Summary

1. Public speaking is a multimedia event in which oral language, vocal characteristics, use of face and body, and employment of various other visual media all combine to create multifaceted messages for audiences.

2. Visual media can boost listener comprehension and memory and add persuasive impact to a speech.

3. There are many types of visual media: actual objects or props, your own body, photographs, videos and films, whiteboard drawings, transparent and computerized overhead projections, graphs, charts and tables, and models.

4. Types of graphs include bar, line, pie, and pictographs.

5. Flipcharts unveil ideas one at a time; flowcharts show the entire process on a single sheet.

6. In selecting and using visual media, consider the audience and the occasion, find ways to integrate verbal and visual materials smoothly, and work on methods to use computer graphics effectively.

### Assessment Activities

Develop at least three different types of visual media for the following topics, along with rationales for why you're using those three. Either present them in class or turn them in to your instructor. You'll be assessed for your adaptation to situation or occasion, the relevance of the visuals to your purpose and speech content, and the likely impact of the visuals on your listeners.

   a. The procedure for gene sequencing
   b. How to do CPR on babies
   c. How to Photoshop pictures of people into settings they've not been in
   d. The layout of bird-feeding stations
   e. The procedure for rotating four crops on a piece of farmland
   f. A method for downloading advertisements from the Internet onto your computer

For more examples, log on to MySpeechLab at www.myspeechlab.com.

### Using the Web

The TLC Seminars are training vehicles for teachers, but the one on making and using visual materials is also useful to students. The work there on relating particular kinds of visual materials to particular senses is interesting and worth trying. You also get hints (right side of the home page) on making visual aids. Go to www.tlcsem.com/bvisualaids.htm.

## References

1. Bruce E. Gronbeck, "Visual Rhetorical Studies: Traces Through Time and Space," in *Visual Rhetoric: A Reader in Communication and American Culture,* edited by Lester C. Olson, Cara A. Finnegan, and Diane S. Hope (Los Angeles: Sage, 2008), xxi.

2. A good summary of research into multiple aspects of visual discourse can be found in Paul Messaris, *Visual Literacy, Mind, & Reality* (Boulder, CO: Westview Press, 1994). A solid textbook that reviews visual vehicles, medium by medium, is Paul Martin Lester, *Visual Communication: Images with Messages,* 4th ed. (Belmont, CA: Thomson Wadsworth, 2005). Such journals as *Visual Communication, Journal of Visual Communication,* and *Visual Communication Quarterly* can be great sources of informative conceptual and practical orientations.

3. William J. Seiler, "The Effects of Visual Materials on Attitudes, Credibility, and Retention," *Communication Monographs,* 38 (1971): 331–334.

4. Joel R. Levin and Alan M. Lesgold, "On Pictures in Prose," *Educational Communication and Technology Journal,* 26 (1978): 233–244. Cf. Marilyn J. Haring and Maurine A. Fry, "Effect of Pictures on Children's Comprehension of Written Text," *Educational Communication and Technology Journal,* 27 (1979): 185–190.

5. The term *scopic regime* refers to cultural practices that are followed so often that they come to be expected and that, without them, a presenter is considered amateurish or unprepared. See Anthony Woodiwiss, *The Visual in Social Theory* (New York: Athlone Press, 2001).

6. See Robert Lindstrom in *Being Visual,* ch. 1, "The Emerging Visual Enterprise," online at www.presentersuniversity.com/courses/cs_visualaids.cfm.

7. Mary Sandro, "How Visual Aids Undermine Presentations—Three Ways You May Be Boring Your Audience to Tears" Available at www.proedgeskills.com/Presentation_Skills_Articles/visual_aids_undermind.htm.

8. *Chartjunk* and *letterjunk* are Denver University's Center for Managerial Communications' words for charts that are overloaded with either too many graphic elements or too many letters, especially decorative ones. See www.du.edu/~emuhovic/2021visualaids.html.

It has become almost a cliché to go to Microsoft PowerPoint for screen-enhanced speeches. This is especially true in the business world, though even educators are making more and more use of it for classroom lectures. With the digital revolution, PowerPoint especially has become wonderfully easy to use: The software package that came with your computer likely had it bundled in (usually in the Excel group of programs), and now that the latest versions make it easy to upload a PowerPoint presentation to a Web site, you can build a presentation at one site and play it at another. Most users with portable computers, however, prefer to use their own machines because of familiarity. The user-friendly versions let you cut in pictures or video, animate aspects of the screen, and drive the whole presentation with one finger.

Just because PowerPoint presentations are easy to do and commonly seen, however, doesn't mean that everyone does them well. Tutorials can make you proficient in a short time, but proficiency doesn't guarantee good judgment when it comes to illustrating a speech with PowerPoint. And that is what we want to address here.

You can quickly learn the basics of the software program by following the tutorial that comes with the software package, but learning to use the software to make effective slides is only the beginning. Even if you have a very polished slide presentation, you must use your own good sense of communication principles to tell you how to use your presentation slides effectively as you give your speech. Following are some basic guidelines for giving effective presentations using slideware:

### 1. Don't compete with the PowerPoint slides.

Insert general slides between those with information or important pictures so that your listeners will stay focused on you. If there are a lot of interesting things happening on the screen, you'll lose your audience. You always should reveal a slide one line or topic at a time so that listeners don't race ahead. Stay in charge.

### 2. Don't overload the slides with words or visual stimuli.

Resist the temptation to use all the bells and whistles that come with the PowerPoint program. Your slide presentation should complement your presentation, not overwhelm it. Decide on one overall style and color scheme to use throughout your presentation. For a presentation that will be projected on an LCD screen, keep in mind that a light color for the words of your text works best against a dark background. Make sure you choose a font that is easy to read so that your listeners won't have to work to read it instead of listening to you. A general rule suggests that you limit the number of lines of type on any one slide to six—and fewer if you are also using a graphic element on the slide. Don't use your slide presentation to reproduce your speech word for word. The most effective slide presentations give only the major topics or basic explanations that will reinforce your spoken words and allow you to elaborate on and illustrate your message. Figure 1 illustrates an overwhelming slide. Figure 2 illustrates an effective slide.

### 3. Experiment at home, not at the lectern.

A contemporary PowerPoint program allows you to add graphics or other objects to slides, change fonts and their size, fiddle with alignment and spacing, try various forms of bulleting or numbering, play with size/rotation/ordering, bring in shadows and animation, hyperlink slides together for online presentations, and endlessly change backgrounds. Try different effects on your home computer, and imagine how you'll be able to talk over or with each slide when you deliver your speech.

### 4. Practice, practice, practice.

Match slides to your speech outline to make sure that you're not stuck on one for a long period of time. What you need to find is a rhythm, one where the slides go by in an orderly, regular manner, allowing an audience to feel—and to see—progress through the speech and giving you the sense of security you get from knowing it will work well.

### 5. Just to be safe, check out the speaking location and its equipment ahead of time.

Nothing ruins a PowerPoint presentation like discovering that the program is not on the computer you have available at the speech site! If you can, arrive with a backup portable computer and the cables you need to hook into the room's system.

Knowing how to use PowerPoint well enough to make it seem almost invisible while you're speaking should be your goal. That takes experience and good taste—work on them both.

**Figure 1**

This slide uses a very busy background that competes with the message.

**Figure 2**

This straightforward slide supports the speaker and does not overwhelm the message.

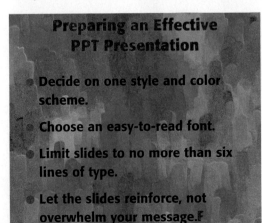

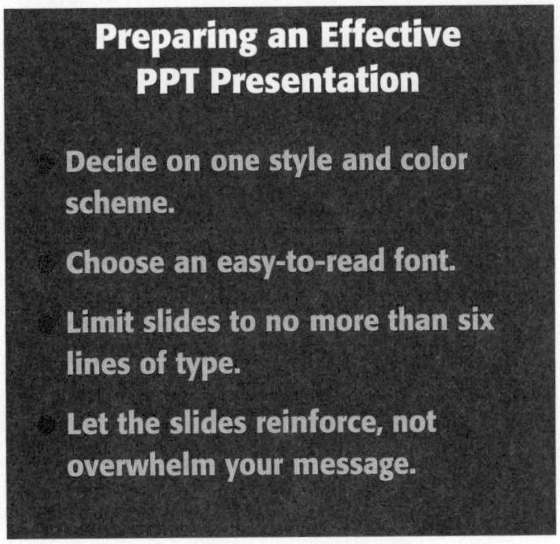

# Speeches to Inform

From business executives to day care providers and parents, speaking to inform is an important part of communication. As a public speaker, you must compete with the mountain of information that is available to your listeners. You have to find ways to get them to sit up and take notice. You can do this by packaging facts and ideas in ways that they can understand and remember. That's what informative speaking is all about.

One theme will be reinforced throughout this chapter: *Mere information is useless until you put it together in a way that makes it clear and relevant to others. Informative speeches select, arrange, and interpret facts and ideas for audiences.* Without selection, structure, clarification, or interpretation, information is meaningless. The informative speaker's job is to adapt data and ideas to both personal interests and listener needs. In this chapter, we discuss various types of informative speeches, outline the essential features of informative talks, and then review some ways of structuring each type of informative speech.

## CHAPTER OUTLINE

Facts, Knowledge, and the Information Age

Types of Informative Speeches

Essential Qualities of Informative Speeches

*Speaking of . . . Skills: Choosing a Topic*

*Speaking of . . . Apprehension: Information Overload*

Sample Outline for a Demonstration Speech: Power Tennis Comes with the Western Stroke

Tips for Developing Informative Speeches

Sample Outline: What's So Special About 1968?

Sample Speech: "The Geisha," *by Joyce Chapman*

Assessing Your Progress

**Information vs. Persuasion**

## KEY TERMS

# Facts, Knowledge, and the Information Age

Our society almost worships facts. A staggering amount of information is available to us, particularly because of such technological developments as electronic media, photostatic printing, miniaturized circuitry, fax machines, and computerized data storage and retrieval systems. Jumping onto the Web puts you on the Information Superhighway, which has more lanes than the Santa Monica Freeway. Entire libraries are available online, as are huge collections of words, pictures, and sounds from around the world. Detective Joe Friday from the old (and new) *Dragnet* TV series would never dare say "Just the facts, ma'am" today, for he would immediately drown in data.

By themselves, mere facts tell us nothing. **Information** is but a collection of facts, figures, observations, and real-world inferences until human beings shape, interpret, and act on it. Public speakers often serve as interpreters of information. They are called on to assemble, package, and interpret information for other human beings—to turn *information* into *knowledge*. To actually create **knowledge**—information that has been given human significance—you have to relate it to people's interests, needs, curiosities, and orientations to the world.

# Types of Informative Speeches

Informative speeches take many forms, depending on the situation, the level of knowledge possessed by listeners, and your own abilities as a presenter of data. Three of these forms—explanations or lectures, demonstrations, and oral reports—occur so frequently, however, that they merit special attention. They represent three common ways in which people package information to meet the needs of others.

## Explanations or Lectures

"Mommy, what's a 'skinhead'?" "Professor Martinez, what's the difference between 'informative speeches' and 'persuasive speeches'?" "Alina, before I sign this purchase agreement, I want to know what a 'joint agency' is." You've been asking questions like these all of your life. A speech of explanation doesn't just offer a dictionary definition. Rather, **explanations** define concepts or processes in ways that make them relevant to listeners. Once five-year-old Sarah knows what a skinhead is, she'll know better how to relate (or not) to that person; once you know what kind of speech you're giving, you'll know something about how to build one; and once you know that a joint agency can represent both you and the seller or buyer, you'll have the information you need to know whether you should sign a purchase agreement.

**Lectures,** which usually involve more extended explanations and definitions, also increase an audience's understanding of a particular field of knowledge or activity. For instance, a business executive might define "lean manufacturing" and go on to show how it can make the company work better. A historian might tell a group of students what sociocultural forces converged to create the Vietnam War. A social worker could lecture an audience of government officials on the continuing local impact of the 1996 federal welfare reform package.

## Demonstrations

Throughout your life, you've heard classroom instructions, seen job demonstrations, and read instructions for the performance of special tasks. Not only have you gone through many "tell" sessions, you've also had people "show" you how to execute actions—how to sort various kinds of plastics for recycling, how to manage stoves and microwaves at a fast-food shop, or how to sharpen the teeth of a chain saw. Generally, **demonstrations** explain processes and illustrate them. Demonstrations involve the serial presentation of information, usually in steps or phases. They require clarity, because your listeners are expected to learn how to reproduce these steps themselves.

## Oral Reports

An **oral report** is a speech that arranges and interprets information gathered in response to a request made by a group. Academic reports, committee reports, and executive reports are examples of oral reports. Scientists and other scholars announce their research findings in oral reports at professional conventions. Committees in business, industry, and government carry out special tasks and then present oral reports to their parent organizations or constituencies. You might have been asked to present a report on possible community projects for a campus organization. An oral report can be controversial: Remember Secretary of State Colin Powell's report to the United Nations on weapons of mass destruction six weeks before the United States invaded Iraq, or the hoopla surrounding Gen. David Petraeus's reports to Congress on progress in Iraq.

## ▌ Essential Qualities of Informative Speeches

Your goal as an informative speaker is to make it easy for your listeners to retain new information. There are five things you can do to ensure that your listeners remember what you say: (1) strive for clarity, (2) associate new ideas with familiar ones, (3) package or cluster ideas, (4) construct strong visualizations, and (5) provide motivational appeal.

### Striving for Clarity

Informative speeches achieve maximum clarity when listeners can follow and understand what the speaker is saying. **Clarity** is largely the result of two factors: effective organization, and the careful selection of words.

**Achieving Clarity Through Effective Organization** The ideas in your speech will be clearer if you limit your points, use transitions to show relationships among ideas, and keep your speech moving forward:

   1. **Limit your points.** Confine your speech to three or four principal ideas, grouping whatever facts or ideas you wish to consider under these main headings. Even if you know a tremendous amount about the sinking of the ocean liner *Titanic,* you can't make everyone an expert with a single speech. Stick to the basics—the sequence of events and the tragic aftermath. Leave out the

### Choosing a Topic

If you're searching for informative speech topics, you can develop possible topics by brainstorming (see Chapter 2), or you can develop your ideas from standard subject areas. Consider these subject areas as you generate your own informative speech topics:

1. *People.* We're all curious about the lives of others. Build on this curiosity by focusing on someone you know, someone you admire, or someone unique. You might investigate the lives of the Wright brothers or Blanche Scott, the first American woman to fly. Or, what about famous people, such as Bill Cosby or Clara Barton? Perhaps villains, such as Rasputin or John Dillinger, fascinate you.

2. *Places.* This might be an opportunity to talk about a place you've visited or would like to visit—a city, museum, park, or another country. Cities such as Rome or your hometown, museums like the Louvre or the local football hall of fame, parks such as the Everglades or your favorite state park, and countries like Tanzania or Argentina can be intriguing speech topics.

3. *Things.* The possibilities are endless. Begin with what you already know. You could talk about your baseball card collection, the architectural style of your neighbor's house, or your uncle's antique automobile.

4. *Events.* Famous occurrences make good speech topics. These include recent events, such as political elections, natural disasters, and armed conflicts. In addition, you might talk about historical events, such as famous battles, unusual discoveries, natural disasters, or memorable celebrations. Of course, you should narrow these broad topics to a subject suitable for a short speech, such as the most recent bond issues, Hurricane Dennis, Pickett's Charge, the discovery of helium, the Stonewall riot, or Cinco de Mayo.

5. *Ideas.* Theories, principles, concepts, theologies, and traditions can make excellent informative speeches. You could explain the traditions of Taoism, the theory of relativity, the principles of capitalism, the concept of aging, or the funereal doctrines of Catholicism. Better yet, narrow the topic further to discuss yin and yang in Taoism, the principle of supply and demand, or the symbolism of incense.

6. *Procedures.* Descriptions of processes can be fascinating. Your listeners may have wondered how watches work, what enables microwave ovens to cook food, or how ballets are choreographed.

discrepancies between the movie depiction and historical facts, the design of the main staircase, and the fate of other White Star ocean liners.

**2. Use transitions to show relationships among ideas.** Word your transitions carefully. Make sure to indicate the relationship of the upcoming point to the rest of your ideas. You might say, "Second, you must prepare the chair for caning by cleaning out the groove and cane holes," or "The introduction of color to

*Informative speakers achieve clarity through effective organization and the careful selection of words.*

television sports in 1964 was followed by an equally important technology, the slow-motion camera." Such transitions allow listeners to follow your thoughts.

**3. Keep your speech moving forward.** Rather than jumping back and forth between ideas, develop a positive forward direction. Move from basic ideas to more complex ones, from background data to current research, or from historical incidents to current events. If you're explaining why 1968 was one of the most important years in American political-cultural history, you'll want to discuss the assassinations of Martin Luther King, Jr., and Robert Kennedy before getting into the summer's Democratic convention in Chicago or the fall election, because this will create a sense of the pressure-cooker atmosphere that built through the summer and fall.

**Achieving Clarity Through Word Choice** The second factor in achieving clarity is being understood. You can develop understanding through careful selection of your words. Recall the discussion about the use of oral language in Chapter 9. For now, think about the following ways to achieve clarity:

**1. Keep your vocabulary precise and accurate but not too technical.** In telling someone how to finish remodeling a basement room, you might be tempted to say, "Next, take one of these long sticks and cut it off in this funny looking gizmo with a saw in it and try to make the corners match." An accurate vocabulary will help your listeners remember what supplies and tools to get when they approach the same project: "This is a ceiling molding; it goes around the room between the wall and the ceiling to cover the seams between the paneling and the ceiling tiles. You make the corners of the molding match by using a miter box, which allows you to cut 45-degree angles. Here's how you do it."

## Information Overload

You're in the library, getting together materials for a speech, when suddenly you're overwhelmed by supporting materials stacking up around you like a vegetable gardener with too much zucchini. What to do? Consider doing the following:

1. *Sample it.* Even if you've found thirteen great examples, pick out only two or three of them. Use the ones you think are most relevant to the audience's needs and desires.

2. *Rotate it.* Use some of the examples this time and some other ones when talking to friends about the topic.

3. *Table it.* If you have too much information to deliver orally, put some of it on a graph or table, and either project it or hand it out to your listeners. That way, you won't have to recite all of the numbers, yet they won't go to waste.

4. *Distribute it.* Lots of juicy quotations? Use them not only in the body of the speech as supporting materials but also in the introduction to set the tone and in the conclusion to wrap up your ideas.

If you do a good job at finding supporting materials, you'll have much too much at your disposal. That's all right. Better than having too little. Be happy in the knowledge that the opposite problem is much, much worse.

---

**2. Simplify when possible.** If your speech on the operation of the Toyota Prius' gas tank and its rubber diaphram begins to sound like a repair manual, you've gone too far. Include only as much technical vocabulary as you need to explain why and how it saves fuel. For a speech on the Heimlich maneuver, you will want to exclude its history and a discussion of the breathing process. Stick to the key ideas—how to detect signs of choking, where to exert pressure, and what to expect if you've completed the procedure correctly.

**3. Use reiteration to clarify complex ideas.** Rephrasing helps solidify ideas for those who didn't get them the first time. You might say, for example, "Unlike a terrestrial telescope, a celestial telescope is used for looking at moons, planets, and stars; that is, its mirrors and lenses are arranged to focus on objects thousands of miles—not hundreds of feet—away from the observer." In this case, the idea is rephrased; the words aren't simply repeated.

### Associating New Ideas with Familiar Ones

Audiences grasp new facts and ideas more readily when they can associate them with what they already know. In a speech to inform, try to connect the new with the old. To do this, you need to know enough about your audience to choose relevant experiences, images, analogies, and metaphors to use in your speech.

Sometimes such associations are obvious. A college dean talking to an audience of manufacturers about the problems of higher education presented his ideas under the headings of Raw Material, Casting, Machining, Polishing, and Assembling. He translated his central ideas into an analogy that his listeners, given their vocations, would understand. If you cannot think of any obvious

**association**, you might have to rely on common experiences or images. For instance, you could explain a cryogenic storage tank by comparing it to a thermos bottle, showing that it's like the construction of that thermos.

## Packaging of Clustering Ideas

You can help listeners make sense of your speech by providing them with a well-organized package of tightly clustered ideas. Research on memory and organization has demonstrated that the "magic number" of items we can remember is in the range of three to seven.[1] This research suggests that you should group items of information under three, five, or seven headings or in three, five, or seven **clusters.** You might, for example, organize a lecture on the four most important recent developments in American television around four key technologies—cable, satellite, HDTV, and low-resolution streaming video—rather than covering every innovation. College registration may be presented to freshmen as a five-step process: (1) secure registration materials, (2) review course offerings, (3) see an adviser, (4) fill out the registration materials, and (5) enter the information into the computer.

Mnemonic devices (memory aids) in your outline also can provide memory triggers. CPR instructors teach the ABCs of cardiopulmonary resuscitation: (a) clear the *airways,* (b) check the *breathing,* and (c) initiate chest *compressions.* A speaker giving a talk on the Great Lakes can show listeners how to remember the names of the lakes by thinking of HOMES: Huron, Ontario, Michigan, Erie, and Superior. These memory devices also help you remember the main points in your outline. Information forgotten is information lost, so package your data and ideas in memorable clusters.

## Constructing Relevant Visualizations

As we've been emphasizing, relevance is a key to speechmaking success. Using **visualizations**—recreations of events that people can "see"—can be a powerful technique for engaging listeners; if they can be made to see a process or event, they perhaps can be induced to project themselves mentally into it. So, for example, a student audience might know about the Iraq War only through the mass media. That's where they have seen coverage, so references to movies and TV programs would be a good way for you to get into the topic. *Syriana, Jarhead,* and *Stop-Loss* would provide three radically different approaches to Iraq. You could use the first to visualize the money-and-power game of war, the second to explore the emotions of battle, and the third to show the trauma that far too many soldiers carry into civilian life. Word pictures—reinforced with photos of video clips—help listeners get into the world of your informative speech. However, visualizing oral language works by itself as well:

> Picture this: You're walking down the Coleman Street in Collegeville, enjoying a sunny afternoon, when you come across a man who looks desperate, and says " Ca-oo-elp-mee-plee-plee-ahm-hafin', ahm-ahm-ahm-hafin'." What do you do? Is this person drunk? Crazy? Sick? In diabetic shock? Having a heart attack? Or maybe simply participating in a psych experiment? How are you going to handle this situation? Well, in my speech today, I'm going to tell you how to handle it. Today, I want to talk to you about. . . .

Notice that the speaker tries to depict a familiar locale, and a plausible event in that locale, to set up a speech on the new kinds of first aid training currently offered to students at her school. If she's successful in conveying a sense of fear, uncertainty, and mistrust, then she's likely going to have her listeners following the rest of her talk.

## Motivating Your Audience

Finally, and perhaps most important, you must be able to motivate your audience to listen. Unfortunately, many people ignore this essential feature of good informative speeches. Many of us assume that because we are interested in something, our audience will want to hear about it as well. You may be fascinated by collecting all fifty states' worth of American quarters, but your listeners may yawn through your entire speech unless you motivate them. You need to give them a reason to listen. To make them enthusiastic, you might explain how the coins individualize the states while assembling them into a common medium, illustrating some of the choices that were made for some states by describing the art competitions.

Keep in mind what we said about attention in Chapter 8. You can use the factors of attention getting to engage the members of your audience and draw them into your speech.

Thinking through the essential qualities of informative speeches might result in a speaking outline like this one:

## ■ Sample Outline for a Demonstration Speech

### Power Tennis Comes with the Western Stroke[2]
#### Introduction

I. Today, the Grand Slam events of tennis—the Australian, French, and U.S. Opens, together with Wimbledon—get serious coverage and large viewing audiences on ESPN and the major networks.

II. The stars of the game who have shone so brightly over the last forty years, the so-called "modern era" of tennis after professionals were finally let into the Grand Slam events, have grown rich and have become celebrities—think Roger Federer or the Williams sisters today.

III. One of the keys to the contemporary power game of tennis, however, came from a thirteen-year-old phenom and his father, and today, I'd like to show you what Jimmy and Antonio Arias gave to the tennis world and to your enjoyment of the great tennis athletes back in 1977.

#### Body

I. In 1977, Jimmy and his father drove to the Colony Beach & Tennis Resort near Sarasota, Florida, to see if the now-fabled coach, Nick Bollettieri, would work with Jimmy.

  A. Bollettieri took one look at a small thirteen-year-old, and not only let him into the program but used him as a model for all other young junior players.

  B. "That's the new Nick Bollettieri forehand," he cried, and the stroke swept tennis the world over.

    C. Today, I'll demonstrate for you what came to be called the "semi-Western grip" and the three other parts of the stroke that little Jimmy Arias introduced in 1977.

II. Here are the four parts of the tennis stroke popularized in 1977.

    A. First comes the grip of the racket. [*bring up a Web site showing different grips*]

        1. If you grab a racket as though you were shaking hands with it, your palm over the top of the racket as you hold it with its strings facing the net, you're using the classic Continental grip.

        2. Notice that a racket handle is an octagon, meaning it has eight surfaces, called "bevels"; if you move the palm of your hand one bevel to the right for righties, you have what's called the Eastern grip.

        3. But, move it one, two, or even three more bevels so that the palm is getting further and further behind and even under the racket, you're using the Western grips. [*show each grip with both a racket in your hand and the Web site up on the screen*]

        4. Jimmy Arias' palm was directly behind his racket in what now is called the semi-Western grip.

            a. With his hand behind the racket, it naturally rolled over the ball during the swing, producing much more top spin than the old Eastern grip. [*show*]

            b. That meant that Jimmy could swing harder, using the extra top spin to force the ball to dive into the court.

            c. And, to swing harder, he started the swing almost directly behind his body, like this. [*show*]

    B. Next is the stance and rotation.

        1. Jimmy started his swing with the racket behind him, his left foot in front of his right.

        2. Then, as he swung, his feet left the ground and his body rotated a full 180 degrees so that he'd land with his right foot in front, followed by a bounce, adjusting his feet so he'd be ready for the next shot. [*demonstrate the swing, body rotation, and footwork*]

    C. The third part of the Western shot is the extension.

        1. To the nonplayer, Jimmy's forehand looked a lot like a roundhouse punch a wild boxer might use—and it was.

        2. With the arm fully extended, the racket makes a wide, sweeping arc, starting and ending behind the player.

        3. The name of the game here is racket speed, and even a thirteen-year-old without a lot of muscle can generate a tremendous amount of speed with a roundhouse swing. [*show*]

    D. The fourth and final part of the shot is, simply, the finish.

        1. Jimmy's roundhouse swing finished with his racket passing over his left shoulder, like this.

        2. That high finish helped him generate the top spin that the grip was aiming for, so that as he got stronger and faster, he still could keep the ball on the court because of the exaggerated spin.

        3. Today's players finish with the racket going around the hip, not over the shoulder, with what we call Roger Federer's "wiper finish."

        4. The lower finish helps with control, and besides, players are able to get extra top spin by moving their grip further around the racket, even with their palms underneath the racket. [*show the differences between the Arias swing and the Federer swing*]

*(Continued)*

### Conclusion

   I.  To the casual viewer, contemporary tennis, as you'll see it at the Grand Slams or on the Tennis Channel, is modern dance worthy of Twyla Tharp, with players leaping to hit forehands, dipping and gliding to one- or two-handed backhands, and sliding into shots, especially on clay or grass, to be in position to get the next ball.

   II.  That style of play goes back to Jimmy Arias' father, Antonio, and the wisdom of a tennis coach, Nick Bollettieri, who was willing to revolutionize his instructional techniques when he saw a powerful innovation in the grip, the bodily movement, the extension of the racket, and the wraparound finish.

   III.  With the new athleticism and physical training regimens that came with the Western forehands and then the two-handed backhands, tennis grew into a major sport that now has spread throughout an amazing range of tennis clubs and instructional facilities across the country. Thanks, Jimmy!

## ▌ Tips for Developing Informative Speeches

Because informative speeches treat large amounts of information, both familiar and unfamiliar, there are some special considerations that you should take into account. One of your primary jobs, whether lecturing, demonstrating, or reporting, is to bring coherence, focus, and listener relevance to the information being presented. In addition, you must consider your listeners as learners. To that end, you should think about the ways in which people acquire new information most easily.[3] Here are some ways to adapt information to listeners:

**1. Create curiosity.** Often, listeners don't realize the full impact of new information or its potential for improving their lives. You need to pose this possibility for them, creating enough curiosity that they will stick with you through the acquisition of new ideas or concepts. Pretend that you've decided to provide your classmates with information about mole rats. Think about what attracted you to mole rats. Was it the blind, pink, and hairless bodies of the mole rat that first caught your eye in the zoo display? Or was it the intricate patterns of their subterranean tunnels that intrigued you? As you think about what first caught your attention, you may discover the key to creating curiosity in your listeners. You can hook your listeners by starting with the appearance of the mole rat or its tunneling behavior—that is, by visualization. Once they get a glimpse of the creature and its maze of tunnels, your job will be easier.

Apathetic audiences are a special challenge in speeches on unfamiliar concepts, because we're tempted to say, "Well, if I've made it this far in life without knowing anything about quarks or double-entry bookkeeping or knuckleballs, why should I bother now?" You need to make people wonder about the unknown. Use new information to intrigue them. How could you start a speech on knuckleballs? Obviously, most of your listeners will never make it to the major leagues. Most of them will never even throw a knuckleball. But some of them will watch baseball, and others can be fascinated by the reason knuckleballs tumble

*The job of an informative speaker is to consider the needs of the listeners.*

and skitter across home plate. Explain the physics of imbalance—when the stitches on one side of the baseball catch the air while the smooth surface on the other side offers less resistance, you get an erratic flight pattern—otherwise known as a knuckleball.

**2. Adapt to what your listeners already know.** Most of us approach learning situations not as blank slates, but with all sorts of preexisting categories of facts, theories of relationships, and attitudes toward learning. We have notions about how the world works, how history happened, and how we fit into all of this. Understanding these predispositions can be critical in developing informative speeches, because all learning involves the merging of new facts and ideas into the framework that already exists in listeners' minds. If your listeners believe that men are better at math, you might disagree, but you'll still have to deal with this predisposition if you want everyone in your audience to think about quadratic equations. If your listeners have "math phobia," then you are dealing with an entirely different predisposition toward your topic. In either case, you should consider what your listeners already think as you construct your speech.

New information often is retained more easily when we know that it can be useful. When we're convinced that we need to know something, we're more likely to learn it. Think about taking your first test for an automobile license. The rules of the road might have seemed somewhat arbitrary, but realizing that you needed to know this information to get a license probably made learning them easier. Besides, it's useful to know who has the right-of-way. You could say, "Understanding right-of-way rules at a four-way stop can save you time and trouble. It sure beats ending up in a fender-bender!"

**3. Use repetition.** Researchers have demonstrated that repetition is critical to increasing recall of ideas and facts. Think about your own experiences. You probably won't learn a new word such as *intrepid* if you repeat it once, but you're more likely to remember *intrepid* with two or three repetitions. Use it in a sentence or repeat it for the fourth time, and research tells us that you're 90 percent more likely to remember it. (So what does *intrepid* mean? Courageous or fearless or bold. Try using *intrepid* in a sentence.)

Repetition is important when you're learning a single fact, but this concept also applies when you're learning more complex material. People remember more information when it is packaged in a way that emphasizes repetition. If you're going to take your listeners through the steps involved in refinishing a bookcase, for example, give them an overall picture of the process before you start detailing each procedure. Then, your listeners will know where you're headed, and they'll be more likely to go with you. After you've detailed the refinishing process, you should summarize the main ideas in your conclusion. Consider your conclusion a final chance to repeat your main ideas. Your summary will increase the chances that your listeners will retain information for a much longer period of time. Repeat the main points. You might say, "Remember the 4 S's: strip, sand, stain, and seal . . . " Notice that the main steps in the process are easier to remember, because they all begin with "s."

**4. Involve your listeners.** Recall the factors of attention discussed in Chapter 8. Each of these factors offers a way to capture the attention—and thus the involvement—of your listeners. Although we discussed how you can use the nine factors of gaining attention at the beginning of your speech, it doesn't need to stop there. Your listeners should be engaged during the entire speech. A process such as tombstone rubbing, for example, looks easier than it is; many people are tempted to quit listening and give up somewhere along the way. If you forewarn them that you'll expect them to try the basic techniques in a few minutes, however, they will be more likely to listen intently, because you've appealed to activity and the vital.

Remember, too, that we learn new information in multiple ways. Think about how a young child discovers the world: Any new object is touched, tasted, smelled—and probably thrown! The more ways you can offer your listeners for interacting with a new idea, the more likely it is that they'll retain it.

**5. Choose an appropriate organizational pattern.** Speeches that demonstrate a process or technique often follow a natural chronological or spatial pattern. Consequently, you generally will have little trouble organizing the body of a speech that is primarily a demonstration. For example, it's clear that if you're demonstrating how to make homemade bread, you'll need to show your viewers how to mix the ingredients before showing them how to knead the dough.

Most explanations and lectures use a topical pattern, because such speeches usually describe various aspects of an object or an idea. It seems natural, for example, to use a topical pattern to structure a speech on careers in television around such topics as careers in broadcast TV, careers in cable and satellite TV, and careers in industrial TV. There are occasions, however, when other patterns might serve your specific purpose better than topical patterns. You might use an effect-cause pattern, for example, when preparing an informative speech on the laws of supply and demand. You could enumerate a series of effects with which people are already familiar—changing prices at the gas pumps—and then discuss the laws of supply and demand as well as forecasting and speculation that account for such changes.

In many cases, there will be competing information and conflicting conclusions. The key to packaging this information lies in the way in which the speaker constructs a *viewpoint* or *rationale.* Suppose that you wanted to explain the discovery of the New World. Traditional Eurocentric histories stress the discovery of uncharted lands by men such as Christopher Columbus, Vasco da Gama, or Ponce de Leon, but how would native North Americans see the arrival of these Europeans? Clearly, their viewpoint offers a different way to understand historical events.

**6. Use multiple channels.** Many informative speakers take advantage of the power of visual channels to capture quantities of information quickly and forcefully. Work across communication channels in ways adapted to your purpose and speech content. By reinforcing ideas with another channel—the visual, the auditory, or the kinesthetic—you increase the chances that the information you present will be remembered. Here are some special considerations for incorporating multiple channels:

- *Coordinate verbal and visual material.* Demonstrating processes, concepts, or steps often demands that speakers "show" while "telling," as we saw in the outline for the Western stroke. Be sure to practice demonstrating your material while explaining aloud what you're doing. Decide where you'll stand when showing a digital picture so that the audience can see both you and the image. Practice talking about your yoga exercise positions while you're actually doing them. Do a Web search for your speech in practice sessions so that you'll be ready to do it for a real audience.

- *Adapt your rate.* If you need to let a cream pie cool before adding meringue, what do you do? You can't just wait for the pie to cool. Instead, you should have a cooled pie ready for the next step. You also need to plan some material for filling the time—perhaps additional background or a brief discussion of

*Practice coordinating verbal and visual materials while speaking so that you can do it smoothly and professionally.*

what problems can arise at this stage. Plan your remarks carefully for those junctures so that you can maintain your audience's attention.

- *Adjust the size.* How can you show various embroidery stitches to an audience of twenty-five people? When dealing with tiny operations, you often must enlarge them so that everyone can easily see. In this example, you could use a large piece of cloth, an oversized needle, yarn instead of thread, and stitches measured in inches instead of millimeters. You can adapt your techniques to make them visible to all your listeners. At the other extreme, in a speech on how to make a homemade compost frame, you should work with a scaled-down model.

**7. Suggest additional resources.** If you've done your job, your listeners should be excited about what you've told them and eager to learn even more than you can present in a short speech. Give them the opportunity to pursue new information on their own. For example, a speaker who is discussing diabetes might conclude by offering listeners public service booklets containing more information, the URL of the American Diabetes Association, the address of a local clinic that does free testing, or the meeting time and place of a diabetics' support group. Be sure to include Internet as well as print sources. Screen the material you recommend to be sure that it is both appropriate and of high quality.

Include experts, such as yourself and others, as additional resources. Sometimes what sounds simple in demonstrations may be much more complicated in execution. If possible, make yourself available for assistance: "As you fill out your application form, just raise your hand if you're unsure of anything, and I'll be happy to help you." Or, point to other sources of further information and assistance: "Here's the address of the U.S. Government Printing Office, whose pamphlet X12344 is available for only three dollars. It will give you more details," or "If you run into a problem retrieving computer files that I haven't covered in this short orientation, just go over to Maria McFerson's desk, right over here. Maria is always willing to share her expertise." Such statements not only offer help but also assure your listeners that they won't be labeled as stupid if they actually have to ask for it.

## Sample Outline

### What's So Special About 1968?[4]

**Introduction**

I. History may seem old, which it is, and passé, which it definitely is not.
   A. The past is past, but history—and our memories of the past—provide us with a direct connection between now and then.
   B. You and even your parents may be too young to remember 1968, for example, but it affects in tangible ways how you understand and experience the world today.
   C. The past, as Victor Hugo said, is prologue, and being prologue, it is a key part of the story of today—the today of your lives.

II. I may not actually convince you that Victor Hugo knew what he was talking about, though he inspired me to offer you today a series of explanations: explanations of how the world of 1968, a world forty years old and more, affects how you think about and act in your own world of the twenty-first century.

III. I cannot reproduce the whole of life as your grandparents experienced it in 1968, but I can talk about three facets of life then—the life of sports, of social relations, and of politics—that modified the life of sports, social relations, and politics today in very serious and important ways.

## Body

I. Let me begin by reviewing some of the key events in sports of 1968.

   A. It would be fun to concentrate on something my grandfather personally experienced—Dennis McLain's 30-game winning season in baseball, the last such season in recorded baseball history.

   B. While that's interesting given that McLain spent the rest of his professional life in disgrace and never pitched like that again, it doesn't affect us today.

   C. Rather, I want to spend my time on the world-changing sporting events of 1968 in tennis, as well as boxing and the Olympics.

   D. Tennis may seem like an odd place to look for significant changes in sporting culture, but that's exactly what happened in 1968.

      1. The coming of expanded sports coverage via television, together with the noisy introduction of touring professionals, were putting tremendous pressure on the so-called Grand Slam tournaments—the Australian, French, and U.S. biggest amateur tournaments as well as Wimbledon—to admit professionals, to be "open" tournaments.

      2. The International Lawn Tennis Federation—now the International Tennis Federation—held a meeting in March '68 of representatives from 47 countries at the Place de la Concorde, site of the famous tennis court where the common people of France took their oath to take over government in 1789.

      3. The site could not have been more symbolic: The people were crying for a mixing of all players, regardless of status, to be given a chance to play together—the old elitists from the ancient aristocratic clubs together with the new kids coming up through city and private-sponsored camps and clubs.

      4. On March 30, 1968, the big tournaments were designated as "open," and the Australian Open, the French Open, the U.S. Open, and Wimbledon were staged as open tournaments.

        a. No longer did so-called "amateurs" have to be paid under the table to keep them playing in the marquee events.

        b. The pros could still run their independent leagues and tours even while lending their names and skills to the most prestigious events—the open tournaments.

   E. Boxing was the next sport that made 1968 a memorable year.

      1. Heavyweight champion Muhammad Ali was put on the April cover of *Esquire* magazine, in his boxing regalia and with arrows sticking in his skin from every angle.

*(Continued)*

2. Late in the previous year, he had been stripped of his heavyweight title by the World Boxing Association, because he had refused to serve in Vietnam.
   a. He had joined the Nation of Islam, changed his name from Cassius Clay to Ali, and was charged with draft evasion by the Selective Service.
   b. Stripped of his title for his religious-political convictions, he paid the price.
   c. He was sentenced to jail, but that conviction was overturned in 1970.
3. In Ali's stand as a conscientious objector and antiwar advocate, he demonstrated that even professional athletes are allowed to have social and political convictions.

F. The values that Muhammad Ali was living out were articulated even more startlingly during the Mexico City Olympics.
   1. There, African Americans Tommie Smith and John Carlos took the medal stand together after winning the gold and bronze in the 200-meter run.
   2. As the "Star Spangled Banner" was played, both raised their glove-covered fists with the "Black Power" salute.
   3. The assassination of Martin Luther King, Jr., earlier that year, together with the riots in various cities that spring and fall, had made "Black Power" a battle cry for serious reform in ghetto life, and they were recognizing that fact.

II. Second, Smith and Carlos remind us that, socially, 1968 also was the year of social revolutions.
   A. In the United States, that revolution was marked by two notorious assassinations—first of Martin Luther King, Jr., in April, and then of Robert Kennedy in June.
      1. King's assassination as he was supporting the Memphis sanitation workers' strike enflamed the country and added tremendous emotion and media coverage to the so-called "poor people's march" on Washington.
      2. While the poor people's march was not deemed a legislative success, it in fact visibly demonstrated that poverty crossed the color line, as blacks and whites stayed with each other in the tents that were pitched on the Washington Mall.
      3. As well, King's assassination drove home the point that hatred had to be resisted actively by citizens of all colors if the country was going to avoid being destroyed by the race issue: "Black Power" was basically economic power, and it was soon demanded by poor citizens of all ethnic backgrounds.
   B. Equally disruptive of social-political relations in 1968 were the strikes in France.
      1. When students striking against the governance of universities by Charles de Gaulle's party were rebuffed, a general strike of more than 10,000 workers took place across the country.
      2. The confrontation lasted a month and drew together the collection of forces that brought down the Gaullists, as the World War II hero was humiliated.
      3. The "68ers," called *le soixante-buitard* in French, so strongly attacked all large, bureaucratic institutions that we entered a period of what often is called "post-modernism"—a period of stress on individual thought and localist controls and of distrust of large-scale generalizations about how to get things done in society.

III. And finally, 1968 was one of the most culture-changing and mind-bending years ever in American politics. Consider this sequence of events.
   A. Antiwar activist Eugene McCarthy did so well in New Hampshire that Robert Kennedy, running on a similar platform, decided to oppose President Lyndon Johnson, the man his brother Jack picked as a running mate in 1960.

B. On March 31, President Johnson announced that he would not run for re-election so that he could devote all of his time to the Vietnam War and to healing the nation.

C. First Martin Luther King, Jr., and then Robert Kennedy were assassinated, one campaigning for sanitation workers trying to challenge the city of Memphis and the other trying to move the country to a more supportive place—and so the nation became even further divided and frustrated.

D. Next, the Democratic National Convention in Chicago was swamped in riots, with even the presidential candidate, Hubert Humphrey, roundly booed.

E. Richard Nixon won the presidency, beginning a six-year pair of terms that ended in the disgrace we call "Watergate. "

   1. Nixon was believed to be a middle-of-the-road answer to the country's progressive or even revolutionary politics in that year.
   2. Yet, he left office in disgrace when threatened with impeachment for obstruction of justice and fraud.

## Conclusions

I. So, what do we see in the changes in sports, social life, and politics flowing from the world of 1968?

   A. Looking at only these three arenas of human activity, we see the commercialization of sport and its place even in the political limelight, changing sport forever by taking away its innocence and the pretense of amateurism.

      1. Big-time professional sports turns into big-time economics for teams and their players in the age of television.
      2. Amateurism inevitably leads extraordinary athletes to seek even more extraordinary professional careers, as collegiate freshmen and even high school players become highly paid workers in the NBA—just think of LaBron James.
      3. With media exposure as well comes chances for athletes to use their celebrity to work the political side of the street or even run for the presidency, as former NBA star Bill Bradley did in 2000—something pros in the '20s and '30s never would have done.

   B. Popular revolutions both inside and outside the United States created opportunities for thinking of social change as coming from the bottom up, from people, rather than from the top down, from governmental institutions.

      1. Exploring the political powers in individuals also puts a stress on local rather than on national or international action.
      2. Such thinking gives birth to thousands of NGOs—non-governmental organizations—working to change the world.

   C. And, the breaking of a president's hold on his party and his office, the gunning down of future hope in the form of a movement leader and a political candidate, and the presidential election of a seemingly unpopular man, Richard Nixon, because of his experience all show us that the citizen has the power to respond in a variety of ways when political chaos demands it.

      1. After the assassinations and riots, the country began working, if slowly, on local reform.
      2. After international strife, we finally put Vietnam behind us and even opened the People's Republic of China to American commerce and influence.

*(Continued)*

II. So, 1968 was a pivotal year in the history of the United States, one whose problems are still being worked on more than forty years later.
   A. Our values, paradoxically, changed to celebrate both economic individualism and the collective power of the people's voice.
   B. Those seemingly contradictory impulses, one other-directed and the other self-directed, form the heritage of 1968 in our lives.

## Sample Speech

The following speech, "The Geisha," was delivered by Joyce Chapman when she was a freshman at Loop College in Chicago. It illustrates most of the virtues of a good informative speech: (1) It provides enough detail and explanations to be clear; (2) it works from familiar images of geishas, adding new ideas and information in such a way as to enlarge listeners' frames of reference; (3) its topical organization pattern is easy to follow; and (4) it gives listeners reasons for listening.

### The Geisha *Joyce Chapman*[5]

As you may have already noticed from my facial features, I have Oriental blood in me and, as such, I am greatly interested in my Japanese heritage. One aspect of my heritage that fascinates me the most is the beautiful and adoring Geisha.

I recently asked some of my friends what they thought a Geisha was, and the comments I received were quite astonishing. For example, one friend said, "She is a woman who walks around in a hut." A second friend was certain that a Geisha was, "A woman who massages men for money and it involves her in other physical activities." Finally, I received this response, "She gives baths to men and walks on their backs." Well, needless to say, I was rather surprised and offended by their comments. I soon discovered that the majority of my friends perceived the Geisha with similar attitudes. One of them argued, "It's not my fault, because that is the way I've seen them on TV." In many ways my friend was correct. His misconception of the Geisha was not his fault, for she is often portrayed by American film producers and directors as: a prostitute, as in the movie *The Barbarian and the Geisha;* a streetwalker, as seen in the TV series *Kung Fu;* or as a showgirl with a gimmick, as performed in the play *Flower Drum Song.*

A Geisha is neither a prostitute, streetwalker, nor showgirl with a gimmick. She is a lovely Japanese woman who is a professional entertainer and hostess. She is cultivated with exquisite manners, truly a bird of a very different plumage.

I would like to provide you with some insight to the Geisha, and, in the process perhaps, correct any misconception you may have. I will do this by discussing her history, training, and development.

The Geisha has been in existence since A.D. 600, during the archaic time of the Yakamoto period. At that time the Japanese ruling class was very powerful and economically rich. The impoverished majority, however, had to struggle to survive. Starving fathers and their families had to sell their young daughters to the teahouses in order to get a few yen. The families hoped that the girls would have a better life in the teahouse than they would have had in their own miserable homes.

During ancient times only high society could utilize the Geisha's talents, because she was regarded as a status symbol, exclusively for the elite. As the Geisha became more popular, the common people developed their own imitations. These imitations were often crude and base, lacking sophistication and taste. When American GIs came home from World War II, they related descriptive accounts of their wild escapades with the Japanese Geisha. In essence, the GIs were only soliciting with common prostitutes. These bizarre stories helped create the wrong image of the Geisha.

Today, it is extremely difficult to become a Geisha. A Japanese woman couldn't wake up one morning and decide, "I think I'll become a Geisha today." It's not that simple. It takes sixteen years to qualify.

At the age of six a young girl would enter the Geisha training school and become a Jo-chu, which means housekeeper. The Jo-chu does not have any specific type of clothing, hairstyle, or make-up. Her duties basically consist of keeping the teahouse immaculately clean (for cleanliness is like a religion to the Japanese). She would also be responsible for making certain that the more advanced women would have everything available at their fingertips. It is not until the girl is sixteen and enters the Maiko stage that she concentrates less on domestic duties and channels more of her energies on creative and artistic endeavors.

The Maiko girl, for example, is taught the classical Japanese dance, Kabuki. At first, the dance consists of tiny, timid steps to the left, to the right, backward and forward. As the years progress, she is taught the more difficult steps requiring syncopated movements to a fan.

The Maiko is also introduced to the highly regarded art of floral arrangement. The Japanese take full advantage of the simplicity and gracefulness that can be achieved with a few flowers in a vase, or with a single flowering twig. There are three main styles: Seika, Moribana, and Nagerie. It takes at least three years to master this beautiful art.

During the same three years, the Maiko is taught the ceremonious art of serving tea. The roots of these rituals go back to the thirteenth century, when Zen Buddhist monks in China drank tea during their devotions. These rituals were raised to a fine art by the Japanese tea masters, who set the standards for patterns of behavior throughout Japanese society. The tea ceremony is so intricate that it often takes four hours to perform and requires the use of over seventeen different utensils. The tea ceremony is far more than the social occasion it appears to be. To the Japanese, it serves as an island of serenity where one can refresh the senses and nourish the soul.

One of the most important arts taught to the Geisha is that of conversation. She must master an elegant circuitous vocabulary flavored in Karyuki, the world of flowers and willows, of which she will be a part. Consequently, she must be capable of stimulating her client's mind as well as his esthetic pleasures.

Having completed her sixteen years of thorough training, at the age of twenty-two, she becomes a full-fledged Geisha. She can now serve her clients with duty, loyalty, and most important, a sense of dignity.

The Geisha would be dressed in the ceremonial kimono, made of brocade and silk thread. It would be fastened with an obi, which is a sash around the waist and hung down the back. The length of the obi would indicate the girl's degree of development. For instance, in the Maiko stage the obi is longer and is shortened when she becomes a Geisha. Unlike the Maiko, who wears a gay, bright, and cheerful kimono, the Geisha is dressed in more subdued colors. Her makeup is the traditional white base, which gives her the look of white porcelain. The hair is shortened and adorned with beautiful, delicate ornaments.

As a full-fledged Geisha, she would probably acquire a rich patron who would assume her sizable debt to the Okiya, or training residence. This patron would help pay for her wardrobe, for each kimono can cost up to $12,000. The patron would generally provide her with financial security.

The Geisha serves as a combination entertainer and companion. She may dance, sing, recite poetry, play musical instruments, or draw pictures for her guests. She might converse with them or listen sympathetically to their troubles. Amorous advances, however, are against the rules.

So, as you can see the Geisha is a far cry from the back-rubbing, streetwalking, slick entertainer that was described by my friends. She is a beautiful, cultivated, sensitive, and refined woman.

## ▌ Assessing Your Progress

### Chapter Summary

1. Speeches to inform seek to package information or ideas so as to create knowledge in listeners.

2. In this era of the information explosion, selecting and arranging information for others is a necessary skill for survival.

3. Three types of informative speeches are explanations or lectures, demonstrations, and oral reports.

4. No matter what type of informative speech you're preparing, you should strive for five qualities: (a) ensuring clarity, (b) associating new ideas with familiar ones, (c) clustering ideas to aid memory and comprehension, (d) constructing relevant visualizations to aid in audience comprehension, and (e) motivating your audience.

5. To maximize your ability to reach your audience, you should create curiosity, adapt to what listeners already know, use repetition, involve listeners, choose an appropriate organizational pattern, use multiple channels, and suggest additional resources.

### Assessment Activities

Indicate and defend the type of arrangement (chronological sequence, spatial sequence, cause-effect, and so on) you think would be most suitable for an informative speech on the following subjects:

   a.   The status of international or area studies on campus
   b.   Recent developments in stem cell research
   c.   Mayan excavations in Central America
   d.   Annuity, IRA, and SRA savings for retirement
   e.   Key sections of rental leases
   f.   Censorship of video games
   g.   Diet fads of the 1980s and 1990s
   h.   Residential colleges and universities

Your instructor will assess your rationales as underdeveloped, competent, or exceptional.

For additional exercises, log on to MySpeech Lab at www.myspeechlab.com.

### Using the Web

In an era of information overload, we need summaries—even summaries of summaries—to help us understand the picture before we look at its details. To survive in many professional settings, you will need to know how to make an "executive summary." Go to oregonstate.edu/dept/eli/buswrite/Executive_Summary.html. to learn about them and to see one. The trick, of course, will be to include enough information to be useful and understandable without becoming too long. Being good at executive summaries may be a requirement for promotion!

## References

1. The classic study of information processing is G. A. Miller, "The Magic Number Seven Plus or Minus Two: Some Limits on Our Capacity for Processing Information," *Psychological Review*, 63 (1956): 81–97. For exploring cognitive structures for information, see Carl Shapiro and Hal R. Varian, *Information Rules: A Strategic Guide to the Network Economy* (Boston, MA: Harvard Business School Press, 1999). To look at idea packaging in TV programming, see Elizabeth Grabe, Shuhua Zhou, Annie Lang, and Paul David Bolls, "Packaging Television News: The Effects of Tabloid on Information Processing and Evaluative Responses," *Journal of Broadcasting & Electronic Media* 44 (2000): 581–98.

2. The story in this speech outline taken is from Asad Raza, "The Way to Hit the Ball," Tennis, May 2008, 40–42. For the visuals, see tennis.about.com/od/forehandbackhand/ss/fhgripclosewt_3.htm.

3. For additional research on learning, see National Research Council, *How People Learn: Brain, Mind, Experience, and School* (Washington, D.C.: National Academy Press, 2000).

4. Information for this outline is taken from Stephen Tignor, "A Port in a Storm," *Tennis*, May 2008, 51–55; Clay Risen, "The Unmaking of the President," *Smithsonian*, April 2008, 68–78 [from a forthcoming 2009 book]; and Editors of Time-Life Books with Richard B. Stolley, *Turbulent Years: The 60s* (Our American Century series; Richmond, VA: Time-Life, Inc., 1998).

5. Joyce Chapman, "The Geisha," in *Communication Strategy: A Guide to Speech Preparation*, edited by Roselyn Schiff et al. (Boston: Allyn & Bacon, 1982). Copyright © 1982 by Pearson Education. Reprinted by permission of the publisher.

Now that you have completed the chapter on **informative speaking**, stop and think about the process of informing and how it differs from the topics we'll discuss in the next chapter on **persuasive speaking**. Your role as an informative speaker is to make information useful to other human beings. Let's review the broad steps that make up that informative speechmaking process:

1. You first select a topic about which you will speak with your purpose to inform your listeners.
2. You research the facts about the subject and select the relevant information.
3. You arrange the facts in a way to make them understandable for your audience.
4. You interpret the facts for your listeners.

So long as your purpose is informative—that is, to explain, to show, to report findings to others—then you are working within cultural guidelines for informative speaking. If in stage two you select information that shows only one side of the story, it's bad information, but information nonetheless.

However, if you carefully package that information, interpret it, and describe problems that need an urgent solution or require specific actions of the listeners, then you have likely crossed the line from informative speaking to persuasive speaking. It likely has been prepared to specifically affect listeners' beliefs, attitudes, values, and behaviors, and therefore is persuasive.

Both your purpose as a speaker and the degree to which you attempt to psychologically imbed the information in your audience's beliefs, attitudes, and value statements determine whether you are giving an informative or persuasive speech.

However, sometimes the line between informative and persuasive speaking is not clear. Your own personal experiences as a listener and your own common sense will tell you that the simple process of learning about new information can influence you to change your mind and your behavior. Even if the speaker has followed the accepted standards for informational speaking and has no intent to persuade the audience, that speaker may still get you to change your mind about his or her topic. In such a case, however, it is not so much the speaker as the listeners themselves who are responsible for belief, attitude, and value change; so, the speech itself still can be considered informative even if the effects are persuasive.

## Consider the following example:

Cho Seung-Hui went on a killing rampage on the Virginia Tech campus in April of 2007. The following two facts came out in the public media shortly after the event:

- Seung-Hui was suffering from paranoid delusions.
- He had been scheduled for psychotherapy sessions but did not attend them.

We conclude from this example that if a law permitting preventive involuntary out-patient commitment (IOC) had been in effect, the tragedy would never have happened. Seven of the U.S. states, New Zealand, Australia, and Scotland already have such laws in place to protect the public, and they should be enabled in Virginia as well.

But now, consider the "involuntary" part of the proposal together with the fact the courts already have the power, in extreme cases, to order confinement of danger-ous individuals. Would an IOC law that takes away the free rights of another person really be a good thing for our society?

When you attempt to find unbiased information about the effectiveness of such laws, you discover that only two large, randomized studies have ever been con-ducted: one at Duke University and one in New York. The Duke study found only small reductions in violence among IOC patients. The New York study found no ben-efit for IOC. That information causes us to reconsider. Should a person's civil rights be violated if the treatment doesn't help?[1]

Here, new and seemingly scientifically valid information is pressuring your belief structure that appropriate political-governmental action to enforce IOC laws would be a good thing.

Was the information persuasive? In the sense that it affected your belief system, it was. Yet, the information per se came from two scientific studies conducted in as disinterested a way as possible. Furthermore, the article cited did not advocate the elimination of IOC laws—it only suggested that involuntary commitment might not be effective for most people who could end up committing violent acts during some psychotic episode.

**The question is this:** Is there really a distinct line between information and persuasion?

### References

1. Rachel Nowak, "When Getting Lands You in Court," NewScientist, March 22, 2008, 8–9; Cf. www.newscientist.com.

# Speeches to Persuade

We encounter **persuasion** nearly every day of our lives—from the advertisements that invade our e-mail boxes to the commercials that interrupt our favorite television programs. And we're not just the receivers of persuasive messages. We use them to convince our employers to give us raises, to influence our city government to lower our taxes, and to bargain on purchases like cars.

The speaker who persuades makes a very different demand on an audience than the speaker who informs (see Chapter 12) or argues (see Chapter 14). Informative communicators are satisfied when listeners understand what has been said. Speakers who form arguments aim to construct logically compelling reasons for change. They seek to alter their listeners' thoughts or behaviors, appealing primarily through rational means. Persuaders, however, attempt to influence listeners' thoughts or actions primarily through motivation. Whatever the specific purpose, the general purpose of all persuaders is to move audiences to thought or action. Broadly, persuasion encompasses a wide range of communication activities, including advertising, marketing, sales, political campaigns, and interpersonal relations. *Persuasion is the process of changing thinking or behavior in others. The persuasive speaker seeks to produce change in listeners' thinking or behavior through an oral message.*

At the dawn of the twenty-first century, it is very clear that the world of persuasive speaking has changed radically over the last 100 years. We're a fragmented society in many ways. This means that you have to think of audiences as *segmented,* with the different segments—clusters or cultures—often requiring their own motivational appeals to act. That is why we'll begin this chapter with various approaches to understanding and thinking about motivational appeals before talking about *persuasive* speechmaking.

## Selecting Motivational Appeals

The key to audience analysis for persuaders is understanding listeners' needs and desires. Needs and desires, of course, are psychological constructs—perceptions people have of themselves, their plight in life, their fantasies, and their nightmares. Insofar as these perceptions drive people to think and act in particular ways, they are motive needs. A **motive need** is an impulse to satisfy a psychological-social want or a biological urge. Such needs may arise from physiological considerations—pain, lack of food, or surroundings that are too hot or cold—or they may come about for sociocultural reasons, such as when you feel left out of a group. If you feel the need deeply, your feelings may compel you to do something about your situation. You might eat, adjust the thermostat, or join a group—you're motivated.

Once you recognize the power of motive needs to propel human action, you may ask, "How can I identify and satisfy these needs in a speech? How can I use these basic needs, wants, and desires as the basis for effective public speaking?" The answer to both of these questions is "With the use of motivational appeals." A **motivational appeal** is either a visualization of a desire and a method for satisfying it or an assertion that an entity, idea, or course of action holds the key to fulfilling a particular motive need. This is the cornerstone of persuasion.

*The key to audience analysis begins with the speaker's understanding of listeners' needs and desires.*

### Some Common Motivational Appeals

If you attempted to list the potential motivational appeals for every audience, you might never finish. The task is endless. Rather than trying to list each individual appeal, consider the general thrust of each motive cluster. A **motive cluster** is a group of individual appeals that are grounded in the same fundamental human motivation. Table 13.1 shows the three motive clusters—affiliation, achievement, and power—as well as some motivational appeals within each cluster.[1] **Affiliation motives** include the desire to belong to a group or to be well liked or accepted. This cluster also includes love, conformity, dependence on

## Basic Human Needs

Decades ago, psychologist Abraham H. Maslow argued that human needs function in a prepotent hierarchy. That is, lower-level needs must be largely fulfilled before higher-level needs become operative. While Maslow's hierarchy does not automatically predict human behavior, it does allow us to understand that human needs do not act in isolation; rather, they are intertwined. You may be hungry, for example, but unless you are truly starving, you will probably not grab food and gobble it down. Instead, you will adhere to the customs of good table manners, because you seek social acceptance and approval.

The following categories of needs and wants impel human beings to think, act, and respond as they do:

1. *Physiological needs:* for food, drink, air, sleep, sex—the basic bodily "tissue" requirements.

2. *Safety needs:* for security, stability, protection from harm or injury; need for structure, orderliness, law, predictability; freedom from fear and chaos.

3. *Belongingness and love needs:* for abiding devotion and warm affection with spouse, children, parents, and close friends; need to feel a part of social groups; need for acceptance and approval.

4. *Esteem needs:* for self-esteem based on achievement, mastery, competence, freedom, independence; desire for esteem of others (reputation, prestige, recognition, status).

5. *Self-actualization needs:* for self-fulfillment, actually to become what you potentially can be; desire to actualize your capabilities; being true to your essential nature; what you *can* be you *must* be.

**Self-Actualization**
Self-fulfillment: to be what one can be

**Esteem Needs**
Self-esteem from achievement, competence, mastery, confidence, reputation, recognition, status

**Belongingness and Love Needs**
Love and affection with family, friends; acceptance and approval by social groups

**Safety Needs**
Security, stability, protection, structure, orderliness, law, predictability, freedom from fear and chaos

**Physiological Needs**
Food, drink, sleep, sex

See Abraham H. Maslow, *Motivation and Personality* (New York: HarperCollins, 1970, 1987) and Abraham H. Maslow, *Dominance, Self-Esteem, Self-Actualization: The Germinal Papers of Abraham H. Maslow* (New York: Brooks/Cole Publishing Company, 1973).

**TABLE 13.1** Motive Clusters

| Individual motivational appeals fall into clusters that share a common theme. Think of a current television advertisement, and identify the motive clusters in it. | | |
|---|---|---|
| **Affiliation** | **Achievement** | **Power** |
| Companionship | Acquisition/saving | Aggression |
| Conformity | Success/display | Authority/dominance |
| Deference/dependence | Prestige | Defense |
| Sympathy/generosity | Pride | Fear |
| Loyalty | Adventure/change | Autonomy/independence |
| Tradition | Perseverance | |
| Reverence/worship | Creativity | |
| Sexual attraction | Curiosity | |
| | Personal enjoyment | |

others, sympathy toward others, and loyalty. **Achievement motives** are related to the intrinsic or extrinsic desire for success, adventure, creativity, and personal enjoyment. **Power motives** primarily concern the desire to exert influence over others.

As you think about your audience, begin with this list—because then you'll be in a better position to choose the best motivational appeals for speech. Remember this guideline as you make your choices: *Motivational appeals work best when they are associated with the needs and desires of your listeners.* Analyze your audience, and then choose your motivational appeals on the basis of what you've learned about your listeners.

**The Affiliation Cluster** Affiliation motives are dominated by a desire for acceptance or approval. They're more focused on the social or interpersonal bonds attributed to people than with personal success or power over others. A social desire to be part of a group is an affiliation motive. What follows are some examples of appeals to listeners' affiliation desires:

1. **Companionship and affiliation.** "A friend in need is a friend indeed." "Birds of a feather flock together." The fear of loneliness or separation from others is strong.

2. **Conformity.** "AARP—It's for People Like You." "To get along, you need to go along." We fear not only isolation, but also being too different from others.

3. **Deference/dependence.** "Nine out of ten doctors recommend . . ." "America's deepest thinking president, Abraham Lincoln, has said . . ." You can be made to feel dependent on either majority rule or extraordinary individuals.

4. **Sympathy/generosity.** "You could be the parent this child has never known for just a dollar a day." "Give that others might live." "Contribute today to help us 'Take Back the Night.'"

**5. Loyalty.** This is how Vietnam combat veteran Ron Mitscher described loyalty in combat: "The camaraderie becomes something that you carry the rest of your life with those individuals. Sometimes you never get a chance to see those individuals again, but in your heart you know you'd do anything for them because they did that for you in a situation which could have gotten them killed."[2]

**6. Tradition.** "It is through our sacred rituals and ceremonies that we are known as a people." The call to collective celebration or worship is a strong affiliative appeal, especially in times of crisis and stress.

**7. Reverence/worship.** "But in a larger sense we cannot dedicate, we cannot consecrate, we cannot hallow this ground. The brave men, living and dead, who struggled here, have consecrated it far above our power to add or detract."[3]

**8. Sexual attraction.** "Don't Be Such a Good Boy" (ad for the men's cologne Drakkar Noir). "Nothing gets between me and my Calvins" (ad for Calvin Klein jeans).

**The Achievement Cluster** Achievement motives are focused on individual urges, desires, and goals—an explicit concern for self and for personal excellence, prestige, and success. The following appeals to achievement motives are aimed at audience members as individuals:

**1. Acquisition/saving.** "Earn good money now in our new Checking-Plus accounts!" "Buy U.S. savings bonds where you work—invest in America!" Both of these are blatant appeals to personal accumulation of wealth, but the second makes the act seem more generous by tying it to patriotic motives (see "Tradition" above).

**2. Success/display.** "Hear the Radio That Woke Up an Entire Industry [Bose—Better Sound Through Research]." "Successful executives carry the Connerton electronic organizer." These ads play off two kinds of success—corporate (a kind of appeal to majority opinion) and personal (it will make you stand out from the rest).

**3. Prestige.** "L'Oréal—Because You're Worth It!" "The U.S. Marines—The Few. The Proud. The Marines." In both cases, the prestige appeal implies special qualities, either of the brand name (L'Oréal) or the organization (the Marines).

**4. Pride.** "Be Proud of America. Support the Troops" (Gulf War slogan). "Lose weight through our diet plan and feel great about your body." Motivational appeals to pride can center on the collective (here, one's country) or on individual characteristics (here, your body, so often a source of anxiety, rather than pride).

**5. Adventure/change.** "The Polo Sport Arena: A place to test yourself and your environment." "Join the Navy and See the World." Again, appeals to adventure can be personal or collective, but they are always centered on self-aggrandizement.

**6. Perseverance.** "It's not the size of the dog in the fight but the size of the fight in the dog." "If at first you don't succeed, try, try again." We want to believe that continual effort will be rewarded, so this appeal can be strong.

**7. Creativity.** "Dare to be different: Design your own major." Appeals to creativity are almost always appeals to an inborn talent that separates you in a good way from everyone else (strongly related to pride).

**8. Curiosity.** Want to know who wins the *American Idol* competition or how this season of *Lost* ends? You have to tune in to find out. "Curiosity killed the cat; satisfaction brought him back," says conventional wisdom, suggesting that curiosity is dangerous but rewarding.

**9. Personal enjoyment.** "Let the good times roll!" There's often a hedonistic element to this appeal.

**The Power Cluster** All appeals in the power cluster focus on influence or control over others or the environment. All motives in this group feature appeals to one's place in the social hierarchy—a dominant place. People with power motives seek to manipulate or control others, but not all uses of power are negative. With power can—(and should)—come social responsibility, the demand that power be used in socially approved ways to benefit the group. Appeals to power also depend heavily on appeals to affiliation, because power is used most constructively when people see it as being in their own best interest to grant it to others. So, motivational appeals from the power cluster often are accompanied by appeals to affiliation. We won't illustrate that in the examples that follow, but you should think of how to do it in your speeches:

**1. Aggression.** "We must fight for our rights—if we are to be heard, we dare not let others silence us." Here, the appeal to power is specifically turned into an affiliative "we."

**2. Authority/dominance.** "If the FDA [Food and Drug Administration] will not protect us, we must protect ourselves." "By the power invested in me, I now pronounce you man and wife." Authority for oneself arises from the need for a leader; institutional authority usually comes from an external source, whether divine, as in the marriage ceremony, or secular, as when the president of the United States begins, "As commander-in-chief, I . . ."

**3. Defense.** "We fight not for our own glory and prestige, but to protect ourselves from ruthless enemies." If aggressive actions are viewed as defending ourselves or others, they're usually thought to be more ethically justified.

**4. Fear.** "Friends don't let friends drive drunk." Here, the appeal to the fear of neglecting one's social responsibility is strong. Use fear appeals cautiously (see "Speaking of . . . Ethics: Using Fear Appeals").

**5. Autonomy/independence.** "Just do it." For a decade, Nike has played on your sense of independent, autonomous action to sell you shoes.

You might have noticed that some of the appeals we've just described seem to contradict each other. For example, fear seems to oppose adventure, and sympathy and conformity seem to work against independence. Remember that human beings are changeable creatures, who at different times might pursue quite different goals and thus can be reached through many different kinds of verbalizations of their wants and desires. The clusters we've described aren't all-inclusive; but this discussion is enough to get you started in your work on persuasion.

## Using Motivational Appeals

In practice, motivational appeals are seldom used alone; speakers usually combine them. Suppose you were selecting a mountain bike. What factors would

## Using Fear Appeals

Common sense tells you that fear appeals are among the most potent appeals to audiences. After all, if you can make your audience feel afraid for the future if a problem is not resolved, your proposal will be just the antidote. Unfortunately, a comprehensive review of decades of research on fear appeals suggests that this common-sense notion is not that well grounded. There is no clear advice about whether the use of fear appeals to gain acceptance of a message outweighs any harms caused by frightening people—perhaps needlessly. The inability to offer such advice raises an ethical question about the use—and potential misuse—of fear appeals.

Consider the following scenarios:

1. You give a speech on the increase of date rape on college campuses. To convince your audience that date rape is wrong and extremely common, you create scenarios that appeal to the fears of your listeners. Your scenarios are so vivid that several of your listeners, who are rape survivors, are visibly overcome with emotion. One of the listeners is so upset that she leaves the classroom during your speech; everyone in the audience sees her leave.

2. You feel very strongly that the college president is wrong to continue investing college money in countries where torture and imprisonment without trial are legal. In a persuasive speech, you appeal to your audience's fears by suggesting that the college president actually is propagating torture and corrupting American values to the point that, someday, torture and imprisonment without trial might be legal in the United States. Your listeners become so incensed as a result of your speech that they march to the president's house and set his car on fire.

3. You're preparing to give a speech on hate crimes in the United States. You want to make sure you have your audience's attention before you begin, so you decide to present the details of a series of grisly murders committed in your town by a psychopath, even though these murders were not motivated by hate but by mental illness (and so are not examples of hate crimes).

influence your decision? One would be price (*saving*); a second certainly would be performance (*adventure*); another might be comfort and appearance (*personal enjoyment*); a fourth probably would be the reputation of the manufacturer (*prestige*) or its uniqueness (*independence*). These factors combined would add up to *pride* of ownership. Some of these influences, of course, would be stronger than others; some might even conflict. All of them, however, probably would affect your choice. You would base your decision to buy the bike on the strongest of the appeals.

Because motivational appeals are interdependent, it's a good idea to coordinate them. You should select three or four appeals that are related and that target segments of your audience. When you work from cluster appeals, you tap multiple dimensions of your listeners' lives.

Consider the following appeal to your classmates to sponsor Mark Todd as he attempts to break the world record for cycling around the perimeter of Australia and raise money to combat the global AIDS crisis. Most of your classmates probably didn't realize there was a world record to be broken. Others might be asking, "Why does AIDS in Africa matter to me?" So, how do you try to reach them? Through combining motivational appeals with visualization, you can raise their awareness and get them to think about their role in the worldwide AIDS epidemic:

> A student just like us (*affiliation*), Mark Todd hadn't really thought about AIDS, especially not in Africa. It was something he didn't have much prior knowledge about until he started investigating the topic online. There's a huge amount of information out there and as he began to learn more and more, Mark knew he had to do something (*perseverence*). He couldn't just sit by while countless children lost their parents to this horrible disease, entire villages were decimated, and millions of lives were shattered (*sympathy/generosity*). So Mark is going to cycle around Australia to raise money to help fight the epidemic. Mile by mile, 8,820 miles in all, Mark's dream is to give hope to others by donating the money he raises to charities in southern Africa.
>
> We can be a part of Mark's dream and ease the suffering of the victims of this horrible disease (*affiliation*). Just think of what we can accomplish if each of us contributes just one dollar and asks a friend to match our contribution (*success/display*). For us, it's not much—hardly the price of a soft drink. But for someone in Africa who has contracted this deadly virus, it may mean that they have better health care in the remaining days of their life. It may mean that a child will have a chance to grow up. And, it may help prevent the further spread of the epidemic. Start today. Go online at challengeaustralia.com and together with Mark, we can change the world! (*pride*)

Notice the interweaving of affiliative and achievement motivational appeals with a specific action step. The speaker hoped that by including his listeners and providing them with a specific action, they would respond positively to his message.

One final piece of general advice: Inconspicuous appeals work best. People rarely admit, even to themselves, that they act on the basis of self-centered motivations—greed, imitation, personal pride, and fear. Be subtle when using these appeals. For example, you might encourage listeners to imitate the actions of well-known people by saying, "Habitat for Humanity counts among its volunteers the former president and first lady, Jimmy and Rosalynn Carter," rather than saying, "If you volunteer to work for Habitat for Humanity, you'll get to associate with famous people."

## Enhancing Your Credibility

Now, consider another essential dimension affecting the persuasive process: credibility, or *ethos*. In Chapter 1, we noted that your credibility as a speaker is determined by listeners' perceptions of you—their sense of your expertise or competency, trustworthiness, sincerity, and personal dynamism. You should work to maximize the potential impact of all these factors whenever you speak. They are especially important, however, when you seek to change someone's mind or behavior. The following guidelines can assist you in making decisions about the use of credibility as an effective tool in persuasion.

First, when speaking to people who are relatively unmotivated and do not have enough background information to critically assess what they hear, *the higher your credibility, the better are your chances of being a successful persuader.* Conversely, if your credibility is low, even strong arguments may not overcome your initial handicap.[4] Sure, this is obvious, but it's amazing how many speakers think they needn't worry about their credibility, especially if their listeners are unmotivated or uninformed.

Second, *your listeners are more likely to trust you if you display knowledge about your topic.* People are unlikely to change their beliefs and values if they think you've done a poor job of researching the issues, because they are less likely to

### Inoculating Audiences Against Counterpersuasion

In this chapter, we've concentrated on the issue of persuading—increasing or otherwise changing people's acceptance of certain beliefs, attitudes, and values. We have not, however, focused on the ways in which you can increase your listeners' resistance to ideas or counterpersuasion—attempts by others to influence listeners away from your position.

Just as vaccines are used to ward off diseases, you may inoculate your audience against your opponents' arguments. Studies of political advertising found that voters were more resistant to an opponent's message if they were warned of the attack. Voters who received arguments to refute an attack were far more resistant to the opponent's message. This suggests that forewarning (letting audience members know in advance that they'll be exposed to a counterpersuasive attempt) an audience may help them resist counterpersuasion. Further research concludes that it does not appear to matter whether the forewarning is general ("My opponent will attack me.") or more precise ("My opponent will tell you that I'm wrong about Social Security."). Nor does it appear to matter whether the attack really is imminent or comes later.

Another strategy that increases resistance involves the amount of knowledge that people bring to a situation. For example, Hirt and Sherman found that individuals who have greater knowledge are more resistant to refutational arguments. Thus, you can increase potential resistance to messages that are contrary to your own by adding to the audience's knowledge about the issues involved.

For further reading, see William L. Benoit, "Forewarning and Persuasion," *in Forewarning and Persuasion: Advances Through Meta-Analysis*, edited by Mike Allen and Roy W. Preiss (Dubuque, IA: Brown and Benchmark, 1994), 159–184; E. R. Hirt and S. J. Sherman, "The Role of Prior Knowledge in Explaining Hypothetical Events," *Journal of Experimental Social Psychology*, 21 (1985): 591–643; Michael Pfau, "The Potential of Inoculation in Promoting Resistance to the Effectiveness of Comparative Advertising Messages," *Communication Quarterly*, 40 (1992): 26–44; Michael Pfau, and Michael Burgoon, "Inoculation in Political Communication," *Communication Monographs*, 15 (1988): 91–111.

trust your ideas. So, (1) carefully set forth all of the competing positions, ideas, and proposals relevant to a topic before you come to your own judgment; (2) review various criteria for judgment—criteria that others can also apply—to show that your positions flow from accepted measures; and (3) show that the recommendations you offer actually will solve the problems you have identified in your speech.

Third, *mimic the response you want from your listeners when you seek their commitment or action.* People will be more likely to follow your lead if they believe you know what you're talking about, have their best interests in mind, and are excited about your own proposal.

An audience's sense of your dynamism can be enhanced if you speak vividly by drawing clear images of the events you describe; using sharp, fresh metaphors

*Your mode of delivery should reflect your own speech habits, audience expectations, and the demands of the physical setting within which you are speaking.*

and active rather than passive verbs; and expressing your ideas with a short, hard-hitting, oral style rather than a long, cumbersome, written style. Your physical delivery should mirror your own enthusiasm as well. You can use direct eye contact rather than reliance on notes, varied vocal patterns, emphatic gestures, and a firm, upright stance.[5]

When you speak in public, you are a living, active human being behind the lectern—a person who embodies a message and whose own values are expressed both in and through the message. Your presence will command more attention and interest than written words, and unlike films and videos, you can interact with your listeners, creating a sense of urgency and directness. Your personal credibility may be your most important asset as you persuade others.

## ▌ Organizing Persuasive Speeches: The Motivated Sequence

Now, it's time to think about organizing your appeals into a persuasive speech. As we've suggested, an important consideration in structuring appeals is your listeners' psychological tendencies—ways in which individuals' own motivations and circumstances favor certain ways of structuring ideas. You must learn to sequence supporting materials and motivational appeals to form a useful organizational pattern for speeches as a whole. Since 1935, the most popular such pattern has been called **Monroe's motivated sequence** (see Figure 13.1).[6] We will devote the rest of this chapter to it.

SPEAKING OF . . .
S K I L L S

**Persuading the Diverse Audience**

One of the most difficult tasks a speaker faces is trying to convince a diversified audience to act together. How can you get racially diversified, bigendered, class-stratified audiences of young and old people to work in harmony?

The advice offered in that chapter bears repeating (and rereading if necessary):

- Recognize diversity even while calling for unity.
- Show that particular values are held in common even if they're operationalized differently by various groups of people.
- Encourage different paths to a goal they all can share.
- Exhort people to adjust some of their own lifestyle choices for the greater good of all.
- Assure people that they can maintain their self-identity even when working with people of different values, lifestyles, and cultures.

All of this is good advice, *but can you actually execute it? And if so, how?* Well, the bottom line is courage—the courage to recognize differences in explicit ways, to force people to confront and deal with their differences, and to make joint progress on problems caused by those very differences.

• • • • • • • • • • • • • • • • • •

The motivated sequence ties problems and solutions to human motives. The motivated sequence for the presentation of verbal materials is composed of five basic steps:

1. **Attention.** Create interest and desire.
2. **Need.** Develop the problem by analyzing wrongs in the world and relating them to the individual's interests, wants, or desires.
3. **Satisfaction.** Propose a plan of action that will alleviate the problem and satisfy the individual's interests, wants, or desires.
4. **Visualization.** Depict the world as it will look if the plan is put into action or if it's not.
5. **Action.** Call for personal commitments and deeds.

The motivated sequence provides an ideal blueprint for urging an audience to take action. That's what it was designed for, because it was used originally as the basis for sales presentations. Let's look first at some ways in which you might use Monroe's sequence to structure a speech to seek action from listeners.

## Step 1: Get Attention

You must engage your listeners at the very beginning of your speech if you hope to get them to move. Remember that startling statements, illustrations, questions, and other factors focus attention on your message. You can't persuade people without their attention.

**FIGURE 13.1** The Motivated Sequence

Notice how the audience should respond to each step of the motivated sequence.

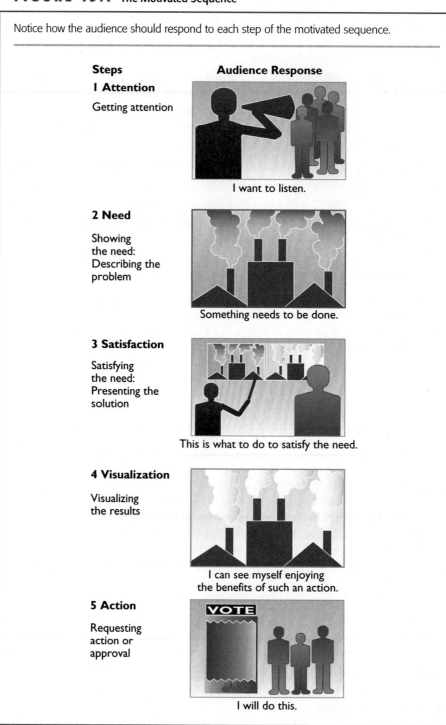

| Steps | Audience Response |
| --- | --- |
| **1 Attention**<br>Getting attention | I want to listen. |
| **2 Need**<br>Showing the need: Describing the problem | Something needs to be done. |
| **3 Satisfaction**<br>Satisfying the need: Presenting the solution | This is what to do to satisfy the need. |
| **4 Visualization**<br>Visualizing the results | I can see myself enjoying the benefits of such an action. |
| **5 Action**<br>Requesting action or approval | I will do this. |

## Step 2: Show the Need: Describe the Problem

Once you've captured the attention of your listeners, you're ready to explain why change is needed. To do this, you must show that a definite problem exists. You must point out, through facts and figures, just how bad the present situation is: "Last month our fund-raising drive to support the campus radio station fell $3,500 short of its goal. If we can't gain those dollars in this week's emergency drive, we'll have to close down two work-study positions. That will not only make it difficult for those students to stay in school, but also we'll have to shut down our Friday night live coverage of local music."

In its full form, a need or problem step has four parts:

1. **Statement.** Give a definite, concise statement of the problem.
2. **Illustration.** Give one or more examples that explain and clarify the problem.
3. **Ramification.** Offer additional examples, statistical data, testimony, and other forms of support that show the extent and seriousness of the problem.
4. **Pointing.** Offer an explanation of how the problem directly affects the listener.

*Statement* and *pointing* should always be present, but the inclusion of *illustration* and *ramification* will depend on the amount of detail required to convince the audience. Whether you use the complete development or only part of it, the *need* step is critical in your speech. Here, your subject is first tied to the needs and desires of your listeners.

## Step 3: Satisfy the Need: Present the Solution

The solution or satisfaction step urges the adoption of a policy. Its goal is to get your listeners to agree that the program you propose is the correct one. Therefore, this step consists of presenting your proposed solution to the problem and proving that this solution is both practical and desirable.

Five items are usually contained in a fully developed satisfaction step:

**1. Statement.** State the attitude, belief, or action you wish the audience to adopt. This is a statement of action: "We need to adopt an incentive system for our Littleton carburetor plant."

**2. Explanation.** Make sure that your proposal is understood. Visual aids, such as charts and diagrams, can be very useful here. In our example, you would define the incentive system: "By *incentive system,* I mean that workers at the Littleton plant should be paid by the actual number of carburetors completed rather than the hours worked."

**3. Theoretical demonstration.** Show how your proposed solution meets the need. For example, you could say, "Worker productivity will rise because workers are paid not just for putting in time but for completing carburetors."

**4. Reference to practical experience.** Supply examples to prove that the proposal has worked effectively where it has been tried. Facts, figures, and the testimony of experts support your contention: "Production at our New Albany plant increased by 42 percent after we instituted this compensation schedule."

**5. Meeting objections.** Forestall opposition by answering any objections that might be raised against the proposal. You might counter the objections of the labor union by arguing, "Increased plant productivity will allow us to expand the medical benefits for plant workers."

Just as certain phases can sometimes be omitted from the need step, one or more of these phases can be left out of the satisfaction step. Also, the foregoing order does not always have to be followed exactly. Occasionally, you can best meet objections by answering them as they arise. In other situations, the theoretical demonstration and reference to practical experience can be combined. If the satisfaction step is developed properly, then at its conclusion, the audience will say, "Yes, you're right; this is a practical and desirable solution to the problem you identified."

## Step 4: Visualize the Results

The function of the visualization step is to intensify desire. It should picture for the audience future conditions if your proposal is or is not adopted. In the visualization step, ask your listeners to project themselves into the future. This projection can be accomplished in one of three ways—by the *positive method,* the *negative method,* or the *method of contrast.*

1. **Positive method.** Describe how conditions will improve under your proposal. Make this description vivid and concrete. Select a situation that you are quite sure will arise. Then, picture your listeners actually enjoying the conditions your proposal will produce. For example, if plant productivity allows better medical benefits, describe the advantages for everyone—lower deductibles, dental care, free eye examinations, and hospice services.

2. **Negative method.** Describe conditions as they will be in the future if your proposal is *not* carried out. Picture for your audience the evils that will arise from failure to follow your advice. Select the most undesirable conditions, and show how they will be aggravated if your proposal is rejected. Describe plant employees being laid off, losing their pension plan, and experiencing the trauma of finding new jobs in a tight market.

3. **Method of contrast.** Combine the two preceding methods. Use the negative approach first, and then use the positive approach. In this way, the benefits of the proposal are contrasted with the disadvantages of the present system. The following illustration shows how one speaker, urging an audience to get regular blood pressure checkups before problems are apparent, used visual contrasts:

> So what happens when you don't take that simple little step of getting your blood pressure checked regularly? You know what happens. Given how badly Americans eat, how little most of them exercise, and how tense the world of work becomes for too many of us, arteries begin a buildup of fatty deposits, openings narrow, blood flow becomes constricted, breathing becomes more difficult, and sooner or later—boom! You're on the ground in terrifying pain, hoping against hope that the person next to you can call 911 and knows some CPR well enough to sustain your life until professional help arrives.
>
> With proper and periodic blood pressure checks, however, you needn't face the prospect of open heart surgery. When Drs. Andrea Foote and John Erfurt established a worker health program, 92 percent of the hypertensive workers at four different industrial sites controlled their blood pressure. When the Hypertensive Education Program in Michigan and in Connecticut went into effect, insurance rates were cut in both states. Back in 1970, Savannah, Georgia, had the infamous title of "Stroke Capital of the World." But today, with fourteen permanent blood pressure reading stations and special clinics, its stroke rate's been cut in half. And, of course, if you take advantage of the blood pressure monitoring program at Student Health or even at the Walgreen's drug store downtown, you'll be

secure in the knowledge that you're not one of America's 11 million people who have high blood pressure and don't even know it.[7]

Whichever method you use—positive, negative, or contrast—remember that the visualization step must stand the test of reality. The conditions that you picture must be vivid and reflective of the world as your listeners know it. Let your listeners actually see themselves enjoying the advantages or suffering the evils you describe. The more realistically you depict the situation, the more strongly your listeners will react.

## Step 5: Request Action

The function of the action step is to call for explicit action. You can do this by offering a challenge or appeal, a special inducement, or a statement of personal intention. For examples, review the conclusions discussed in Chapter 8. Your request for action should be short and intense enough to set your listeners' resolve to act. It should also be specific enough so that listeners will know exactly how to implement their newfound resolution.

The motivated sequence is flexible. You can adapt it to various situations once you are familiar with its basic pattern. Like cooks who alter good recipes to their personal tastes, you can adjust the formula for particular occasions—changing the number of main points from section to section, sometimes omitting restatement from the attention step, and sometimes omitting the positive or negative projections from the visualization step. *Like any recipe, the motivated sequence is designed to give you a formula that fits many different situations*. It gives you an excellent pattern but does not remove the human element; you still must think about your choices. Consider the choices made in the following outline of an actuative speech using the motivated sequence.

*Senator John McCain used his record as a war hero to enhance his credibility in the 2008 presidential campaign.*

## Sample Outline of a Persuasive Speech

To see how the motivated sequence can work for you, examine the following outline. Notice that the speaker is concerned with accurately reflecting the usual behavioral patterns of people living in retirement communities, with making sure that listeners know he or she is a credible Internet user, and with seeking motivational appeals that will get at least a significant segment of this group to try out computer-based distance learning.

### You're Never Too Old to Learn—Virtually!

**The Situation.** As a project for a community education class, you decide to work with the recreation and education center at a local housing project for elderly residents. The center currently offers only crafts classes and is woefully short of educational materials.

**Specific Purpose.** To persuade people attending the education center to take Web-based classes.

**Attention Step**

> *Work against stereotypes of the elderly's lifestyles. Engage them, and improve your credibility (trustworthiness).*

I.  It's too easy to assume that just because you're retired, you only want to play checkers and make Christmas presents out of plastic milk jugs.

II. In fact, you haven't given up living and learning. You're still curious, and now you have time for a broad range of educational experiences.

**Need Step**

> *Work with power cluster motives (especially defense and fear) to make them want to hear more.*

I.  Yet the elderly often have trouble traveling to three-times-a-week classes at a local college to get that stimulation.

II. Today's retirees are going to live longer than ever and so must keep learning to keep from falling significantly far behind the rest of society.

**Satisfaction Step**

> *Tie your proposal to environmental elements in the center as well as to achievement motives (pride, success, adventure).*

I.  The growing number of high-quality, Web-based classes—thousands are available online—create great opportunities for you.
    A. You have plenty of computer terminals with browsers.
    B. Because Internet courses often are less expensive than traditional classes, you can afford college-level schooling.
    C. You're chatters—good conversationalists—and that makes a good Web-based class into a rewarding experience.

II. I will spend this semester as a resource person and tutor for you.
    A. I'll provide technical help for any of you who're new to computer work.
    B. I'll help you surf the Internet to find a course that interests you.
    C. We can set up some discussion groups for people who are studying similar kinds of things.

**Visualization Step**

> *Blend appeals to achievement (prestige, creativity, curiosity, personal enjoyment) and to power (autonomy/ independence) using lifestyle characterizers sensitive to some of the usual interests of active elderly people.*

I.  Think of what you have available on the Internet.
    A. The California Virtual Campus has over 2,000 courses available online.
    B. You can earn a bachelor's degree in General Studies electronically at Indiana University Online.

C. The Rochester Institute of Technology has science and technology courses available to those of you who come out of technical backgrounds.

D. The University of California at Berkeley lets you start courses anytime.

E. Western Governors University will even give you credit for life experience.

II. Virtual connections with faculty and fellow students can be very rewarding.

A. Think of the pleasure you can have in chatting about Charles Dickens' *Oliver Twist* in an Introduction to Victorian Literature course.

B. Just consider what your life will be like when you can tune into a lecture by a professor working in Cairo while you stay home but are listening alongside a fellow classmate living in Tokyo.

C. And the variety available at just a keystroke is amazing—you can take a course in World Politics from the New School for Social Research in New York, a basic course in midwifery from the University of Pennsylvania, and a course in architectural design from the University of Washington.

### Action Step

I. You all know the value of education; otherwise, you wouldn't have come to this meeting.    ⟵ Final appeals to self-achievement and the credibility of the speaker.

A. You all know the value of thinking, understanding, and evaluating for your own enjoyment and mental health.

B. You all know that we can make more productive use of this facility and these computers.

II. I hope that today's the day you sign up for the virtual ride of your lifetime down the Information Highway![8]

## Sample Outline of an Actuative Speech

The motivated sequence works especially well on actuative speeches because of the action step. Demands for action can be issued and defended very efficiently by using the motivated sequence. In fact, the desire to structure speeches that move people to action (e.g., to buy a product or engage in another specified behavior) was the impetus behind Alan Monroe's development of this organizational scheme. Read the outline here to get a clear sense of how the motivated sequence can be used in developing an actuative speech. Notice the adaptation of supporting materials and motivational appeals to a student audience.

### The Chain Never Stops

**The Situation.** You are attending college at Buena Vista University in Storm Lake, Iowa—also home to a large meat-processing plant run by IBP (Iowa Beef Producers, Inc.). You know that wages are low and that the local plant, like others nationwide, is notorious for accidents and lack of support for injured workers. You want your classmates to help do something about the problems you see.

**Specific Purpose.** To convince your classmates to join you in helping IBP workers get fair compensation for their injuries.

*(Continued)*

## Attention Step

*Use authoritative imagery to create a sad, even fearful illustration, followed by orienting statements about the meat industry.*

I. "In the beginning he had been fresh and strong, and he had gotten a job the first day; but now he was second-hand, a damaged article, so to speak, and they did not want him. . . . They had worn him out, with their speeding-up and their carelessness, and now they had thrown him away!"

II. Though written 100 years ago, these words from Upton Sinclair's novel *The Jungle* still apply to the same places they originally described: slaughterhouses.

III. The meat-processing industry in the United States has grown in efficiency but at a tremendous cost to the average laborer.

IV. Today, I want to review the safety record of meat-packing plants and suggest some changes we can make right here in Storm Lake, Iowa, as part of our education at Buena Vista University.

## Need Step

I. First, you need to understand something about the history of meat processing in this country and the role of IBP in modernizing it.

   A. Begun as Iowa Beef Packers, Inc., in 1961, IBP revolutionized the meat-packing industry.

*Historical background, organized chronologically.*

      1. It moved slaughterhouses out of the cities and into the countryside, nearer supplies, to save money.

      2. It automated the process through division of labor using less-skilled, lower-paid workers. It shipped smaller cuts of prepackaged meats instead of whole carcasses to grocery outlets.

   B. The rest of the meat-processing industry imitated IBP's processing and distribution system.

II. Along with these great innovations, however, came other changes.

   A. The top four meat packers—IBP, ConAgra, Excel, and National Beef—gained control of 85 percent of the market.

   B. Wages in the meat-packing industry fell by as much as 50 percent over the last three decades, making it one of the lowest-paying industrial jobs in the United States.

III. All of these changes have adversely affected workers in the industry.

*Detailing of current needs.*

   A. In 1999, over one-quarter of all meat packers—40,000 workers—suffered a job-related industry or illness.

      1. Up to 400 animals an hour must be processed by workers cutting meat at lightning speeds.

      2. Workers are regularly cut, hit, hooked, caught in meat tenderizers, burned, and even killed.

   B. Those who are hurt are encouraged to waive their right to sue for damages in exchange for medical treatment.

      1. If workers want treatment by the company, they must sign the waiver.

      2. The waiver allows companies in some states to get around the workmen's compensation law.

   C. Workers who are seriously injured are encouraged to quit or are forced to take low-paying, menial jobs.

      1. If you quit, you lose health benefits and have to go on welfare.

      2. If you stay, you might get a job like Michael Grover did. IBP had him picking up dropped dirty towels and toilet paper from the restroom floor all day, every day.

    D. Furthermore, some politicians with connections to the meat-processing industry are lobbying to reduce levels of workmen's compensation.
        1. Texas Senator Phil Gramm's wife Wendy Lee sits on the board of IBP.
        2. Vice President of ConAgra, Kathy Norton, is the wife of Colorado Senator Tom Norton, who sponsored a bill to limit worker compensation.

## Satisfaction Step

I. What can a class of college students in northern Iowa do about any of this?
    A. We can volunteer at the local meat cutters' union hall and the recreation center downtown.       *← Tie solutions to specific skills groups of students have, appealing especially to pride and creativity.*
    B. Someone can get hooked up with ICAN—the Iowa Citizens Action Network—to check on the status of workmen's compensation law reform (proposed limitations) in Iowa.
    C. Others can counsel families of workers directly.
        1. You can commit a few hours per week at the counseling desk we're setting up at the recreation center.
        2. You even can earn research practicum credit for graduation in the Department of Communication.

## Visualization Step

I. If the meat-processing industry does not change, workers will continue to suffer.
    A. Kenny Dobbins' story about being hit by a ninety-pound box of meat while at Monfort Beef Company.       *← Use personal anecdotes to make the needs more vivid, with mostly positive visualization.*
    B. Albertina Rios' story about her life with IBP in Lexington, Nebraska.
    C. Rual Lopez's story about being hung on a chain and crushed at a ConAgra plant in Greeley, Colorado.

II. If the industry even allows worker compensation under state laws, workers' lives will improve.
    A. Workers who have been injured will not be so easily fired.
    B. They'll be able to go to arbitration for compensation in cases of debilitating injury.

## Action Step

I. "The chain never stops"—that's the cry of workers who kill, skin, clean, cut up, box, and finally ship the meat that appears on our tables every morning, noon, and evening.       *← Summarize, call for personal commitment and action.*
    A. When the chain doesn't stop, people get hurt.
    B. Those of us who enjoy the products of their labor—bacon, burgers, a nice steak—have a moral obligation, it seems to me, to make their lives in service to us as good as we can.

II. Come join me tonight at 7:30 in Room 123 to talk about the kinds of help you can provide.
    A. I'll tell you how you can volunteer to meet with families.
    B. I'll show you some research projects we need to pursue if you'd rather do that.
    C. I'll give you a list of Buena Vista University instructors who will give you academic credit for your work.

III. It's time for all of us—at least five of us if you'll join me—to make sure that Upton Sinclair's *The Jungle* no longer reflects factory life in Storm Lake, Iowa, and all of the other packer towns of this country.[9]

## Assessing Your Progress

### Chapter Summary

1. Speeches to persuade and actuate have psychological and behavioral changes as their primary goals.
2. As you prepare your speech to persuade or actuate, you should consider adapting to your listener's behavioral patterns, enhancing your credibility, and selecting effective motivational appeals.
3. Analysis of audience segments can provide speakers with motivational appeals to use in persuading listeners.
4. Listeners are more likely to respond to your persuasive message if you are credible. You should demonstrate expertise, trustworthiness, and dynamism.
5. Motivational appeals visualize human desires and offer ways to satisfy those desires.
6. Commonly used motivational appeals can be grouped into three clusters: affiliation, achievement, and power.
7. Monroe's motivated sequence is an organizational pattern based on people's natural psychological tendencies.
8. The five steps in Monroe's motivated sequence are attention, need, satisfaction, visualization, and action.

### Assessment Activities

Choose a position on a topic with which your classmates disagree. Identify at least two motivational appeals from each motive cluster, and use them to develop a persuasive speech. After you've delivered your speech, ask your classmates which appeals they found most persuasive. Would other appeals have worked more effectively? Why or why not?

For additional suggestions and activities, log on to MySpeechLab at www.myspeechlab.com.

### Using the Web

Go to **www.creativity-online.com**, sign in, and find an ad to analyze. What motivational appeals make it work? How would you characterize the audience (demographically, by lifestyle) that it's aimed at? Does it work or not? Why or why not?

### References

1. The clusters that we're using are developed from the work of David McClelland. See Katharine Blick Hoyenga and Hemit T. Hoyenga, *Motivational Explanations of Behavior: Psychological and Cognitive Ideas* (Monterey, CA: Brooks/Cole Pub., 1984), ch. 1; Abigail J. Stewart, ed., *Motivation and Society: A Volume in Honor of David C. McClelland* (San Francisco: Jossey-Bass, 1982); and Janet T. Spence, ed., *Achievement and Achievement Motives* (San Francisco: W. H. Freeman, 1983).

2. From an interview with Ron Mitscher, Vietnam veteran, for *Parallels: The Soldiers' Knowledge and the Oral History of Contemporary Warfare*, edited by J. T. Hansen, A. Susan Owen, and Michael Patrick Madden (New York: Aldine de Gruyter, 1992), 137.

3. Abraham Lincoln, "Gettysburg Address," speech delivered in 1863, reprinted in *Lincoln at Gettysburg: The Words that Remade America,* edited by Garry Wills (New York: Simon & Schuster, 1992), 261.

4. Robert B. Cialdini, *Influence: The Psychology of Persuasion* (New York: Quill, 1993), 205.

5. The most complete summary of credibility research is still found in Stephen Littlejohn, "A Bibliography of Studies Related to Variables of Source Credibility," *Bibliographical Annual in Speech Communication: 1971,* ed. Ned Shearer (Washington, D.C.: National Communication Association, 1972), 1–40.

6. To see how Alan Monroe originally conceived of the motivated sequence—as much, then, a psychological theory as an organizational pattern—see especially the Foreword to Alan H. Monroe, *Principles and Types of Speech* (Chicago: Scott Foresman, 1935), vii–x.

7. These paragraphs draw their material from Todd Ames, "The Silent Killer," *Winning Orations.* His materials were used by special arrangement with Larry Schnoor, Director, Interstate Oratorical Association, Mankato, MN.

8. Information for this outline gathered from Eyal Press and Jennifer Washburn, "Digital Diplomas," *Mother Jones,* January–February 2001, 34–39, 82–85; Jon Spayde, "College @ home," *Modern Maturity,* July–August 2001, 60–62, and Don Steinberg, "The Lowdown on Online: Everything You Need to Get Plugged In," 63.

9. Information from this outline is taken from Eric Schlosser, "The Chain Never Stops," *Mother Jones,* July–August 2001, 38–47, 86–87; www.ibpinc.com/index.htm; and www.ibpinc.com/about/IBPNewHistory.stm.

# 14 | Argumentation and Critical Thinking

The ability to think critically is central to your survival in our complex world. You're constantly bombarded with requests, appeals, and pleas to change your beliefs or behaviors. Sorting through all those appeals to determine which are justified and whether you should alter your thoughts or actions requires a cool head, not emotional responses. Before committing yourself, you've got to be able to analyze appeals to determine if the reasons fit the claim being made. Skilled speakers, too, must be able not only to construct motivational appeals but also to work from facts to logical conclusions. They must cultivate a critical spirit—the ability to analyze others' ideas and requests.[1]

*Criticism* is a process of careful assessment and judgment of ideas. It's also a matter of supporting your evaluation with reasons. As you engage in evaluation—assessing reasons or offering counter-reasons—you become a critical thinker. You also employ critical skills when you advance a claim and then offer reasons why others should accept it. Finally, a critical spirit requires fair-mindedness, an important dimension of a person's credibility.[2] Both speakers and listeners need to cultivate the critical spirit.

**Argumentation** is a process of advancing claims supported by good reasons and allowing others to test those claims and reasons or offer counter arguments. Through argumentation, people hope to come to reasonable conclusions about matters of fact, value, and

## CHAPTER OUTLINE

Rational Thinking and Talking: Argumentation

Evaluating Arguments

*Speaking of . . . Skills: Evaluating Arguments*

Sample Outline for an Argumentative Speech: The Dangers of Chewing Tobacco

Detecting Fallacies in Reasoning

*Speaking of . . . Ethics: Name-Calling*

Tips for Developing Argumentative Speeches

*Speaking of . . . Skills: Responding to Counterarguments*

Assessing Your Progress

## KEY TERMS

policy. The act of arguing does not consist merely of offering an opinion or stating information—and certainly not of screaming. An act of arguing is an act one step beyond the act of persuading by appealing to motives.

Both persuasion and argumentation seek to convince audiences. Persuasion works largely through emotion, while argumentation acts through reasoning. Argumentation commits you to communicating by using good reasons. Consider the differences between televised political advertisements for two candidates and a debate between those same candidates. Usually, an advertisement relies most heavily on appeals to listeners' emotions, such as patriotism or outrage, while a debate requires candidates to develop reasons for their positions.

You probably engage in argument in many ways. In public forums, such as city council meetings, you might provide reasons why your community should preserve a marshland rather than allow condos to be built, or you might advocate better community regulation of local day care facilities. You might write a letter to the editor of a newspaper proposing a community center. In conversations with friends, you probably argue over sports teams and players. In each of these cases, you'll be more effective if your arguments are sound, with clearly identifiable reasons given for each claim you make. In this chapter, we'll examine the structure of arguments, then offer ways for you to critically evaluate the arguments of others. We'll finish with some tips to help you argue effectively.

## ▌ Rational Thinking and Talking: Argumentation

To tap the power of rational thought, you've got to learn how to construct an argument. An **argument** is built out of three essential elements that must work together: (1) the claim or proposition you advance, (2) the relevant evidence that you provide in support of that claim, and (3) the reasoning pattern that you use to connect the evidence with the claim (see Figure 14.1).

### Types of Claims

Most argumentative speeches assert that (1) something is or is not the case, (2) something is desirable or undesirable, or (3) something should or should not be done. Such judgments or assessments are the speaker's **claims** or propositions. Your first task as an arguer or a listener is to determine the type of claim being argued.

**Claims of Fact**  A **claim of fact** asserts that something is or is not the case. If you're trying to convince listeners that "Using compact fluorescent light bulbs will reduce your utilities cost significantly," you're presenting a factual claim asserting

**FIGURE 14.1** The Elements of Argument

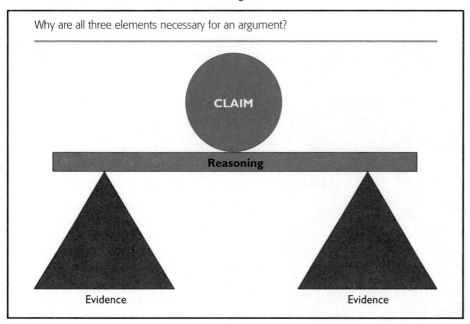

that a given state of affairs exists. When confronted with this sort of claim, two questions can occur to the critically aware listener:

**1. How can the truth or accuracy of the claim be measured?** If you're asked to determine someone's height, you immediately look for a yardstick or other measuring tool. Similarly, listeners look for a standard by which to measure the accuracy of a factual claim. Before agreeing with your claim, the critical thinker asks what you mean by "reduce your utilities costs significantly." What percentage reduction in your electrical bill is considered significant? Against what standard, precisely, is the accuracy of the claim to be judged? As a speaker, you need to build those criteria for judgments into your speeches.

**2. Do the facts of the situation fit the criteria?** Now, then, to the replacement of light bulbs: How many have to be replaced to achieve the utility bill reduction you're after? First, get listeners to agree to certain standards of judgment, and then present evidence that a given state of affairs meets those standards. In these ways, you work to gain the assent of listeners to your factual claims.

**Claims of Value** When your claim asserts that something is good or bad, desirable or undesirable, justified or unjustified, you're advancing a **claim of value**—a claim about the intrinsic worth of the belief or action in question. Here, too, it is important to ask the following questions:

**1. By what standards is something to be judged?** For example, you can measure the quality of a college by the distinction of its faculty (intellectual value), the excellence of its building program (material value), the success of its graduates (practical value), the size of its endowment (monetary value), or the reputation it enjoys according to surveys of education excellence (educational value).

*Different sorts of arguments appeal to different segments of your audience.*

**2. How well does the item in question measure up to the standards specified?** Suppose you were considering attending either Apple Valley Community College or State University. You can assess the worth of each institution by the standards you've identified—intellectual, material, practical, monetary, or educational. Your rating is not merely an assertion of personal preference ("I like Apple Valley Community College best.") if can be argued for on the basis of established standards.

**Claims of Policy** A claim of policy recommends a course of action that you want the audience to approve. Typical examples are "State standards for welfare eligibility should be tightened," or "A test for English competency should be instituted as a graduation requirement." In both instances, you're asking your audience to endorse a proposed policy or course of action. Four questions are relevant to the judgments your listeners are being asked to make when analyzing a policy claim:

**1. Is there a need for such a policy or course of action?** If your listeners don't believe that a change is called for, they're not likely to approve your proposal. If, for example, students are already required to pass four English courses before graduation, is a test for English competency necessary?

**2. Is the proposal practical?** Can we afford the expense the proposal would entail? Would it really solve the problem or remove the evil it is designed to correct? Does such a policy stand a reasonable chance of being adopted? If you can't show that your proposal meets these and similar tests, you can hardly expect it to be endorsed.

**3. Are the benefits of your proposal greater than its disadvantages?** People are reluctant to approve a proposal that promises to create conditions worse than the ones it is designed to correct. Burning a barn to the ground, for example, may be an effective way to get rid of rats, but it's hardly a desirable one. The benefits and disadvantages that will result from a plan of action must always be carefully weighed along with considerations of its basic workability. Would an English proficiency test, for instance, be expensive and cumbersome to administer and grade?

**4. Is the proposal superior to the alternatives?** Listeners are hesitant to approve a policy if they have reason to believe that another course of action is more practical or more beneficial. A program of job training may be a better way than new qualifications tests to remove people from the welfare rolls.

**TABLE 14.1** Types of Claims

Notice how each type of claim can be analyzed.

| Claim | Description | Analysis |
|---|---|---|
| Claim of fact | Assertion of truth or that something exists | 1. By what criteria is the truth or accuracy of the claim measured?<br>2. Do the facts of the situation fit the criteria? |
| Claim of value | Assertion that something is good or bad; desirable or undesirable; justified or unjustified | 1. By what standards is something to be judged?<br>2. How well does the thing measure up? |
| Claim of policy | Recommendation of a course of action | 1. Is there a need for this policy or course of action?<br>2. Is the proposal practicable?<br>3. Are the benefits of the proposal greater than its disadvantages?<br>4. Is the proposal better than other courses of action? |

Different types of claims make varying demands on you as an arguer (see Table 14.1). You should tell your listeners how to assess your claims. Articulating criteria or standards for judgment is essential if you want to win an argument. For example, if you think tuition waivers should be tied to financial need rather than academic performance, you must show your listeners why financial need is a better standard for waiving tuition.

Unless there are sound reasons for delay, you should announce your claim early in your speech. If listeners don't see where you're going in your argument, your strongest arguments may be lost on them. Take time to say something like "Today, I want to convince you that increases and decreases in student tuition should be coupled with the Consumer Price Index. If the Board of Regents takes this action, the cost of education will be more fairly distributed between the state and the students."[3]

## Types of Evidence

As you discovered in Chapter 6, supporting materials clarify, amplify, and strengthen the ideas in your speech. They provide evidence to strengthen your ideas and, in doing so, provide the base from which an argument is built. It can be presented in any of the forms of supporting materials with which you are already familiar: comparisons and contrasts, illustrations, examples, statistics, and testimony.

There's no single or easy rule for selecting relevant evidence. Supporting material that's relevant to one claim may be irrelevant to another, or it may provide logical proof but not compelling reasons for action. You should consider both the rational and the motivational characteristics of evidence as you select it: Is it reasonable? Is it convincing?

**Rationally Relevant Evidence** The type of evidence you choose should reflect your claim. For example, if you're defending the claim that controls on the content of

Internet chat rooms violate the First Amendment guarantee of freedom of speech, you'll probably choose testimony by noted authorities or definitions of terms to advance your claim. On the other hand, examples, illustrations, and statistics work better for showing that a problem exists or a change is needed. For example, if you argue that the speed limit in your state should be lowered by 10 miles per hour on interstate highways and have statistics indicating that lives will be saved, you'll be providing a compelling reason for a change. The claim you present requires a rationally relevant type of evidence. As you plan your arguments, ask yourself "What type of evidence is logically relevant in support of my claim?"

**Motivationally Relevant Evidence** If you hope to convince listeners to adopt your attitudes or actions, your claim must supply more than logically relevant evidence. You must get your listeners emotionally involved, as we saw in Chapter 13. That is, your evidence must be motivationally relevant to them. So, you should ask two questions:

**1. What type of evidence will this audience demand?** If you want to argue that your city needs to build a new sewage plant, many people will demand that you demonstrate the problems with the present system, a financial plan that won't bankrupt the city, incentives that the new plant will provide for new jobs, and even a plan for laying the lines that won't paralyze neighborhoods. On the other hand, if you're reviewing a new film release for friends, an example from the plot, an analogy to similar films, or an illustration of dialogue would be more forceful as proof than statistical word counts, box office receipts, or testimony from published movie critics. Careful audience analysis, as we discussed earlier, will help you determine what type of evidence is needed to move your listeners psychologically.

**2. What specific evidence will generate the best response?** You should pose this question once you've determined the type of evidence required by your argument. For example, if you've decided to use expert testimony to support your argument, whom should you quote? Or, if you're using an illustration, should you use a factual example or develop one of your own? Will listeners be more moved by a personalized story or a general illustration?

To answer these and similar questions, you need to analyze your listeners. A homogeneous audience of local residents may be suspicious of outsiders. They might react best to local experts or examples from the local community or common experiences: the mayor, a reference

*Speakers should ask what type of evidence their listeners will demand as well as what evidence will generate the best response.*

to a particular neighborhood, or the town's experience in the flood of 2009. A heterogeneous audience of college students who do not share a common background with the community, on the other hand, will not know those local experts and probably will prefer geographically varied examples. Such an audience will probably respond better to a nationally known expert and references to well-known communities across the country. You should consider your listeners' demographic or psychological characteristics to choose the most effective evidence for them.

## Forms of Reasoning

**Reasoning,** or inference, is a process of connecting something that is known or believed (evidence) to a concept or idea (claim) that you wish others to accept. **Patterns of reasoning** are habitual ways in which a culture or society uses inferences to connect what is accepted to what it is being urged to accept. There are five generally accepted reasoning patterns: (1) from examples, (2) from generalization, (3) from sign, (4) from parallel case, and (5) from cause.

Often called *inductive reasoning*, **reasoning from examples** involves examining a series of examples of known occurrences (evidence) and drawing a general conclusion (claim). The inference of this reasoning pattern is that what is true of particular cases is true of the whole class. This inference represents a kind of mental inductive leap from specifics to generalities. For example, the National Cancer Institute has studied hundreds of individual case histories and discovered that people with high-fiber diets are less prone to develop cancers of the digestive tract. With an inductive leap, the Institute then moved to the factual claim "High-fiber diets help control certain types of cancer." Commuters use a similar pattern of reasoning every time they drive during rush hour. After trial and error, they decide that a residential street is the best route to take home before 5:30 P.M. and the expressway after 5:30 P.M. In other words, after experiencing enough instances, they arrive at a generalization and act on it.

**Reasoning from generalization** (sometimes called deduction) means applying a general truth to a specific situation. It is essentially the reverse of reasoning from examples or induction. In a high school consumer education class, you might have learned that buying goods in large quantities saves money (the generalization). Today, you might shop at discount stores because they purchase goods in quantity, thereby saving money and passing those savings on to you (the claim deduced from the evidence). Or, you might believe that getting a college education is the key to a better future (the generalization). Therefore, if you get a college degree, you will get a better job (claim). This inference gathers power because of experience (you learned it through observation) or by definition (one of the characteristics of education is self-improvement). You ultimately accept this inference because of the uniformities you believe exist in the world.

**Reasoning from sign** uses an observable mark or sign as proof for the existence of a state of affairs. You reason from sign when you notice the tickle in your throat (the evidence) and decide that you're getting a cold (the claim). The tickle in your throat doesn't cause the condition; rather, it's a sign of the virus that does cause it. Detectives are experts at reasoning from sign. When they discover that a particular suspect had motive, means, and opportunity (the signs), they make the claim that he or she might be the murderer. Your doctor works the same way every time he or she examines your respiration and heart rhythms for signs of ailments. Reasoning from sign works well with natural occurrences (ice on the pond is always a sign that the temperature has been below 32°F). In the world of human beings, however, reasoning from sign can be troublesome. Signs, of course, are circumstantial evidence—and could be wrong. Just ask detectives and doctors. Yet, we often must use signs as indicators; otherwise, we couldn't project our economy, predict our weather, or forecast the success of political candidates.

Another common reasoning pattern, **reasoning from parallel case**, involves thinking solely in terms of similar things and events. You probably designed your first homecoming float by looking at others; they served as models of what people expect of homecoming floats in your area. Those floats functioned as evidence; the claim was that you should make a similar mark of pride and identification. The inference that linked the evidence and the claim was probably something like "What was acceptable as a homecoming float last year will be acceptable/expected this year." Your instructors might use parallel reasoning every time they say, "Study hard for this exam. The last exam was difficult; this one will be, too." Obviously, this is not a generalization, because every exam will probably not be exactly the same. Your instructors are asserting, however, that the upcoming examinations and past examinations are similar cases—they have enough features in common to increase the likelihood that careful study habits will benefit you.

Finally, **reasoning from cause** is an important vehicle for reaching conclusions. The underlying assumption of causal reasoning is that events occur in a predictable, routine manner, with causes that account for occurrences. Reasoning from cause involves associating events that come before with events that follow (see Table 14.2). When substance abuse appears to be increasing across the country, people scramble to identify causes: the existence of international drug cartels, corrupt foreign governments, organized crime inside our

**TABLE 14.2**   Kinds of Reasoning

Try to think of additional examples of each kind of reasoning.

| Reasoning | Description | Examples |
| --- | --- | --- |
| Reasoning from examples (inductive reasoning) | Drawing a general conclusion from instances or examples | I enjoy the music of Bach, Beethoven, and Brahms. I like classical music. |
| Reasoning from generalization or axiom (deductive reasoning) | Applying a general conclusion to a specific example | Irish Setters are friendly dogs. I think I'll get an Irish Setter puppy for my niece. |
| Reasoning from sign | Using an observable mark or symptom as proof of a state of affairs | The petunias are all dead. Someone forgot to water them. |
| Reasoning from parallel case | Asserting that two things or events share similar characteristics or patterns | North Korea is developing nuclear technology. South Korea won't be far behind. |
| Reasoning from causal relation | Concluding that an event that occurs first is responsible for a later event | The engine won't start because the carburetor is flooded with gasoline. |

own borders, lower moral standards, the breakup of the nuclear family, and lax school discipline. What the arguer must do is assert causes that might reasonably be expected to produce the effects—to point to material connections between, for example, the actual policies of foreign governments and the presence of drugs in Los Angeles or other American cities. Overall, the inference in causal reasoning is simple and constant: Every effect has a cause.

# Evaluating Arguments

The reasoning process is the fulcrum on which argument pivots. You must test reasoning to protect yourself, both as a speaker and as a critical listener, from embarrassment when you're arguing and from faulty decisions when you're listening to others. For each kind of reasoning, there are special tests or questions that help you determine the soundness of arguments. Consider the following questions as you construct arguments and evaluate those of others:

## Reasoning from Examples

**1. Have you looked at enough instances to warrant generalizing?** If you live in Minnesota, you don't assume that spring has arrived after experiencing one warm day in February.

**2. Are the instances fairly chosen?** You certainly hope that a teacher doesn't judge your speech skills by listening only to your first speech, when you were confused and nervous. You want to be judged only after being observed in several speaking situations.

**3. Are there important exceptions to the generalization or claim that must be considered?** While presidential elections show that, generally," "As Maine goes, so goes the nation," there have been enough exceptions to this rule to keep presidential candidates who lose in Maine campaigning hard.

## Reasoning from Generalization

**1. Is the generalization true?** Women are more emotional than men; woolly caterpillars come out when winter's about to arrive; private universities provide better education than public universities. Each of these statements is a generalization. You need to determine whether sufficient evidence exists to support the truth of the statement.

**2. Does the generalization apply to this particular case?** Usually, discount stores have lower prices, but if a small neighborhood store has a sale, it might offer better prices than a discount house. While the old saying "Birds of a feather flock together" certainly applies to birds, it might not apply to human beings.

## Reasoning from Sign

**1. Is the sign fallible?** As we've noted, many signs are merely circumstantial. Be extremely careful not to confuse reasoning from sign with causal reasoning.

If reasoning from sign were infallible, the weather forecaster would never be wrong.

**2. Is the observation accurate?** Some of us see what we want to see, not what's there—children see ghosts at night, drivers miss stop signs, and people fall in love at first sight. Be sure that the observation is reliable.

## Reasoning from Parallel Case

**1. Are there more similarities than differences between the two cases?** College A and College B may have many features in common—size, location, programs, and so on. Yet, they probably also have many different features, perhaps in the subgroups that make up their populations, the backgrounds of their faculty, and their historical development. Too many differences between two cases rationally destroy the parallel.

**2. Are the similarities you have pointed out the relevant and important ones?** There are two children in your neighborhood who are the same age, go to the same school, and wear the same kinds of clothes; are you therefore able to assume that one is well-behaved simply because the other is? Probably not, because more relevant similarities than their clothing and age would include their home lives, their relationships with siblings, and so forth. Comparisons must be based on relevant and important similarities.

## Reasoning from Cause

**1. Can you separate causes and effects?** We often have a difficult time doing this. Does stress lead to a propensity to drink too much, or does excessive alcohol consumption lead to stress? Does a strained home life make a child misbehave, or is it the other way around?

**2. Are the causes strong enough to have produced the effect?** Did George W. Bush's appearance on *Oprah* really win the 2000 election for him, or was that an insufficient cause? There probably were much stronger and more important causes.

**3. Did intervening events or persons prevent a cause from having its normal effect?** If a gun is not loaded, you can't shoot anything, no matter how hard you pull the trigger. Even if Nigeria cuts off oil sales to the United States, there may not be shortages if U.S. consumer gas consumption drops.

**4. Could any other cause have produced the effect?** Although crime often increases when neighborhoods deteriorate, increased crime rates can be caused by any number of other changes—alterations in definitions of crime, increased reporting of crimes that have been going on for years, or closings of major industries. We must sort through all of the possible causes rationally before championing one.

The heart of critical thinking is idea testing. You must learn to use what you have available—the evidence others have presented, your own experience, your wits, and sometimes, a trip to the library when the decision's particularly important— to test the rationality and force of others' arguments.

SPEAKING OF . . .
S K I L L S

### Evaluating Arguments

Undoubtedly, you'll participate in disputes or arguments many times as an advocate or a bystander. Often, you'll have to determine if your arguments or those of others were effective. Here are four questions you can ask to help discover the effectiveness of an argument:

1. *What was the argument's effect?* Did it convince people to vote? To boycott? To donate canned goods? Clearly, if your argument results in a desired response, it was effective. However, this is only one way of judging the effectiveness of arguments. You must also ask the next three questions.

2. *Was the argument valid?* Did the arguer follow a logical order of development? Did he or she use supporting materials to prove the points? Were those supporting materials relevant to the claim advanced? If the argument was sound, it can be judged valid.

3. *Was the argument truthful?* Did it meet the test of reality? If an argument doesn't correspond to the way things really are, then it fails the truthfulness test.

4. *Was the argument ethical?* Did it advocate what is morally good? Did the arguer use ethical means to achieve results? This is an especially important test in this age of ethical malaise.

## Sample Outline for an Argumentative Speech

### The Dangers of Chewing Tobacco[4]

**Introduction**

I. When he was 12 years old, Ricky Bender tried his first plug of chewing tobacco. After all, he was a Little Leaguer, and all his heroes in the major leagues chewed tobacco. Fourteen years later, Ricky found out he had oral cancer. The cancer cost him most of his tongue, half of his jaw, and the use of his right arm.

*The speaker uses motivationally relevant evidence to gain attention.*

II. Little Ricky Bender's case isn't an isolated one. Every day children like little Ricky Bender start using "spit tobacco." It's estimated that 10 percent of teenage males are regular users.

*The growing scope of the problem is explained with rationally relevant evidence.*

III. It's important that we recognize the dangers of this addictive drug, because health problems related to its use are rising dramatically in this country.

*Audience motivation to listen is developed.*

IV. Let's examine the addictive nature of spit tobacco, the health problems it causes, and the myths that surround it.

*The speech structure is previewed*

Body

I.  The addictive nature of spit tobacco.

The uses of spit tobacco are explained. ➤ A.  Spit tobacco is leaf tobacco that comes in two forms.
1.  Chewing tobacco comes in a pouch in a coarsely shredded form.
2.  More finely shredded snuff is packaged in a tin and is sometimes flavored.
3.  Both forms are put between the cheek and the gum. Nicotine is absorbed through the tissues of the mouth.

Reasoning from parallel case establishes the similarities between cigarette and spit tobacco use. ➤ B.  Nicotine dependency results from the use of spit tobacco.
1.  Studies reveal that blood levels of nicotine for smokers and spit tobacco users are identical.
2.  Psychological dependency on tobacco results in both users.
3.  The only difference between the two forms is that nicotine enters the bloodstream more slowly when it is absorbed through the skin.

II. The health problems caused by spit tobacco.

Causal reasoning is supported with statistical evidence. ➤ A.  Dental problems are rampant among spit tobacco users.
1.  Habitual users injure the linings of their mouths where the tobacco is held.
    a.  The first signs of deterioration are halitosis or bad breath and tooth discoloration.
    b.  Then, teeth begin to decay, and gingivitis sets in.
    c.  Finally, users begin to lose their teeth prematurely.
2.  Statistics reveal the toll spit tobacco takes on dental health.

Causal reasoning links nitrosamines to oral cancer. ➤ B.  The risk of oral cancer increases.
1.  Nitrosamines, known carcinogenic agents, are formed when spit tobacco is manufactured.
2.  These carcinogens enter the user's bloodstream along with nicotine.
    a.  The risk of oral cancer is four to six times higher than that for nonusers.
    b.  The risk of oral cancer is higher than that for cigarette and pipe smokers.
    c.  There is also a risk from the expelled tobacco when it comes into contact with skin.

Nicotine is identified as a cause of heart disease. ➤ C.  Heart disease increases with the use of spit tobacco.
1.  Systemic problems result from spit tobacco use.
    a.  Within minutes, nicotine causes blood pressure to increase.
    b.  The heart is required to pump harder, increasing the heart rate.
2.  The strain on the cardiovascular system over a period of time leads to coronary problems and heart disease.

III. The myths surrounding spit tobacco.

Reasoning from generalization applies overall rates of cancer to spit tobacco users. ➤ A.  It's often called "smokeless tobacco," fostering the perception that it is less harmful than smoking.
1.  The fact is that spit tobacco is just as likely to cause cancer as cigarette smoking is.
    a.  Oral cancer rates are higher among spit tobacco users.
    b.  Other cancer rates exceed those of nonusers.
2.  Heart disease is another result of using spit tobacco.

Reasoning from sign uses advertising and peer pressure to explain spit tobacco use among teenagers. ➤ B.  Some people argue there is less pressure among teens to use spit tobacco, but the opposite is true. Peer pressure spirals during the adolescent years.
1.  Companies spend millions of dollars advertising spit tobacco at sponsored rodeos, NASCAR, and other popular events.
2.  Potential users frequent these events.

3. Studies reveal that peer pressure induced by pervasive advertising is the chief reason for the initial use of spit tobacco.

Conclusion

I. Remember little Ricky Bender? What started as an innocent attempt to emulate his major league heroes cost him most of his face and threatened to take his life.

II. The threat to young people, especially teenaged males, is on an upward spiral.

III. It's important for us to recognize that spit tobacco is addictive—and not only that, it kills.

*Return to introductory example reaches closure by reminding listeners of motivationally relevant example.*

*Listeners are warned about the lethal nature of spit tobacco.*

# Detecting Fallacies in Reasoning

Your primary job as a critical listener and arguer is to evaluate the claims, evidence, and reasoning of others. On one level, you're looking for ways that the ideas and reasoning of others are important to your own thinking; and on another level, you're examining the logical soundness of others' thinking. A **fallacy** is a flaw in the rational properties of an argument or inference. There are many different fallacies. Let's look at eight common ones:

**1. Hasty generalization.** A **hasty generalization** is a claim made on the basis of too little evidence. You should ask, "Has the arguer really examined enough typical cases to make a claim?" If the answer is no, then a flaw in reasoning has occurred. Urging a ban on ibuprofen because some people have had liver problems with it and closing a pedestrian mall because of an armed robbery are examples of hasty generalization.

**2. Genetic fallacy.** A **genetic fallacy** occurs when someone assumes that the only "true" understanding of some idea, practice, or event is to be found in its origins—in its "genes," either literally or metaphorically. People sometimes assume that if an idea has been around for a long time, it must be true. Many people who defended slavery in the nineteenth century referred to biblical practices of slavery to support their claim. Studies of origins can help us understand a concept, but they're hardly proof of present correctness or justice.

**3. Appeal to ignorance.** People sometimes appeal to ignorance by arguing with double negatives: "You can't prove it won't work!" They may even attack an idea because information about it is incomplete. "We can't cure AIDS so let's just stop therapies until we learn more." Both of these illogical claims **appeal to ignorance**, because they depend on what we don't know. Sometimes we must simply act on the basis of the knowledge we have, despite the gaps in it. In countering such claims, you can cite parallel cases and examples. So, you might say,

OK, so we don't have all of the answers to the AIDS puzzle. That doesn't mean we don't work with what we know. Consider the case of tuberculosis. The vaccines against it weren't developed until the 1950s, and yet thousands of lives were saved earlier in the century because TB sanitariums used the physical and pharmacological regimens they had available. Of course, they couldn't save everyone, but they relieved suffering and even prevented the deaths of many with the partial knowledge they had. Give HIV-positive people the same chance—to use what we have now even while we're waiting for the cure.

**4. Bandwagon fallacy.** A frequent strategy is to appeal to popular opinion or urge people to jump on the bandwagon. The **bandwagon fallacy** assumes that if everyone else is doing something, you should, too: "Everyone enjoys bowling!" or "But Dad, all my friends are going!" While these appeals may be useful in stating valuative claims, they're not the basis for factual claims. The world has witnessed hundreds of widely believed but false ideas, from the belief that night air causes tuberculosis to panic over an invasion by Martians.

**5. Sequential fallacy.** Often present in arguments based on evidence from causal relations, the **sequential fallacy** arises from the assumption that if one event follows another, the first event must have caused the second. Thunder and lightning do not cause rain, although the phenomena often occur sequentially. Even if you usually catch colds in the spring, the two occurrences are not causally related. The season of the year does not cause your cold—a virus does.

**6. Begging the question.** Rephrasing an idea and then offering it as its own reason is known as **begging the question.** This kind of reasoning is circular thought. If someone asserts "Abortion is murder because it is taking the life of the unborn," he or she has committed a fallacy by rephrasing the claim (it is murder) to constitute the reason (it is taking life). Sometimes questions can be fallacious, such as "Have you quit smoking on weekends?" The claim, phrased as a question, assumes that you smoke during the week; therefore, whatever your answer to the question, you're guilty. Claims of value—such as "Democracy is the best form of government because it involves everyone" or "Foreign films are hard to understand"—are especially prone to begging the question.

**7. Appeal to authority.** When someone who is popular but not an expert urges the acceptance of an idea or a product, this is an **appeal to authority.** Television advertisers frequently ask consumers to purchase products because movie stars or sports heroes endorse them. Michael Jordan promotes everything from underwear to telephone services. The familiar figure provides name recognition but not expertise. You can detect this fallacy by asking, "Is he or she an expert on this topic?"

**8. Name-calling.** The general label for attacks on people instead of on their arguments is known as **name-calling.** Name-calling may take the form of an attack on the special interests of a person: "Of course you're voting for O'Casey, you're Irish." Or, it may be an attack on a personal characteristic rather than on ideas: "You're just a dweeb (or nerd, or retrograde male)." Even dweebs, nerds, and retrograde males, however, sometimes offer solid claims. Claims ought to be judged on their own features, preferably their objective features, and not on the characteristics of the person who makes them.

These are some of the fallacies that creep into argumentation. A good book on basic logic can point out additional fallacies.[5] Armed with knowledge of such fallacies, you should be able to protect yourself against unscrupulous demagogues, sales personnel, and advertisers. The Latin phrase *caveat emptor*—"let the buyer beware"—should be a part of your thinking as an audience member. You share with speakers the responsibility of cultivating the sort of critical spirit discussed in the opening of this chapter.

### Name-Calling

Arguments often threaten to degenerate into fights—not always physical clawing and punching but certainly symbolic assaults, such as attacks on an opponent's intelligence, parentage (or lack thereof), associations, motives, or appearance. Is that ethical? Where do you draw the line?

Consider the following situations:

1. You're having a class argument about ways to control hate speech. You know that your opponent is gay. Do you reveal that information in the debate?

2. During the 2008 presidential primaries, several candidates and their supporters were charged with making comments that were racist or sexist. How relevant were those charges to the issues?

3. "Well, you're over thirty, so how would you understand?" "You're a girl, so of course . . ." "Now, you're Jewish, and so I'd expect you to . . ." "When you lived in the ghetto, didn't you . . .?" Is it ethical to make statements like these when arguing with someone?

Name-calling—or *argumentum ad hominem* (arguments to the person)—has been used since Homer wrote *The Iliad*. But is it ethical? Anytime? Sometimes? When?

## Tips for Developing Argumentative Speeches

As you get ready to pull all of your claims, kinds of evidence, and reasoning patterns together into coherent argumentative speeches, consider the following pieces of advice:

**1. Place your strongest arguments first or last.** This strategy takes advantage of the **primacy-recency effects.** Arguments presented first set the agenda for what is to follow, and a strong opening argument often impresses an audience with its power, thereby heightening the credibility of the arguer (the primacy effect). We also know that listeners tend to retain the most recently presented idea (the recency effect). Therefore, you might put your strongest argument at the end of your speech so that listeners will remember your best shot.[6] Decide which position will help most with the particular audience you face, and then place your best argument there (but then, of course, summarize all of the arguments in your conclusion).

**2. Vary your evidence.** Different listeners are likely to prefer different kinds of evidence, and most listeners want supporting materials that are both logically relevant and psychologically motivating. For example, if you're arguing that more Americans must invest in solar power units for their home electrical needs, general statistics on energy savings and average reduction in costs of utilities are good, but a good, clear illustration with details on what it's like to live in a solar-assisted environment will more likely clinch the argument.

**3. Avoid personal attacks on opponents.** Maintain arguments on an appropriate intellectual level. This tactic enhances your credibility. If you can argue well

*As a member of your community, you will need to critically examine the claims of others.*

without becoming vicious, you'll earn the respect—and perhaps the agreement—of your listeners; most know that the more someone screams, the weaker his or her arguments are. Hold your opponent accountable for arguments and reasoning, yes, but without name-calling and smear tactics (see "Speaking of . . . Ethics: Name-Calling").

**4. Know the potential arguments of your opponents.** The best advocates know their opponents' arguments as well as their opponents do; they have thought about those arguments and ways of responding to them ahead of time. Having thought through opposing positions early allows you to prepare a response and feel confident about your own position. Notice how presidential candidates are able to anticipate each other's positions in their debates.

**5. Practice constructing logical arguments and detecting fallacious ones.** Ultimately, successful argument demands skill in performing the techniques of public reasoning. You need to practice routinely constructing arguments with solid relationships between and among claims, evidence, and reasoning patterns, and you need to practice regularly detecting the fallacies in proposals of others. Critically examine product advertisements, political claims, and arguments that your neighbors make in order to improve your communication skills—both as a sender and as a receiver of argumentative messages.

SPEAKING OF . . .
**S K I L L S**

## Responding to Counterarguments

Constructing an argument is often not enough. You might have to respond to the objections of others who oppose your ideas. Here are some suggestions for developing an effective response:

1. *Listen and take notes.* You need to understand your opponent's position before you can refute it.

2. *Decide whether to answer the objection.* Many times, people just want to vent frustration or be heard by others. Their comments may not be relevant to your argument.

3. *Organize your response.* Here's a four-step process to help:

   a. *Restate your opponent's claim.* "Mary said learning a foreign language is useless."
   b. *Explain your objection to it.* "I think learning a foreign language can be beneficial in your career and in your personal life."
   c. *Offer evidence to support your position.* "Studies show that . . ."
   d. *Indicate the significance of your rebuttal.* "If you want faster career advancement and more satisfying international travel experiences, take a foreign language."

4. *Keep the exchange on an intellectual level.* Name-calling or emotionally charged ranting harms your credibility.

## ▌Assessing Your Progress

### Chapter Summary

1. Argumentation is a process of advancing propositions or claims supported by good reasons.
2. Criticism is a process of careful assessment, evaluation, and judgment of ideas and motives.
3. Arguments are built from three elements: (a) the claim, (b) the evidence, and (c) the reasoning pattern.
4. The types of claims common to arguments are claims of fact, claims of value, and claims of policy.
5. Evidence for arguments can be chosen to reflect the rational quality of the claim (rationally relevant evidence) or to stimulate audience involvement (motivationally relevant evidence).
6. Five forms of reasoning connect evidence and claims: (a) reasoning from examples, (b) reasoning from generalization, (c) reasoning from sign, (d) reasoning from parallel case, and (e) reasoning from cause.

7. A fallacy is a flaw in the rational properties of an argument or inference.

8. Common fallacies are hasty generalization, genetic fallacy, appeal to ignorance, bandwagon fallacy, sequential fallacy, begging the question, appeal to authority, and name-calling.

9. In developing argumentative speeches, (a) organize your arguments by putting the strongest first or last, (b) vary the evidence, (c) avoid personal attacks on opponents, (d) know the potential arguments of your opponents, and (e) practice constructing logical arguments and detecting fallacious ones.

## Assessment Activities

Fallacies are often present in assertions made by advertisers. Think of as many assertions made in current television and print advertisements as you can. Choose a member of the class to list them on the chalkboard, and then assess the claims. What kinds of fallacies can you detect? Explain why the reasoning in the advertisement is flawed.

For additional suggestions and activities, log on to MySpeechLab at www.myspeechlab.com.

## Using the Web

Individuals and organizations often post their views on the Internet. Locate a Web page that develops an argument. You might look for a highly controversial person or group, especially those seeking recruits or financial donations. Assess the argument. Is the claim clearly stated? Is supporting material provided to substantiate the claim? Is the supporting material rationally or motivationally relevant? What reasoning patterns are present in the argument? Are they logical?

## References

1. Harvey Siegel, *Educating Reason: Rationality, Critical Thinking, and Education* (New York: Routledge, 1988), 1–47. The importance of critical thinking has been underscored in two national reports on higher education: The National Institute of Education, *Involvement in Learning: Realizing the Potential of American Higher Education*, 1984; and the Association of American Colleges, *Integrity in the College Curriculum: A Report to the Academic Community*, 1985. For a summary of research on critical thinking in the college setting, see James H. McMillan, "Enhancing College Students' Critical Thinking: A Review of Studies," *Research in Higher Education*, 26 (1987): 3–29.

2. Fairness or fair-mindedness is one dimension of a primary factor underlying positive source credibility, trustworthiness. See James B. Stiff, *Persuasive Communication* (New York: Guilford Press, 1994), esp. 90–92.

3. A full discussion of the logical grounding of claims in evidence and reasoning is presented in the classic book on argumentation: Douglas Ehninger and Wayne Brockriede, *Decision by Debate*, 2nd ed. (New York: Harper and Row, 1978).

4. Information for this sample outline was drawn from the Johns Hopkins Health Information Web site (www.intelihealth.com/IH/ihtlH) and from Marjike Rowland, "Man Without a Face to Talk on Dangers of Chewing Tobacco," *Modesto Bee* (2 February 1999).

5. See Irving M. Copi and Keith Cohen, *Informal Logic*, 10th ed. (Upper Saddle River, NJ: Prentice Hall, 1998); and Frans H. VanEemeren and Rob Grootendorst, *Argumentation, Communication, and Fallacies* (Hillsdale, NJ: Lawrence Erlbaum Associates, 1992).

6. The debate over primacy-recency effects continues. For the position that primacy and recency are equally potent, see Stephen W. Littlejohn and David M. Jabusch, *Persuasive Transactions* (Glenview, IL: Scott Foresman, 1987), 235–236; for the arguments championing the primacy position, see Robert E. Denton, Jr., *Persuasion and Influence in American Life* (Prospect Heights, IL: Waveland Press, 1988), 299–300.

PART FOUR

# 15 Speaking in Community Settings

Some situations—often called **special occasions**—call for speeches that are particularly sensitive to community or group needs and expectations. Such special occasions have a ritualistic air to them. Members of societies learn that there are generally acceptable—almost *required*—ways to speak at funerals, weddings, graduations, conferences, or breakfasts honoring community leaders. A **community** is a group of people who think of themselves as bonded together—whether by blood, locale, nationality, race, culture, religion, occupation, gender, or other shared attributes. The phrase *who think of themselves* is the key here. Communities are bonded by shared characteristics or commitments, and those shared characteristics and commitments often are recognized—celebrated, probed, redefined—on "special occasions."

In this chapter, we will explore **community-based special occasion speeches.** We'll look in particular at speeches of introduction, speeches of courtesy (welcomes, responses, acceptances, toasts), speeches to entertain (because the humorous exploration of group beliefs or attitudes often becomes the basis for changing member behavior), and speeches to stimulate (speeches that create examination of special community challenges in emotional terms).

# Speeches of Introduction

**Speeches of introduction** are usually given by members of the group that will hear the speech. They're designed to prepare the community (the audience) to accept the featured speaker and his or her message. In a way, a speech of introduction asks permission for an outsider to speak. The decision to grant that permission is based on what the nonmember can contribute to the group: The group must *want* to hear the outsider before the featured speaker can be successful. Or, if the speaker is a member of the group, the introduction may serve as a reminder of his or her role and accomplishments within the community or organization.

## Purpose

If you're invited to give a speech of introduction, remember that your main objective is to create in others a desire to hear the speaker you're introducing. Everything else should be subordinate to this aim. You're the speaker's advance agent; your job is to sell that person to the audience. Your goals should be (1) to arouse curiosity about the speaker and the subject in the minds of the listeners, so it will be easy to capture their attention, and (2) to motivate the audience to like and respect the speaker, so they'll tend to respond favorably to the forthcoming information or proposal.

## Formulating the Content

Usually, the better-known or more respected a speaker is, the shorter your introduction needs to be; the less well-known the person is, the more you'll need to arouse interest in the speaker's subject and build up the person's prestige. When presenting a speech of introduction, do the following:

**1. Be brief.** To say too much is often worse than to say nothing at all. For example, if you were to introduce the president, you might simply say, "Ladies and gentlemen, the president of the United States." The prestige of the person you introduce won't always be great enough for you to be so brief, but it's always better to say too little than to speak too long.

**2. Talk about the speaker.** Anticipate the audience's questions: "Who are you? What's your position in business, education, sports, or government? What experiences have you had that qualify you to speak on the announced subject?" Build up speakers' identities and tell what they know or have done, but do not praise their abilities as speakers. Let them demonstrate their own skills.

**3. Emphasize the importance of the speaker's subject.** For example, in introducing a speaker who will talk about the oil industry, you might say, "In one way or another, the oil industry is in the news every day—prices at the pump, Middle East concerns, ethanol research, tanker spills, our energy needs for the twenty-first century. To help us make sense of the industry and the ways it impacts our daily lives, today's speaker . . ."

**4. Stress the appropriateness of the subject or the speaker.** If your town is considering a program to rebuild an abandoned factory lot, a speech by a city planner is likely to be timely and appreciated. References to relevant aspects of a speaker's background or the topic can tie speaker and speech to the audience's interests.

**5. Use humor if it suits the occasion.** Nothing puts an audience at ease better than laughter. Take care, however, that the humor is in good taste and doesn't negatively affect the speaker's credibility. The best stories usually are those shared by the introducer and speaker and told to illustrate a positive character trait of the speaker.

## Sample Introduction

The four primary virtues of a speech of introduction are tact, brevity, sincerity, and enthusiasm. These virtues are illustrated in the following introduction.

---

### "Introducing a Classmate" *by Randolf Brown*

A popular sport in the student union cafeteria is reading through lists of ingredients in prepared foods and candies, especially the chemical additives. One of the best players of this sport I've seen is our next speaker, Angela Vangelisti. Angela is amazing. Even with products like coffee whitener, which contains only one or two things I've even heard of, Angela can identify most of the emulsifiers, stabilizers, and flavor enhancers that make up fake food.

While identifying chemical food additives passes the time in the cafeteria, there's also a serious side to the game. As Angela knows, there's a difference between blue dye nos. 1 and 2, and between good old yellow no. 5 and yellow no. 6; the cancer risk varies from one to the other. For example, the red dye no. 3 that you'll find in maraschino cherries is related to thyroid tumors. These are some of the reasons I was gratified to learn that Angela would share some of her technical knowledge as a nutrition major in a speech entitled, "How to Read Labels and Live Longer."

---

## Speeches of Courtesy: Welcomes, Responses, Acceptances, and Toasts

**Speeches of courtesy** explicitly acknowledge the presence or qualities of the audience or a member of the audience. When you extend a welcome to a political candidate who is visiting your class, for example, or when you accept an award, you are giving speeches of courtesy.

### Typical Situations

Speeches of courtesy fulfill social obligations, such as welcoming visitors, responding to welcomes or greetings, accepting awards from groups, and toasting individuals with short speeches recognizing achievements.

**Welcoming Visitors**  When guests or visiting groups are present, someone extends a public greeting to them. For example, your field hockey announcer might greet the opposing team, or a fraternity chapter president might greet the representative from the national office who is visiting your campus. The speech of welcome is a way of introducing strangers into a group or organization, giving them group approval, and making them feel more comfortable.

**Responding to a Welcome or Greeting**  Responses are ways for outsiders to recognize their status as visitors and to express appreciation for acceptance by the group or organization. Thus, the representative from the national office who is visiting a fraternity might respond to a greeting, in turn, by thanking the group for its welcome or by recognizing its importance and accomplishments.

**Accepting Awards**  An individual who has received an award usually acknowledges the honor. Sometimes the award is made to an organization rather than to an individual, in which case someone is selected to respond for the group. In all cases, the acceptance of awards via a speech is a way of thanking the group and acknowledging the importance of the activity being recognized.

**Offering Toasts**  While toasts offered to bridegrooms or others can become silly, the act of toasting is usually an important ritual. Toasts are acts of tribute: Through them, a group recognizes the achievements of an individual and expresses the hope that this person will continue to achieve distinction. After negotiations, heads of state usually toast each other's positive personal qualities, accomplishments, and desire for future good relations. Ceremonially, toasts can unite fragmented peoples.

## Purpose

The speech of courtesy has a double purpose. The speaker not only expresses a sentiment of gratitude or hospitality but also tries to create an aura of good feeling in the audience. Usually, the success of such a speech depends on satisfying the listeners that the appropriate thing has been said.

## Formulating the Content

The scope and content of a speech of courtesy should by guided by the following principles:

1. **Indicate for whom you're speaking.** When you act on behalf of a group, make clear that the greeting or acknowledgment comes from everyone and not from you alone.

2. **Present complimentary facts about the person or persons to whom you are extending the courtesy.** Review the accomplishments or qualities of the person or group you're greeting or whose gift or welcome you're acknowledging.

3. **Illustrate; don't argue.** Present incidents and facts that make clear the importance of the occasions, but don't be contentious. Avoid areas of disagreement. Express concretely and vividly the thoughts that are already in the minds of your listeners.

Speeches of courtesy are more than merely polite talk. The courtesies extended in welcoming someone into your midst or in thanking someone for work done are statements of your group's rules for living—its guiding principles. In extending courtesies to others, you're acknowledging the culture you share with them.

What follows is a short toast offered to a retiring professor by those attending a spring dinner in his honor. Notice its conciseness, the qualities of the person that form the basis for the tribute, and the use of illustrations (the honoree's values) not only to celebrate the person but also to suggest to those assembled the nature of the community standards for accomplishment.

## Sample Speech of Courtesy

### A Toast to Leo Brecker

As we prepare to leave the dinner table, I'd like to offer a toast to the man we honor this evening—retiring Professor Leo Brecker.

Leo, you've been a part of this university for 50 years: as an undergraduate student before and after World War II, as a graduate student, and as a professor of speech education, broadcasting, and mass communication. Your life is indistinguishable from the life of this university. You embody the values everyone else reaches for. You constantly pose what you call the "interesting questions" that are the essence of the scholar's life. You often say that no matter how crazy our students are, they're still the reason we come to work every day. You remind us weekly that we are not only *in* the world but are *of* the world; just as the world gives us the opportunity to study and teach, so do we owe it not only our thanks but our attention and good works.

In living out the values that justify the very existence of the state university, Leo, you've been the flesh-and-blood example of all that is good in higher education. For that, I toast you—your vision, your daily life, and your ideals that will guide our future. In you, Professor Brecker, we see the best that we can be. I toast you in the hope that the best is indeed yet to come for all of us.

## Speeches to Entertain

**Speeches to entertain** present special challenges for speakers. As you may recall, in Chapter 2, we identified the speech to entertain as one of the three types embodying an independent general purpose. Discounting the slapstick of the slipping-on-a-banana-peel type, most humor depends primarily on a listener's sensitivities to the routines and morals of his or her own society. This is obvious if you've ever listened to someone tell jokes from a foreign country. Often, humor cannot be translated, in part because of language differences (puns, for example, don't translate well) and, in larger measure, because of cultural differences.

### Purpose

Like most humor in general, speeches to entertain usually work within the cultural frameworks of a particular group or society. Such speeches may be "merely funny," as in comic monologues, but most are serious in their force or demand on audiences. After-dinner speeches, for example, usually are relevant to the group at hand, and the anecdotes they contain usually are offered to make a point. That point may be as simple as deflecting an audience's antipathy toward the speaker or making the people in the audience feel more like a group. Alternatively, it may be as serious as offering a critique of society.

Speakers seeking to deflect an audience's antipathy often use humor to ingratiate themselves. For example, Henry W. Grady, editor of the *Atlanta Constitution,* expected a good deal of distrust and hostility when he journeyed to New York City in 1886 to tell the New England Society about "The New South." He opened the speech not only by thanking the society for the invitation but also by telling stories about farmers, husbands and wives, and preachers. He praised Abraham Lincoln, a northerner, as "the first typical American" of the new age; told another humorous story about shopkeepers and their advertising; poked fun at the great Union General Sherman—"Who is considered an able man in our hearts, though some people think he is a kind of careless man about fire"; and assured his audience that a New South, one very much like the Old North, was arising from the ashes.[1] Through the use of humor, Henry Grady had his audience cheering every point he made about the New South that evening.

Group cohesiveness also can be created through humor. Especially when campaigning, politicians spend much time telling humorous stories about their opponents, hitting them with stinging remarks. In part, of course, biting political humor detracts from the opposition candidates and party; however, such humor also can make one's own party feel more cohesive. Make sure that the humor remains in reasonably good taste. When Stephen Colbert addressed the White House Press Correspondents' dinner in 2006, his jokes about President Bush were so nasty that he ended up embarrassing his audience.[2] Colbert's speech was undoubtedly entertaining for the viewing audience, but likely not so for both the president and the correspondents, whose lack of reporting on key domestic and world issues was satired.

Finally, speeches to entertain can be used not merely to poke fun at outsiders and celebrate membership but even to critique one's society. Humor can be used to urge general changes and reform of social practices.

## Formulating the Content

When arranging materials for speeches to entertain, develop a series of illustrations, short quotations or quips, and stories that follow one another in fairly rapid succession. Most important, make sure that each touches on a central theme or point. An entertaining speech must be more than a comic monologue; it must be cohesive and pointed. The following sequence works well for speeches to entertain:

1. Relate a story or anecdote, present an illustration, or quote an appropriate passage.
2. State the main idea or point of view implied by your opening.
3. Follow with a series of additional stories, anecdotes, quips, or illustrations that amplify or illuminate your central idea; arrange those supporting materials so they're thematically connected.
4. Close with restatement of the central point you have developed; as in Step 1, you can use a quotation or one final story that clinches and epitomizes your speech as a whole.

# Speeches to Stimulate

In this edition, we bring back a speech type that the original author, Alan Monroe, always included in his understanding of community-building: speeches to stimulate. **Speeches to stimulate** are those in which a community—specifically, a spokesperson from a community—asks itself to think seriously about where it's been and where it's going in the face of serious challenges. It's similar to an explanation in that it isolates something not well understand. It goes further, however, by asking listeners to consider what they might do in the face of those challenges—without offering specific courses of action. It's similar to speeches to persuade and actuate in that it hopes listeners will change their minds and behaviors, without calling for any specific changes. Overall, speeches to stimulate are calls for internal dialogues about beliefs, attitudes, values, and behavior, as well as for external dialogues among those who have the power to take action for the public after further reflection.

## Purpose

The purpose of a speech to stimulate is, as Alan Monroe thought,[3] largely to stir audiences deeply enough emotionally so that they can start to think about ways to reform their thoughts and actions. Emotional appeals to self-examination, open and public exploration of problems that have been avoided or hidden, and recommitment to take challenges seriously are all central to speeches to stimulate. Such speeches attempt to initiate public discussion, engage listeners' feelings and thinking, and prepare communities for more sustained dialogues and, ultimately, action.

## Formulating the Content

The attention step of such speeches can follow traditional lines. The need, satisfaction, and visualization steps, however, must contain a more concrete analysis of the problems and enough emotional engagement to force listeners to seriously reconsider their beliefs, attitudes, values, and behaviors. Much of the talk about greenhouse gases and other environmental problems has taken the form of speeches to stimulate. Al Gore's 2007 Academy Award winning documentary, *An Inconvenient Truth,* is a good example of rhetorical stimulation. It relies on scenes of ugly factories, disintegrating glaciers, smog-covered cities, birds without sanctuaries, and so on—all designed to arouse in viewers feelings of sorrow, guilt,

*Senator Barack Obama spoke not only at large rallies but also in small, intimate settings, which allowed him to build a sense of community among his supporters and win the 2008 presidential election .*

awe, anger, and finally, recommitment to environmental ideals and green solutions to problems. It tells us that we *must* take serious steps toward reclaiming air quality, water quality, stable world temperature patterns, and non-polluting energy sources; yet it does not concentrate upon specific solutions that particular countries need to implement. The film instead seeks to raise awareness and stimulate audiences to individual action—not to solve all of the problems.

Barack Obama gave several speeches to stimulate following the various primaries and caucuses of the 2007–2008 presidential campaign season. His actual campaign speeches, like those given by the other Republican and Democratic Party candidates, were persuasive and actuative. Campaign speeches generally are issue- and character-centered. They are constructed to change beliefs, attitudes, and values and to drive citizens to caucus or vote for candidates when the time comes.

Election eve speeches, however, are different. They seek to stimulate the campaign volunteers and paid staffers to stay committed and working; they try to envision a popular understanding of the caucus and primary systems that will help citizens who have not yet voted or caucused to consider doing so. And so they do little with the issues facing the country. They're primarily emotional self-expressions of visions and prods to workers and citizens alike to take their duties and responsibilities in a democracy seriously.

Perhaps Obama's most exquisite speech to stimulate on an election eve came on January 8, 2008, in New Hampshire. He had finished second behind Hillary Clinton only days after beating her in Iowa. He could not allow disappointment to slow staffers or doubt to stop citizens in upcoming states from participating in civic activities. So, his speech was a speech to stimulate.

## ▎Sample Speech to Stimulate

### "New Hampshire Election Eve Address" *by Barack Obama*[4]

I want to congratulate Senator Clinton on a hard-fought victory here in New Hampshire.

A few weeks ago, no one imagined that we'd have accomplished what we did here tonight. For most of this campaign, we were far behind, and we always knew our climb would be steep.

But in record numbers, you came out and spoke up for change. And with your voices and your votes, you made it clear that at this moment—in this election—there is something happening in America.

There is something happening when men and women in Des Moines and Davenport; in Lebanon and Concord come out in the snows of January to wait in lines that stretch block after block because they believe in what this country can be.

There is something happening when Americans who are young in age and in spirit—who have never before participated in politics—turn out in numbers we've never seen because they know in their hearts that this time must be different.

There is something happening when people vote not just for the party they belong to but the hopes they hold in common—that whether we are rich or poor; black or white; Latino or Asian; whether we hail from Iowa or New Hampshire, Nevada or South Carolina, we are ready to take this country in a fundamentally new direction. That is what's happening in America right now. Change is what's happening in America.

You can be the new majority who can lead this nation out of a long political darkness—Democrats, Independents, and Republicans who are tired of the division and distraction that has clouded Washington; who know that we can disagree without being disagreeable; who understand that if we mobilize our voices to challenge the money and influence that's stood in our way and challenge ourselves to reach for something better, there's no problem we can't solve—no destiny we cannot fulfill.

Our new American majority can end the outrage of unaffordable, unavailable health care in our time. We can bring doctors and patients; workers and businesses; Democrats and Republicans together; and we can tell the drug and insurance industry that while they'll get a seat at the table, they don't get to buy every chair. Not this time. Not now.

Our new majority can end the tax breaks for corporations that ship our jobs overseas and put a middle-class tax cut into the pockets of the working Americans who deserve it.

We can stop sending our children to schools with corridors of shame and start putting them on a pathway to success. We can stop talking about how great teachers are and start rewarding them for their greatness. We can do this with our new majority.

We can harness the ingenuity of farmers and scientists; citizens and entrepreneurs to free this nation from the tyranny of oil and save our planet from a point of no return.

And when I am president, we will end this war in Iraq and bring our troops home; we will finish the job against al Qaeda in Afghanistan; we will care for our veterans; we will restore our moral standing in the world; and we will never use 9/11 as a way to scare up votes, because it is not a tactic to win an election, it is a challenge that should unite America and the world against the common threats of the twenty-first century: terrorism and nuclear weapons; climate change and poverty; genocide and disease.

All of the candidates in this race share these goals. All have good ideas. And all are patriots who serve this country honorably.

But the reason our campaign has always been different is because it's not just about what I will do as president, it's also about what you, the people who love this country, can do to change it.

That's why tonight belongs to you. It belongs to the organizers and the volunteers and the staff who believed in our improbable journey and rallied so many others to join.

We know the battle ahead will be long, but always remember that no matter what obstacles stand in our way, nothing can withstand the power of millions of voices calling for change.

We have been told we cannot do this by a chorus of cynics who will only grow louder and more dissonant in the weeks to come. We've been asked to pause for a reality check. We've been warned against offering the people of this nation false hope.

But in the unlikely story that is America, there has never been anything false about hope. For when we have faced down impossible odds; when we've been told that we're not ready, or that we shouldn't try, or that we can't, generations of Americans have responded with a simple creed that sums up the spirit of a people.

Yes we can.

It was a creed written into the founding documents that declared the destiny of a nation.

Yes we can.

It was whispered by slaves and abolitionists as they blazed a trail toward freedom through the darkest of nights.

Yes we can.

It was sung by immigrants as they struck out from distant shores and pioneers who pushed westward against an unforgiving wilderness.

Yes we can.

(Continued)

It was the call of workers who organized; women who reached for the ballot; a president who chose the moon as our new frontier; and a King who took us to the mountaintop and pointed the way to the Promised Land.

Yes we can to justice and equality. Yes we can to opportunity and prosperity. Yes we can heal this nation. Yes we can repair this world. Yes we can.

And so tomorrow, as we take this campaign South and West; as we learn that the struggles of the textile worker in Spartanburg are not so different than the plight of the dishwasher in Las Vegas; that the hopes of the little girl who goes to a crumbling school in Dillon are the same as the dreams of the boy who learns on the streets of LA; we will remember that there is something happening in America; that we are not as divided as our politics suggests; that we are one people; we are one nation; and together, we will begin the next great chapter in America's story with three words that will ring from coast to coast; from sea to shining sea—Yes. We. Can.

In this chapter, we have explored the role of public speaking on special occasions when the special characteristics and commitments of communities are recognized and celebrated. At these times, we honor members of our community with speeches of introduction, speeches of courtesy (welcomes, responses, acceptances, toasts), speeches to entertain, and speeches to stimulate. These speeches serve to bind us together, reinforcing our dedication to each other and celebrating our common rituals.

## ▌Assessing Your Progress

### Chapter Summary

1. Special occasions often call for speeches that reflect community or group interests.
2. Speeches of introduction prepare an audience by arousing their curiosity and motivating listeners to respond positively to the speaker and the message.
3. Speeches of courtesy acknowledge the presence or qualities of special individuals or audiences, such as welcoming visitors, responding to greetings, accepting awards, or offering toasts.
4. While challenging, speeches to entertain can range from speeches that are merely funny to speeches that deflect audience antipathy to speeches that generate greater audience cohesion.
5. Speeches to stimulate require the emotional engagement of an audience with some special challenge in the community, asking people to think about themselves and about ways to meet that challenge in the future.

### Assessment Activities

Examine a special occasion speech at your college or university. Does your president address the student body at the beginning of each new school year? Do speakers address convocations on special occasions? Have speakers dedicated new buildings? Does your college or university celebrate Founder's

Day or pay tribute to persons or groups? Obtain a text (many can be found on a school's Web site or secured from the president's or student government's office), and then analyze it: How was its purpose tied to your community? What segments of the community, both on- and off-campus, were referenced? In what ways were shared values reinforced? Did its conclusions make you happy to be a member of the community? Turn in your analysis, and your instructor will assess the competency level of your analysis. (Alternatively, you might be asked to examine a speech such as those given on the first anniversary in 2008 of the Virginia Tech shootings. If so, you'll have to do a little research on Virginia Tech or another such school to find out more about the audience.)

For additional exercises, log on to MySpeechLab, at www.myspeechlab.com.

## Using the Web

Community-building is a hot topic in our time. As the United States becomes more aware of itself as fragmented and senses the disintegration of some of its connections with other parts of the world in the twenty-first century, community-building rises higher on the agenda of community activists. For some exercises on community-building suitable for various professional and cultural contexts, see www.counselingoutfitters.com/vistas/vistas07/Gelardin2.htm.

## References

1. Henry W. Grady, "The New South," in *American Public Addresses: 1740–1952*, edited by A. Craig Baird (New York: McGraw-Hill, 1956), 181–185.

2. Use a search engine to explore "Colbert correspondents dinner," and you'll come up with YouTube versions of the talk as well as a large amount of commentary. The Wikipedia entry on it gives you useful general background.

3. Alan H. Monroe, *Principles and Types of Speech* (reprinted for the United States Armed Forces Institute; Chicago: Scott Foresman 1944), 295. This book was originally published in 1936, but when World War II came, Monroe prepared a special edition for the training of U.S. officers.

4. Text released by the Obama campaign and reprinted across the country on January 9, 2008. This speech became the basis for the music video "Yes We Can," a four-and-a-half minute, star-studded song by will.i.am of the Black Eyed Peas built around quotations from the speech. By late spring of 2008, the video had over eight million hits in its YouTube versions. The Internet spread Obama's speech to stimulate across the country and the world.

# Index

## Photo Credits

**Chapter 1:** 2, © Bob Daemmrich/PhotoEdit; 4, © J.R. Bale/Alamy; 6, © Bettmann/ CORBIS; 10, © Joanne Ciccarello/The Christian Science Monitor/ Getty Images; 15, © Alberto Pizzoli/Sygma/CORBIS; **Chapter 2:** 18, © Steve Rubin/The Image Works; 22, © Bob Daemmrich/The Image Works, Inc.; 26, © Joe Sohm/The Image Works; **Chapter 3:** 34, © Tony Savino/The Image Works; 37, © Stuart Cohen/ The Image Works; 38, © Culver Pictures, Inc.; **Chapter 4:** 48, © Kayte M. Deioma/PhotoEdit; 51, © Roger Dollarhide; 53, © Jonathan Ernst/Getty Images; 58, © Katy Winn/CORBIS; **Chapter 5:** 66, © Bob Daemmrich/The Image Works; 68, © Marilyn Humphries/The Image Works; 71, © Bettmann/CORBIS; 78, © Jeff Greenberg/The Image Works; **Chapter 6:** 82, © Michael Newman/PhotoEdit; 98, © Syracuse Newspapers/The Image Works; **Chapter 7:** 108, © Fotocronache Olympia/PhotoEdit; 116, © Kayte M. Deioma/PhotoEdit; 119, © Bob Daemmrich/PhotoEdit; **Chapter 8:** 128, © David Young-Wolff/PhotoEdit; 137, © ©Journal-Courier/The Image Works; 140, © Jason DeCrow/AP Images; **Chapter 9:** 146, © Bob Daemmrich Photography; 151, © Steven Starr/Stock Boston; 157, © Chris Windsor/Getty Images; **Chapter 10:** 164, © David Young-Wolff/PhotoEdit; 167, © Jeffrey Greenberg/PhotoEdit; 176, © Kathy Ferguson/ PhotoEdit; **Chapter 11:** 182, © Steve Rubin/The Image Works; 186, Roller Blade, Inc.; **Chapter 12:** 202, © Todd Warnock/Getty Images; 207, © David Young-Wolff/PhotoEdit; 213, © Jeff Greenberg/The Image Works; 215, © Stockbyte/ Getty Images; **Chapter 13:** 226, © Barry Rosenthal/Getty Images; 228, © AP Images; 236, © Joseph Khakshouri/CORBIS; 241, © Bob Daemmrich/The Image Works; **Chapter 14:** 248, © Tony Freeman/PhotoEdit; 252, © Rachel Epsein/PhotoEdit; 24, © Junko Kimura/Getty Images; 264, © AP Images; **Chapter 15:** 268, © Bob Daemmrich/The Image Works; 275, © Bob Daemmrich/PhotoEdit.